CLASSICS FOR PLEASURE

Michael Dirda

CLASSICS
FOR PLEASURE

HARCOURT, INC.

ORLANDO AUSTIN NEW YORK SAN DIEGO LONDON

www.HarcourtBooks.com

Library of Congress Cataloging-in-Publication Data
Dirda, Michael.
Classics for pleasure/Michael Dirda.—1st ed.
p.   cm.
1. Literature—History and criticism. 2. Canon (Literature) I. Title.
PN524.D57   2007
814'.54—dc22   2007003029
ISBN 978-0-15-101251-0

Text set in Adobe Garamond
Designed by Cathy Riggs

Printed in the United States of America
First edition
A C E G I K J H F D B

For Marian

CONTENTS

Words from the Wise

Everyday Magic

Lives of Consequence

INTRODUCTION

CLASSICS for pleasure? To some readers this may seem an oxymoron. Aren't classics supposed to be difficult, esoteric, and a little boring? Yes, teachers and critics claim they're good for you, but so are milk of magnesia and cod-liver oil. Really, after a hard day's work, who wants to settle down with more . . . work? A fast-moving thriller or a steamy romance—those sound more like it.

I sympathize with this common view, even if it is quite wrong. Classics are classics not because they are educational, but because people have found them worth reading, generation after generation, century after century. More than anything else, great books speak to us of our own very real feelings and failings, of our all-too-human daydreams and confusions. Sappho's heartache is that of anyone who has ever been hopelessly in love. Ernst Jünger's *Storm of Steel* starkly reveals both the horror and exhilaration of war. *The Book of Common Prayer* reliably comforts us in times of sorrow, uplifts us in times of celebration.

Truly distinctive voices, once heard, ought never to be forgotten. We should always be shocked by the rage and bile in Céline's view of humanity, appalled by the brutality surrounding the young Frederick Douglass. For years now, Sheridan Le Fanu's ghost stories, Bram Stoker's *Dracula,* and H. P. Lovecraft's tales of cosmic horror have led us deep into the shivery twilight zone of our acknowledged fears—and unacknowledged desires. On those evenings when the world is too much with us, 221B Baker Street, home to Mr. Sherlock Holmes and Dr. John Watson, has long offered a warm fire and a snug refuge. Come April or May, we will always awake some Saturday morning, like Mary Lennox in *The Secret Garden,* to the wonder and beauty of spring.

In *Classics for Pleasure* I encourage you to try some of the great books of the distant and recent past. For roughly ninety authors I've written brief essays of introduction or invitation, hoping through summary, tantalizing quotation, and concise biography to convey a writer's or a book's particular magic. In general, my approach is that of a passionate reader rather than that of a critic or scholar. I love the Icelandic sagas and Thomas Love Peacock's "conversation" novels and the poetry of C. P. Cavafy, and I want you to love them, too.

Why, you might ask, these particular titles? Let me explain how I came to choose the contents of *Classics for Pleasure.*

When I was a boy of twelve or thirteen, I happened to acquire—through what a rigid purist might call larceny—a paperback copy of Clifton Fadiman's *The Lifetime Reading Plan.* At the time, I had no particular interest in "classics." What I liked then—and still like—were stories, tales of mystery and adventure, the kind of entertainment that earlier ages sometimes labeled romance. In my youthful days, however, I would read almost anything and so discovered that this Fadiman guy made great books sound just as exciting as Green Lantern comics or the latest Tarzan paperback. Not at all academic in his approach, he simply talked to you—reader to reader—about the *Odyssey,* the *Inferno* or *Pride and Prejudice.*

Over the years I gradually meandered my way through nearly all the works in Fadiman's "plan." Eventually, perhaps inevitably, I majored in English in college, and later received a Ph.D. in comparative literature (concentrating on medieval studies and European Romanticism). Then, in 1978, I was lucky enough to start work as an editor and staff writer for the *Washington Post Book World.* Twenty years passed and, in 1997, I happened to notice that the original *Lifetime*

Reading Plan was reissued in a fourth edition, this time augmented by John S. Major to include authors from the Middle East and Asia.

Classics for Pleasure deliberately ignores most of the authors discussed in that 1997 revised Fadiman-Major edition. As valuable as that work may be, its canon of 133 great books has grown relatively familiar. Who will argue against the merits of Shakespeare's plays or Dickens's novels? It seemed more useful—and fun—to point readers to new authors and less obvious classics.

What, precisely, is gained by skipping right by so many of the world's established masterpieces? A great deal, I think. *Classics for Pleasure* focuses on several key authors passed over by Fadiman and Major, many important writers of what one might call the popular imagination, and a few seemingly minor figures who deserve to be better known. So in this book you will find essays on Ovid and Petronius, on Rider Haggard's *She* and Jean Toomer's *Cane*, on *The Man Who Was Thursday* and *The Good Soldier Švejk*, on Arthurian romances, the tales of E. T. A. Hoffmann and the fiction of Eça de Queiros, Agatha Christie, and Philip K. Dick.

Nearly all the works covered tell great stories, whether these are fictional, historical, or biographical. I also suggest a few philosophers (including Heraclitus and Spinoza), a number of golden-age children's books (by such authors as E. Nesbit and John Masefield), and a handful of favorite poets (Pope, Meredith, and Akhmatova among others). I could easily have compiled a book just about poets. As much as to story, I gravitate to an original voice, especially one that's idiosyncratic (J. K. Huysmans, S. J. Perelman), elegant (La Fayette, Gibbon), or witty (Goncharov, Ivy Compton-Burnett). Still, many of my favorite authors aren't included in *Classics for Pleasure*. If you wonder why there's no essay on Isaac Babel or Ford Madox Ford or Colette or Flann O'Brien or Marguerite Yourcenar or P. G. Wodehouse or Italo Svevo, it's because I didn't want to repeat what I'd already said about them in *Bound to Please* or *Readings*.

But enough of these cavils and preliminaries. Think of what follows as a guide to good reading, a collection of love letters to favorite books, and an expansion of the canon to include more genre titles, a kind of "Beyond the Lifetime Reading Plan." For convenience, I've arranged the entries thematically, even though few books fit neatly into any one category. So please feel free to dip and browse at whim; there won't be any test. These are, after all, just what the title says: classics for pleasure.

Playful Imaginations

In the immortal words of *A Funny Thing Happened on the Way to the Forum*: Tragedy tomorrow, comedy tonight! Some of the writers in this category whisper, "What fools these mortals be!" while others, perhaps wiser, merely smile and say instead, "What lovable fools these mortals be!" Here is the realm of every sort of laughter—wit, irony, repartee, satire, gallows humor, imaginative exuberance, the fanciful and the surreal. The resulting literary vaudeville show ranges from skits about the outrageous nightlife of the gods to the antic oafishness of a bumbling clown to the manic wordplay of S. J. Perelman. A good time is had by all.

LUCIAN (c. 115–200 B.C.)
The True History; Lucius, or The Ass; Dialogues of the Dead; Essays

Speak of the ancient Greeks, and one immediately thinks of noble philosophers, tragic dramatists, mournful choruses and a fair amount of rape, incest, madness, sacrifice, and blood. No matter what these serious-minded folk undertake, they almost never seem to be doing it just for fun.

Aristophanes is the most obvious exception to this generalization. His plays satirize philosophy, sex, war—anything. The philosopher Diogenes—the one who went searching in vain for an honest man— also possessed a playful spirit and a dry wit. When he observed a beggar drink from the palm of his hand, the philosopher threw away his cup; when Alexander the Great stood over him and offered to grant any wish, Diogenes—who had been working on his tan— simply asked the master of the world to stop blocking the sun's rays.

Arguably the most amusing of all the Greeks, though, is the writer history knows as Lucian. (In fact, there may have been both a Lucian and a Pseudo-Lucian, but scholars have suspected this only in modern times.) *The True History* takes us on the kind of journey we associate with Odysseus or Jason and the Argonauts and turns it into the adventures of a Greek Baron Munchausen. *Lucius, or The Ass* is a picaresque and sometimes bawdy tale about a young man trans- formed into a donkey by witchcraft. It climaxes with a sex-crazed ma- tron wondering what the beast would be like in bed; the next morning Lucius's owner decides he wants to sell tickets for a follow- up performance.

Lucian's numerous dialogues—almost brief playlets—read as if written by a Greek Bernard Shaw. In the *Dialogues of the Dead,* the characters complain about the boring society of Hades. Charon grouses that his boat is too small and, what's more, it leaks; Hannibal and Alexander argue over who was the better general; Socrates assures us that he really did know nothing and wasn't being at all ironic; and Tiresias is asked to describe, in detail, his transformation from woman to man. In the *Dialogues of the Heterae* old whores discuss sex, passion, jealousy, and money with younger women new to the game, while in the *Dialogues of the Gods* Jupiter, like a tired executive, pa- tiently explains Ganymede's new duties as cup-bearer, though the young shepherd cannot quite grasp why he has to sleep with the ruler of the universe.

Lucian refuses to show respect or reverence for anyone or any- thing, and his preferred genres—the dialogue and short essay—offer abundant opportunity for parody and humor, as well as for social commentary. As H. W. Fowler and his brother F. G. Fowler observe in their introduction to a translation of this ancient scoffer's collected works:

> Lucian . . . will supply no one with a religion or a philosophy; but it may be doubted whether any writer will supply more fully both example and precept in favour of doing one's thinking for oneself; and it may be doubted also whether any other intellectual lesson is more necessary . . . He is individualist to the core. No religion or philosophy, he seems to say, will save you; the thing is to think for yourself and be a man of sense.

Little wonder, then, that Lucian's example—his bright analytic intelligence, his savage indignation—can be detected in Erasmus's *Praise of Folly,* Thomas More's *Utopia,* Ben Jonson's play *Volpone,* and Jonathan Swift's *Gulliver's Travels,* especially the voyage to Laputa. Very early on, he may even have influenced the Latin writer Apuleius, whose magic-filled novel *The Golden Ass* essentially reprises the plot of *The Ass* (but also enhances it with the story of Cupid and Psyche, perhaps the most beautiful fairy tale of antiquity).

For modern readers, *The True History* may be the most attractive of all Lucian's works. It is essentially a tall tale, with elements of science fiction (a trip into space) and fantasy (life inside a giant sea monster), and even a dollop of postmodern playfulness: The preface to this "true history" ends with the caution, "I am telling you frankly, here and now, that I have no intention whatever of telling the truth . . . So mind you do not believe a word I say." My own favorite section recounts a visit to the Isles of the Blessed. There the narrator (Lucian himself) meets glorious poets and heroes and, like a crack reporter, promptly interviews several of them, asking Homer, for example, about the precise critical importance of the word "wrath" in the opening sentence of the *Iliad.* Homer blithely answers: "No significance whatsoever. It was the first word that came into my head."

Later, when Lucian is about to leave the Isles of the Blessed, Odysseus surreptitiously slips him a note to deliver to Calypso, which Lucian, naturally, reads. It is, of course, a love letter, one in which Odysseus explains how sorry he is for sailing off and turning down the goddess's offer of immortality and how he promises to sneak away and come see her as soon as he can.

The True History and *The Ass* are among the dozen or so ancient Greek "novels" that have survived to the present day. Most of the others are tales of lovers separated by cruel fortune, who are finally reunited after myriad adventures. The earliest is *Chaereas and Callirhoe;* the longest, Heliodorus's *An Ethiopian Story;* and the most charming is Longus's *Daphnis and Chloe,* the very model for what we think of as pastoral romance. All these are currently being rediscovered and freshly appreciated, but none offers as much fun as Lucian's tall tales.

⇒•◦•⇐

DENIS DIDEROT (1713–1784)
Rameau's Nephew; other works

Of all the polymaths of the French Enlightenment, the most likable and modern is Denis Diderot. Voltaire might be wittier and Rousseau a greater master of prose, but the editor of the *Encyclopedia*—that "systematic dictionary of the arts, sciences, and trades"—possessed the kind of restless, original mind that throws off ideas like a Fourth of July sparkler. He is irresistible.

With equal ease and brilliance, Diderot could analyze the manufacture of steel or stockings, virtually create modern art criticism, dash off a pornographic novel (*The Indiscreet Jewels,* wherein private parts are made to talk), compose a whimsical essay about his old dressing gown, author a play in which a character writes the play the audience is seeing, establish a major theory of acting (that great actors are in fact coolly deliberative when they seem most emotional), defend radical sexual freedom (in the innocently titled *Supplement to the Voyage to Bougainville*), undermine religion while reflecting on the blind, almost invent an encoding machine and a kind of typewriter, out-talk the best conversationalists in Paris at a time when salons were at their most sparkling, pass hours alone with Catherine the Great arguing about a constitution for Russia, compose dizzyingly ahead-of-their-time novels (*The Nun* treats lesbianism with considerable sympathy), and die quietly after eating an apricot.

One might readily view Diderot as the philosophical equivalent of a performance artist. He instinctively prefers dialogue to discourse, repeatedly setting up conversations or playlike situations in his best essays, metaphysical speculations, and fictions. The apotheosis of this technique comes in the urbane *Rameau's Nephew*, a sprightly yet disturbing "satire" that sometimes recalls Dostoevsky's *Notes from Underground*, sometimes Kafka. The nephew himself is one of the great scalawags of French literature. As Diderot begins (in L. W. Tancock's translation):

Come rain or shine, my custom is to go for a stroll in the Palais-Royal every afternoon at about five. I am always to be seen there alone, sitting on a seat in the Allée d'Argenson, meditating. I hold discussions with myself on politics, love, taste or philosophy, and let my thoughts wander in complete abandon, leaving them free to follow the first wise or foolish idea that comes along, like those young rakes we see in the Allée de Foy who run after a giddy-looking little piece with a laughing face, sparkling eye and tip-tilted nose, only to leave her for another, accosting them all, but sticking to none. In my case my thoughts are my wenches.

The narrator, "Diderot," goes on to explain how one rainy day, when he had moved inside to watch the chess players at the Café de la Régence, he was accosted by the strangest man in France, the nephew of the famous composer Jean-Philippe Rameau. Rameau's nephew, gifted with some musical talent, though not enough for real accomplishment, has chosen to live as a professional sponge, toady, and flatterer—all of which he candidly, even blithely, admits. From this unexpected avowal the conversation modulates into a series of arguments about morality, music, sex (Rameau regrets the early death of his wife because he had hoped to prostitute her), genius, education, and much else as the slightly prim "Diderot" verbally fences with this ruthlessly self-aware and intelligent parasite. Rameau readily confesses that he is a fool, but so, he maintains, is everyone else, up to and including the king. "I am jester to Bertin and a host of others—to you, perhaps, at this moment," he says. But then he quietly slips in the kicker: "Or possibly you are mine."

Diderot never published *Rameau's Nephew* (it was written about 1761), though he did show the manuscript to some friends. Eventually a copy made its way into Germany, long after his death, and was given to Goethe, who was so taken by the dialogue that he translated it. Thus it happened that a French masterpiece first appeared in German. Later a superb holograph copy was discovered bound in a volume of eighteenth-century pornography, and since then the dialogue has established itself as one of the more eccentric and provocative glories of French literature.

Other works by Diderot well worth reading are the story titled "This Is Not a Story" (talk about postmodern!) and the Tristram Shandy–like *Jacques the Fatalist,* the latter characterized by a smart-alecky narrator, digressions that regress toward infinity, and lots of sidetracks, detours, and reroutings (as in the constantly interrupted history of Jacques' amours), complex reflections on the nature of relationships (servant-master, narrator-reader), and, at the center, a stunning short story, wherein a spurned upper-class woman revenges herself by manipulating her aristocratic ex-lover into marrying a prostitute. She receives her own come-uppance, however, when the newlyweds discover their genuine love for each other and live happily ever after.

→►◦◄←

THOMAS LOVE PEACOCK (1785–1866)
Crotchet Castle; other novels

We think of nineteenth-century novels as many things, but almost always as long. Phrases like "triple-decker" and "published in parts" hardly dispel this image, nor does the (quite properly) canonical status of such fat cats as *Middlemarch, Bleak House,* and *Vanity Fair.* Yet some nineteenth-century fiction is as pointed and concise as any modern bestseller—*Alice in Wonderland,* for instance, or the seven witty "conversation" novels of Thomas Love Peacock.

In these books—*Nightmare Abbey, Crotchet Castle,* and *Gryll Grange,* in particular—Peacock perfected a kind of fizzy Voltairean comedy in which humorous cranks and eccentrics gather at a country estate and over bibulous dinners argue about society, politics, books, and life, while in the background young people fall in and out of love. We find this same pattern used in Aldous Huxley's early satires, especially *Crome Yellow* and *Antic Hay,* and, more recently, in the many "campus" novels about the theoretical excesses of contemporary academics. As Peacock himself once wrote: "Perfectibilians, deteriorationists, statu-quo-ites, phrenologists, transcendentalists, political economists, theorists in all sciences, projectors in all arts, morbid visionaries, romantic enthusiasts, lovers of music, lovers of the picturesque, and lovers of good dinners march and will march forever."

Although *Nightmare Abbey* (1818), which features characters reminiscent of Coleridge, Shelley, and Byron, may be Peacock's most famous title, and *Gryll Grange* (1860) his most mellow, the true pavonine connoisseur regards *Crotchet Castle* (1831) as the novelist's best all-around work.

The plot is minimal: The well-to-do Mr. Crotchet wishes to marry his children into the nobility, and for his callous son he has his eye on the beautiful daughter of an impoverished knight. As it happens, this Lady Clarinda has recently thrown over a Captain Fitzchrome as being too poor to provide anything but "love in a cottage." But Fitzchrome, unwavering in his puppyish devotion, finagles an invitation to a soirée at the Crotchet estate, where he meets the epicurean Reverend Dr. Folliott, who constantly quotes the ancients; Mr. Trillo, who "maintains that the sole end of all enlightened society is to get up a good opera"; Mr. Chainmail, who is rabid for all things chivalric and medieval, and . . . Well, let the irrepressible Clarinda describe two more of her fellow guests as she sits at table with her one-time lover:

> Next to him is Mr. Henbane, the toxicologist, I think he calls himself. He has passed half his life in studying poisons and antidotes. The first thing he did on his arrival here, was to kill the cat; and while Miss Crotchet was crying over her, he brought her to life again. . . . Next to him sits Mr. MacQuedy, the Modern Athenian, who lays down the law about every thing, and therefore may be taken to understand every thing. He turns all the affairs of this world into questions of buying and selling. He is the Spirit of the Frozen Ocean to every thing like romance and sentiment. He condenses their volume of steam into a drop of cold water in a moment. He has satisfied me that I am a commodity in the market, and that I ought to set myself at a high price.

While these various system-mongers argue away like Samuel Johnson and his circle, Lady Clarinda's own vivacity rivals that of Elizabeth

Bennet. Listen to her exchanges—set off like stage dialogue—with her ever-pining admirer. She is explaining why she may accept young Mr. Crotchet's offer of marriage, despite his personal unattractiveness:

> Lady Clarinda: "Well, I really have very little to say in his favour."
>
> Captain Fitzchrome: "I do not wish to hear any thing in his favour; and I rejoice to hear you say so, because—"
>
> Lady Clarinda: "Do not flatter yourself. If I take him, it will be to please my father, and to have a town and country-house, and plenty of servants, and a carriage and an opera box, and make some of my acquaintance who have married for love, or for rank, or for any thing but money, die for envy of my jewels. You do not think I would take him for himself. Why he is very smooth and spruce, as far as his dress goes; but as to his face, he looks as if he had tumbled headlong into a volcano, and been thrown up again among the cinders."
>
> Captain Fitzchrome: "I cannot believe, that, speaking thus of him, you mean to take him at all."
>
> Lady Clarinda: "Oh, I am out of my teens. I have been very much in love; but now I am come to years of discretion, and must think, like other people, of settling myself advantageously. . . ."

Besides the Jane Austen–like wit, there's a flavor of Gilbert and Sullivan to these pages, not least because Peacock provides several terrific drinking songs:

> *If I drink water while this doth last,*
> *May I never again drink wine:*
> *For how can a man, in his life of a span,*
> *Do any thing better than dine?*

We'll dine and drink, and say if we think
That any thing better can be;
And when we have dined, wish all mankind
May dine as well as we . . .

Among the great virtues of *Crotchet Castle* is that nothing goes on too long. You can read the whole book in three or four hours, even if you pause to reread and underline, as you will. Chapters tend to run to five or six airy pages. And action—such as an attempted robbery of Dr. Folliott—is set down quickly and without fuss. Only late in the novel does Peacock indulge in some deliberate effusions, evoking an isolated lake, a lonely precipice, or a tumbled-down castle in sentences that are clearly meant as romantic pastiche.

The poet Shelley said that his friend Peacock's pages would always charm "chosen spirits," and that the novels would be even more widely appreciated in years to come. That hasn't quite happened, but for readers who respond to Peacock, his humor remains a perennial delight. As the friar says in *Maid Marian:*

> The world is a stage, and life is a farce, and he that laughs most has most profit of the performance. The worst thing is good enough to be laughed at, though it be good for nothing else; and the best thing, though it be good for something else, is good for nothing better.

—✶—

MAX BEERBOHM (1872–1956)
Seven Men; A Christmas Garland; Zuleika Dobson; selected essays

Few writers offer more civilized amusement than Max Beerbohm. As befits one of the world's great dandies, his perfectly bespoke sentences exhibit classically simple diction and a gradual, sly, and inexhaustible wit. In all his work—essays, stories, and a single novel—Beerbohm's voice remains invariably courteous and easygoing, slightly tinged with a midlife wistfulness, regardless of his actual age. As early as 1896, when he was only twenty-four, Beerbohm sounded this plangent note: "Already I feel myself to be a trifle outmoded. I belong to the Beardsley period." And though the Incomparable Max, as George Bernard Shaw dubbed him, lived on well past the century's end, he never did keep pace with his times. Perhaps that's the secret of becoming a classic, or at least a major minor essayist.

Over the years Beerbohm's great admirers have ranged from Oscar Wilde and Virginia Woolf to Evelyn Waugh and Edmund Wilson, to mention only distinguished literary W's. "If you knew how I had pored over your essays," confessed Woolf, "how they fill me with marvel—how I can't conceive what it would be like to write as you do!—This is sober truth." Even the bilious Waugh offered a copy of *Brideshead Revisited* to "the Master," meekly writing that "I can hardly hope you will read it, still less that you will approve any of it. I bring it like a terrier putting a dead rat on the counterpane—as an act of homage."

Max Beerbohm himself believed that he possessed only a small, if pretty, talent for writing. "Very exquisite literary artists seldom are men of genius," he once said. "Genius tends to be careless in its strength. Genius is, by the nature of it, always in rather a hurry. Genius can't be bothered about perfection." What Beerbohm possessed in place of mere genius was perfect pitch, an ability to establish a mood through a tone of voice, to convey irony or self-deprecation with the tiniest flick of a phrase: "To give an accurate and exhaustive account of that period would need a far less brilliant pen than mine."

No matter what the subject, Beerbohm could write about it with Fred Astaire–like elegance. In one wide-ranging collection of his essays (*And Even Now*), he recalls a visit to Swinburne, divides people

into natural-born "hosts" or "guests," reflects on the appeal of unfinished works of art, and imagines the archetypal Russian novelist Kol-
niyatsch ("The smile was haunting. There was a touch of old-world
courtesy in the repression of the evident impulse to spring at one's
throat"). He starts the essay "Going Out for a Walk" this way: "It is a
fact that not once in all my life have I gone out for a walk. I have been
taken out for walks; but that is another matter. Even while I trotted
prattling by my nurse's side I regretted the good old days when I had,
and wasn't, a perambulator."

Such conversational nonchalance might seem easy to bring off,
but just try it. Note, for instance, the neat rhetorical wordplay, suggesting strength held back. By instinct, Beerbohm was a caricaturist,
in prose as well as with a pencil (his drawings are as admired as his
writing), able to mimic, guy, and skewer any author's style, any eminent personage's pretentions. Consider the opening sentences of "The
Mote in the Middle Distance," the best known of the parodies gathered in *A Christmas Garland:*

> It was with the sense of a, for him, very memorable something
> that he peered now into the immediate future, and tried, not
> without compunction, to take that period up where he had,
> prospectively, left it. But just where the deuce had he left it? The
> consciousness of dubiety was, for our friend, not, this morning,
> quite yet clean-cut enough to outline the figures on what she
> had called his "horizon," between which and himself the twi-
> light was indeed of a quality somewhat intimidating.

This is perfect late Henry James—indeed, James once told an admirer that Max apprehended his style better than he did himself.
Beerbohm sustains this Old Pretender prolixity, with astonishing fa-
cility, for three more pages, as Keith and Eva, a brother and his "mag-

nificent" sister, hesitantly try to decide whether to peek into their stockings on Christmas morning.

So much skill at mimicry suggests a storyteller's flair, and Beerbohm did write his own fiction in the stories of *Seven Men* and in *Zuleika Dobson,* a slightly labored comic novel about a fin-de-siècle stunner who visits her grandfather, the warden of Judas College, and eventually causes the mass suicide of every undergraduate at Oxford. That book showcases a variety of styles from Elizabethan oratory to the sentimental effusions of a penny romance. Savor the lovely period clichés when Zuleika confesses her (alas, fleeting and unreliable) passion for the Duke of Dorset (whose family motto, *"Pas si bête,"* means "Not so stupid"):

> I thought you would most likely be rather amused, rather touched, by my importunity. I thought you would take a listless advantage, make a plaything of me—the diversion of a few idle hours in summer, and then, when you had tired of me, would cast me aside, forget me, break my heart. I desired nothing better than that. That is what I must have been vaguely hoping for.

As for "Enoch Soames" and "A.V. Laider"—the two finest stories in *Seven Men*—superlatives are inadequate. In the first, Beerbohm recalls an embittered 1890s writer—the author of *Negations* and *Fungoids*—who, one desperate afternoon, makes an ill-advised deal with the devil to travel one hundred years into the future so that he can visit the British Museum Library and look himself up in the card catalogue. Poor Soames can hardly wait to see the vast number of "editions, commentaries, prolegomenas, biographies" that will have been catalogued under his name. In the second, Beerbohm remembers a visit to a seaside hotel, where he hears seemingly tragic stories about palmistry and the strange beauty, and horror, of seagulls.

Beerbohm lived a long time, but aesthetically never advanced much beyond 1910. In that year, at age thirty-eight, he moved with his new wife, Florence, to Rapallo, Italy, and passed the rest of his years there in a small villa. He stopped writing at fifty, though he continued to make caricatures and the occasional radio broadcast. Except for the war years, when he returned to England, Beerbohm simply spent the days reading, doing crosswords, drawing pictures, and talking with old and new friends about the past.

For some lucky people—and Beerbohm knew that he was lucky—the world brings not only honors but also "a heavenly sameness of peace and happiness." It's hard not to envy such contentment. But anyone can experience a bit of it just by opening *Seven Men, And Even Now,* or any other of the incomparable Max Beerbohm's incomparable books.

JAROSLAV HAŠEK (1883–1923)
The Good Soldier Švejk

Though traditional criticism ranks epic and tragedy as the two highest forms of literature, both tend to focus on heroes, on men and women unlike any we might actually meet in life. Yes, we might share some traits with Achilles, Oedipus, or Phaedra, and we might suffer with them and thrill or weep at their fates, but, at the end of the day, they bestride the world as demigods, while we remain all too human.

Which is why comedy is the genre of the common man, of working stiffs and soccer moms, the genre that depicts life in the world as it really is. From Chaucer and Cervantes to Joyce and Proust, our greatest comic writers don't simply make us laugh, they show us what it means to be human. In short, they help us to carry on, no matter how absurd or desperate things get.

Few books convey more of the zest of living than Jaroslav Hašek's 1921 masterpiece, *The Good Soldier Švejk* (or, as it appears in its first English translation, *The Good Soldier Schweik*). This account of an apparently simple-minded Czech Everyman during World War I has never quite received the attention it deserves from English-speaking readers. Its most recent translator, Cecil Parrott, compares it to the work of Rabelais in gusto—and coarseness. The critic Bernard Levin has said that it has "only one peer in world literature, *Don Quixote*." Modern readers will certainly think of Joseph Heller's equally serio-comic *Catch-22*, to which *Svejk* seems a Slavic cousin.

Hašek's novel is a kind of narrative vaudeville show or revue, lurching from one crazy situation to the next. It opens as a newspaper headline about the assassination of Archduke Ferdinand sets off an absurdist dialogue between the doltish Svejk, a dog trainer by profession, and his landlady. In short order, a bumbling government agent arrests Svejk as a possible spy. Once in custody, the wide-eyed innocent finds himself being examined for possible insanity: Surely no one could be this stupid. But is Svejk really quite as dull-witted as he seems? When he tires of the medical questions, the dog trainer turns on the psychologists:

> Now I'll ask you a riddle, gentlemen. There's a three-storied house with eight windows on each story. On the roof there are two gables and two chimneys. There are two tenants on each story. And now, gentlemen, I want you to tell me in what year the house porter's grandmother died?

Ejected from the lunatic asylum, Svejk decides to join the army, but for complicated reasons he needs to go to the recruitment station on crutches. "Fortunately the confectioner had . . . kept a pair of crutches as a family keepsake to remember his grandfather by." Following some misadventures with draftees who deliberately feign

insanity or mutilate themselves to avoid the army, our hero ends up
in a detention barracks. A special branch of these barracks, we are
told, "comprised the political prisoners, eighty percent of whom were
quite innocent and ninety-nine percent of whom were condemned."
Hašek adds that to make sure that these last percentages are maintained, "there was a magnificent legal staff, a mechanism such as is
possessed by every state before its political, economic and moral
collapse."

Before long, however, Svejk has been appointed aide-de-camp to
an army chaplain, Jewish by birth and a drunkard by conviction.
Hašek's attacks on militarism and Christianity grow increasingly vit-
riolic: "Preparations for the slaughter of human beings have always
been made in the name of God or of some alleged higher being which
mankind has, in its imaginativeness, devised and created." Every time
a Catholic priest comforts a condemned man, says Hašek, he carries
a crucifix, "as if to say: 'You're only having your head chopped off,
you're only being hanged, you're only being strangled, you're only
having 15,000 volts shoved into you, but don't forget what He had to
go through.'"

Hašek can often be deliciously crude and heavy-handed in his
humor, but he can also manage learned pastiche of philosophy and
best-seller fiction. Some of the men are sitting around getting drunk.
One is a soldier named Jurajda who used to edit an occultist period-
ical and a series of books entitled *Secrets of Life and Death*. He speaks
with alcoholic authority to a staff sergeant:

> My friend . . . all phenomena, all shapes, all objects possess dis-
> embodied qualities. Shape is disembodiment and disembodi-
> ment is shape. There is no distinction between disembodiment
> and shape; there is no distinction between shape and disembod-
> iment. What is disembodiment, is shape, and what is shape, is
> disembodiment . . .

Meanwhile, the staff sergeant—a poetic soul—is babbling away like the third-person narrator of a sentimental novel:

The corn vanished from the fields. Vanished. Such was his mood when he received her invitation and went to call on her. The Whitsun holidays come in the spring.

The next day some of these same men rush to an important strategy meeting, mainly because "Colonel Schroder was prompted by his great desire to hear himself orate." When the men assemble, the colonel turns to his war map, which has suffered some unexpected depredations:

The whole of the war areas had been scandalously disarranged in the night by a tomcat, the pet of the military clerks in the regimental office. This animal, after having relieved himself all over the Austro-Hungarian areas, had made attempts to bury the resulting mess and had dragged the little flags from their places and smeared the mess over the positions; whereupon he had wetted on the battle fronts and bridgehead, and soiled all the army corps.

So much for strategy. As these pathetic troops (one is tempted to think of them as troupes) are preparing to head into battle, a new chaplain delivers "an impassioned address, containing material which he had obviously derived from military calendars." Finally en route to the front, all the officers are solemnly allocated copies of *The Sins of the Fathers,* by Ludwig Ganghofer, to use in sending coded messages; there are elaborate instructions on how to indicate certain pages and words in the text for these secret communications. Unfortunately, Ganghofer's novel turns out to have been published in two volumes, and headquarters possesses volume one, while the field officers are carrying volume two.

Jaroslav Hašek never lived to complete his projected six-part novel about a Czech Candide in the Great War. What we possess is nonetheless a comic masterpiece. There are two English translations: The one quoted here is by Paul Selver from 1930; Cecil Parrott's fuller and more scholarly version appeared in 1973. Both have their merits. What matters, of course, is to read Hašeks' novel, which never really ends: "When he got tired of singing, Svejk sat down on a pile of gravel, lit his pipe and after having a rest, trudged on, toward new adventures."

IVY COMPTON-BURNETT (1884–1969)
Brothers and Sisters; Manservant and Maidservant
(a.k.a. *Bullivant and the Lambs*); other novels

Ivy Compton-Burnett has never been a household name in America, but for many readers she stands among the purest novelists of the century, her hallmarks being concision, a highly stylized formality, and an unconventional, subtle wit. Her twenty novels are often described as "unique" or "sui generis"—and they are.

The titles of Compton-Burnett's books suggest both her brisk characterization and her obsession with the politics of family life: *Brothers and Sisters, Daughters and Sons, Parents and Children, A House and Its Head, A Father and His Fate.* Almost all of them are set at largeish country houses in what appears to be late Victorian or Edwardian England. Could anything be more genteel?

But Compton-Burnett's plots concentrate on seduction, murder, incest, bastard children, secret wills, and all the horrors of Greek tragedy and Gothic fiction. What shocks some readers—and delights most—is that these horrors are treated with absolute unflappability, in a tone at once cool, skeptical, and a bit campy. In *Darkness and*

Day, for example, Bridget Lovat causes her mother's death and apparently marries her own father. She is as nearly like Oedipus as a woman can be, the only difference being, in the words of one character, that "she has not put out her eyes." "Perhaps fashions have changed," observes another. Besides, actually putting out one's eyes "would make it very public."

It's little wonder that Compton-Burnett should choose dysfunctional families as the focus for her fiction and surgical wit. Her father produced twelve children by two different wives. Ivy's mother sent all her stepchildren away to boarding school as soon as possible. Guy and Noel, Ivy's adored brothers, both died young, the second in battle during World War I. Two sisters committed suicide in what looked like a lover's pact. Not one of the twelve siblings ever had children, and all eight of the girls remained unmarried. One even became a religious fanatic, Ivy icily observing that "people who believe in the resurrection will believe in anything." Hardly your normal English family.

Ivy Compton-Burnett spent much of her own life as the companion of Margaret Jourdain, England's leading authority on furniture and the decorative arts. For the first ten years of their relationship, Compton-Burnett was an unobtrusive figure in the background, a kind of middle-aged governess always dressed severely in black, quietly pouring tea for museum curators and fashion experts. But in 1925 *Pastors and Masters* appeared—much to the surprise of Jourdain, who claimed to have been unaware that her close friend was writing a novel. In 1929, a second novel—*Brothers and Sisters*—was widely acclaimed the book of the year. Imagine a mix of Oscar Wilde, Wilkie Collins, and Sophocles, or think of a gloomy P. G. Wodehouse.

Eighteen more novels followed at two-year intervals, and in all of them, intelligence shines forth as "the hightest moral principle," just as "relief is the keenest form of joy." Household tyrants manipulate other family members and tragedy unfailingly strikes. There is usually more dialogue than description, with every sentence precise and many epigrammatic: Pessimism, according to a butler, "adds a touch of darkness to the grayness of life." Generally speaking, the Compton-Burnett novel is a stage traversed by the worn-out, the keenly observant, and the disillusioned. ("We have seen some real life, Roberta, a thing I have always wanted to see. But now I don't want to see any more as long as I live.") Servants talk as punctiliously as their masters, and are often even more formidable.

Compton-Burnett claimed that "there are far too many books about sex and far too few about money." Her own characters, despite their marital and domestic improprieties, are largely obsessed with cash and acquiring more of it. "Much that I ought not to have done, I would do again"—greed and treachery included—says the domestic tyrant of *Darkness and Day*. Without disguise, the strong prey on the weak with a ferocious energy. Evil generally goes unpunished, and is often rewarded.

One needs to read Compton-Burnett's pages attentively to pick up the oddly stilted rhythms of the conversation and the nuances that make any of her sentences as pointed as a needle. In *Manservant and Maidservant,* she writes: "Horace was standing in the hall with his cousin and aunt, visualising the situation of waiting for his children, and alert for the moment when a minute's delay should rise to it." Later, Horace looks in on his little boy, whom he recently chastised with undue but typical severity: "Sarah was seated on Avery's bed, reading from the Book of Job, not from any sense of fitness, but because it was her brother's choice. He lay with a convalescent air, his face responding as the words confirmed his memory."

Alongside this kind of pervasive yet subtle humor, Compton-Burnett sharpens her dialogue into a series of steely observations of which any seventeenth-century moralist would be proud: "To know all is to forgive all, and that would spoil everything." "My service is of a kind that cannot be paid for in money. And that means it is paid for in that way, but not very well." In the end, though, this strange novelist's distinctive, highly astringent flavor can't be conveyed by a taste here and there. Read one of her books slowly—either *Brothers and Sisters* or *Manservant and Maidservant* is a good first choice—to see how addictive and satisfying she can be. Ivy Compton-Burnett casts modern fiction's coldest eye on the meanness, hypocrisy, and cruelties of family life. Her diamond-sharp wit spares no one: At the beginning of *The Present and the Past*, a group of children watch a sick chicken being pecked to death.

⇒•◦•⇐

S. J. PERELMAN (1904–1979)
The Most of S. J. Perelman

S. J. Perelman's comic writing has been growing more and more dated as the decades roll by. A writer's worst fear? Not in this case. Just as the Sherlock Holmes stories evoke a gaslit London of fog and hansom cabs, so Perelman's humor, laced as it is with allusions to contemporary magazines, old slang, and forgotten film stars and restaurants, carries the reader right back to the innocent, flamboyant side of the 1930s. Perelman's snappy, quip-filled style feels as much a part of the period as Cole Porter and mah-jongg.

That style, of course, is the writer's glory. Perelman co-wrote a couple of the Marx Brothers films, and much of Groucho's comic manner—fast-talking delivery, Dadaist leaps in logic, leering innuendo—can be found in the breathless pages of Perelman's prose: "Alaunia Alaunova dropped a small curtsy. The young man, a pitying expression on his face, picked it up and quickly returned it to her." "I was living in my own country retreat at the time, and as it happened to be my day to go to the post office (ordinarily the post office comes to me), I welcomed this chance to vary the monotony. Piling my head high with diamond roses and ribbons, I pulled on a pair of my stoutest espadrilles and set off, my cat frisking ahead of me with many a warning cry of 'Here comes my master, the Marquis of Carabas.'. . . ."

An ability to parody anything from romance novels to international thrillers to socialist dramas, a quicksilver syntax and breathless narrative pace, diction in which Hollywood argot, Yiddish, and the rarer words in a good thesaurus brazenly co-habit, and sentences that follow the vertiginous logic of their grammar right into Wonderland—these are the chief elements of Perelman's surreal pages.

Sometimes the writer's humor is almost insanely bizarre. Take the scene in "Strictly from Hunger" in which Perelman—visiting Hollywood for the first time—observes an entire film crew about to commit suttee and immolate itself with a disgraced producer on a pyre of film and movie scripts: "Only the scenario writers are exempt. These are tied between the tails of two spirited Caucasian ponies, which are then driven off in opposite directions." When the moment for his leap into the flames finally arrives, the producer turns to the crowd and "with bowed head . . . made a simple invocation couched in one-syllable words so that even the executives might understand." Happily, he is saved from instant destruction by the arrival of a noted critic, dressed in a Confederate uniform, who apologizes for the negative review: "Ah reckon it was an unworthy slur, suh."

But Perelman is just warming up. Immediately after this, he and his hostess, Violet Hush, are snuggled together in a limousine, cruising through Los Angeles. "Soon we would be in Beverly Hills, and already the quaint native women were swarming alongside in their punts urging us to buy their cunning beadwork and mangoes." As it happens, Perelman's arrival in Hollywood has thrown "international financial centers into an uproar." In fact, "an ugly rumor that I might reorganize the motion picture industry was being bruited about in the world's commodity markets. My brokers, Whitelipped and Trembling, were beside themselves. The New York Stock Exchange was begging them for assurances of stability and Threadneedle Street awaited my next move with drumming pulses. Film shares ricocheted sharply, although wools and meats were sluggish, if not downright sullen."

Perelman then visits a movie set: "Thousands of scantily draped but none the less appetizing extra girls milled past me, their mouths a scarlet wound and their eyes clearly defined in their faces." All too soon, as "a nameless fear clutched at my heart," he is ushered into the waiting room of his future supervisor. He waits for what seems hours. Finally, "my serial number was called, the leg-irons were struck off, and I was shoved through a door into the presence of Diana ffrench-Mamoulian." Let him describe what happens next:

> Diana ffrench-Mamoulian was accustomed to having her way with writers, and my long lashes and peachblow mouth seemed to whip her to insensate desire.

He tries to keep her focused, pleading that he was "engaged to a Tri Kappa at Goucher." To no avail:

> "Just one kiss," she pleaded, her breath hot against my neck. In desperation I granted her boon, knowing full well that my weak defenses were crumbling before the onslaught of this love tigree.

That night he goes to Diana's penthouse for dinner:

> "Have a bit of the wing, darling?" queried Diana solicitously, indicating the roast Long Island airplane with applesauce . . . Our meal finished, we sauntered into the rumpus room and Diana turned on the radio. With a savage snarl the radio turned on her.

Much more happens in the eight pages of "Strictly from Hunger," which somehow concludes with Perelman and a little seamstress named Blanche Almonds in a sleigh skimming over the hard crust of the Russian snow toward Port Arthur and freedom.

Though Perelman never really lets the reader catch a breath, some of his pieces are quieter than others. Many fans particularly relish his series "Cloudland Revisited," in which he rereads favorite books of his childhood or watches the old movies he loved while growing up. These are at once affectionate and hilarious, usually mirroring the style of the chosen book or film. "Tuberoses and Tigers," for example, pays homage to Elinor Glyn's once-scandalous novel *Three Weeks*. Back in the summer of 1919, we learn, a certain unnamed fifteen-year-old was blasted by this account of a searing love affair:

> His behavior during that period, while courteous and irreproachable to family and friends alike, was marked by fits of abstraction and a tendency to emit tragic, heartbroken sighs. When asked to sweep up the piazza, for instance, or bike over to the hardware store for a sheet of Tanglefoot, a shadow of pain would flit across his sensitive features and he would assent with a weary shrug. "Why not?" he would murmur, his lips curling in a bitter, mocking smile. "What else can life hold for me now?"

Of the great American comic essayists, only Robert Benchley and James Thurber rival the dazzling Perelman. You can feel his influence on Woody Allen, *The Simpsons,* Dave Barry, and Garrison Keillor. But Perelman remains the master, the nonpareil:

> How about a spot of whisky and soda?" We entered and Littjohn, Snubbers' man, brought in a spot of whisky on a piece of paper which we all examined with interest . . .

———◆◦◆———

ITALO CALVINO (1923–1985)
Invisible Cities; The Castle of Crossed Destinies;
If on a winter's night a traveler

Throughout his writing, Italo Calvino speaks often of the literary qualities he most admires: "lightness, narrative impetus, and energy." He himself repeatedly sought fresh narrative challenges, then explored and exhausted each of them—or himself. In the opening pages of *If on a winter's night a traveler*, Calvino even goes inside the head of his reader:

> You prepare to recognize the unmistakeable tone of the author. No. You don't recognize it at all. But now that you think about it, who ever said that this author had an unmistakable tone? On the contrary, he is known as an author who changes greatly from one book to the next. And that in these very changes you recognize him as himself.

Being both prolific and uncategorizable, Italy's greatest mid-century author produced fairly realistic novels (*The Path to the Nest of the Spiders*), metaphysical fantasies (*The Baron in the Trees*), science fiction (*Cosmicomics*), prose poems (*Invisible Cities*), highly structured tours de force (*The Castle of Crossed Destinies*), memoirs of childhood, an edition of Italian folk tales, and dozens of short stories, many of them more or less fantastic. When reaching for comparisons, critics speak of Jorge Luis Borges, Vladimir Nabokov, and Raymond Queneau as the contemporaries Calvino most resembles. To all of them writing is, at least in part, a kind of game, and they are as fascinated by the process of storytelling as by the story itself.

What redeems such an approach from dryness or dullness is a

writer's sense of play. Calvino, in particular, is the most amiable and sunny of authors, his work—in the romantic description of Pietro Citati—"all tissue paper and soft lights." Nothing ever goes on too long. "Keep it short," he says, and thus he often builds up quite complicated structures out of brief texts, brought together through a series of "combinations, permutations and transformations."

In *The Castle of Crossed Destinies* a group of travelers, rendered mysteriously mute, use tarot cards to relate their past adventures. Ostensibly, Calvino's written text simply interprets or elaborates on the meaning of each card. So we discover in these painted images of knights and ladies, of fountains and hanged men, a dozen tales of romance and mystery that would enchant us on their own. Yet here the artist in Calvino challenges himself even further. The various stories soon start to crisscross, all of them being, in some sense, part of the others.

As Calvino remarks in one of his essays on storytelling, "Each life is an encyclopedia, a library, an inventory of objects, a series of styles, and everybody can be constantly shuffled and reordered in every way conceivable." Yet art, of course, is a matter of order and design, less concerned with the elements than with their particular conjunctions. Of *The Castle of Crossed Destinies,* the author tells us in an afterword: "I felt that the game had a meaning only if governed by ironclad rules; an established framework of construction was required, conditioning the insertion of one story in the others. Without it, the whole thing was gratuitous."

In what many regard as his masterpiece, Calvino enlarged his theoretical perspective to embrace more than just the artful processes of writing: *If on a winter's night a traveler* is an enthralling meditation on the nature of reading, but is also funny, sexy, and deliciously frustrating. In it, you—the reader—go to a shop to buy the latest novel by Italo Calvino. Of course, you come home with *If on a winter's night a traveler* and open to the first chapter. In it a man known only as "I" stops at a provincial train station, observes the locals hanging out at the railway bar, flirts a little with a doctor's divorced wife, and then is mysteriously ordered to board the next express train out of town. At this point, you discover that your copy of the novel is defective—there is no more of the story, only the first chapter repeated again and again.

With considerable irritation, you return to the bookstore for an intact copy of Calvino's latest, and discover that the chapter you have started to enjoy is actually from *Outside the town of Malbork* by Tazio Bazakbal. The publisher accidentally bound up its first section in the boards of the Calvino. As you are now caught up in the Bazakbal novel, you return home with it and begin reading again. It turns out to be quite different from what you had expected and may not be *Outside the town of Malbork* at all. . . . What to do? Fortunately, at the bookstore, you had met a similarly frustrated reader named Ludmilla, and you phone her up to see if her copy of the novel differs from yours. It goes without saying that you are also strongly attracted to Ludmilla . . .

As *If on a winter's night a traveler* continues, Calvino offers us one-chapter parodies of eastern European novels, erotic fiction, and magic realism. In between these chapters—all of which break off at cliff-hanger moments, like old-time serials—you discover that the boundaries between the real and the read seem to be breaking down. The relationship with Ludmilla intensifies: "What makes lovemaking and reading resemble each other most is that within both of them times and spaces open, different from measurable time and space."

Of Calvino's major works, perhaps the most austerely beautiful is *Invisible Cities*. In it, Marco Polo describes to Kublai Khan the elegant and magical places of his realm. The result is a "carousel of fantasies," of one haunting city after another, since the "catalogue of forms is endless: until every shape has found its city, new cities will continue to be born." The prose here is appropriately dreamlike, incantatory, a shifting play of memory, desire, and illusion.

The city of Armilla, for instance, consists solely of pipes and plumbing; there are no walls, and its only inhabitants are beautiful naiads who arch their backs under its showers or luxuriate in its baths. To the traveler approaching Despina from the desert, its roofs and chimneys call to mind a ship ready to cast off for an ocean voyage; to a sailor entering its harbor Despina resembles a camel "from whose pack hang wineskins and bags of candied fruit, date wine, tobacco leaves and already he [the sailor] sees himself at the head of a long caravan taking him away from the desert of the sea, toward oases of fresh water in the palm trees' jagged shade, toward palaces of thick, white-washed walls, tiled courts where girls are dancing barefoot, moving their arms, half-hidden by their veils, and half-revealed."

At one point in *If on a winter's night a traveler,* Ludmilla says, "The novel I would most like to read at this moment should have as its driving force only the desire to narrate, to pile stories upon stories, without trying to impose a philosophy of life on you, simply allowing you to observe its own growth, like a tree, an entangling, as if of branches and leaves. . . ." Little wonder that Calvino's playful fiction so often seems to be pointing the way toward computer hypertext and the new ways of storytelling awaiting us in the twenty-first century.

EDWARD GOREY (1925–2000)
Amphigorey; Amphigorey Too;
Amphigorey Also; Amphigorey Again

"Beware of this and that," warns a droopy raven in *The Epileptic Bicycle.* Beware, indeed. To open one of Edward Gorey's little albums is to cross into a turn-of-the-century twilight zone, a faded black-and-gray realm where bats—or possibly umbrellas—swoop above the shrubbery, buildings appear as attractive and sturdily built as the

House of Usher, and everything feels autumnal, crepuscular, rain-swept, and more than a little menacing.

In Gorey country, ancestral manors and stately homes are usually inhabited by languid, swooning flappers and mustachioed Edwardian gentlemen with a taste for brocaded dressing gowns or ankle-length fur coats. The decor runs to divans, large urns, gazebos, and allegorical garden sculpture, such as the oft-admired "statue of Corrupted Endeavor." Down lonely hallways one may, from time to time, glimpse a newtlike beast or a poltergeist, or possibly a dogged policeman on the trail of a vampire. For the most part, everyone strikes poses, like the more histrionic characters in one of the gloomier plays of Chekhov.

To describe the contents—plot is usually too grand a word—of Gorey's many illustrated novelettes is to make them sound utterly grim or kitsch, when they actually balance the elusive whimsy of children's nonsense (as in the works of Lewis Carroll or Edward Lear) with the discreet charm of black comedy. Their "feel" is roughly that of the classic British film *Kind Hearts and Coronets,* in which a nice young man intent on acquiring a title and an estate blithely murders eight relatives, all played by Alec Guinness.

In this macabre spirit, Gorey has produced albums devoted to, and titled, *Neglected Murderesses* and *The Deranged Cousins.* Poor Millicent Frastley ends up a sacrifice to *The Insect God,* while *The Loathesome Couple* traces the sanguinary career of a very disturbed pair who meet at "a Self-Help Institute Lecture on the Evils of the Decimal System." In *The Blue Aspic,* an opera fan goes insane and murders rivals and admirers of his favorite diva. For *The Hapless Child* Gorey throws in every possible juvenile misfortune: An Edwardian girl is unexpectedly orphaned (or so she thinks), sold to a drunken lout, forced to make paper flowers until she loses her eyesight, and finally run over in the street by her own father, who doesn't recognize her. The book incorporates elements from Shirley Temple tearjerkers, half the corpus of Victorian melodrama, and scores of silent-film weepies.

While everyone speaks admiringly of Gorey's meticulous cross-hatching and melodramatic, gothicky vision, not enough praise has been awarded to the artist's superb prose. Gorey possesses the ear of a great parodist, and virtually all his little albums offer pastiches of some previous literary genre or book: the classic mystery (*The Awdrey-Gore Legacy*), turn-of-the-century melodrama (*The Green Beads*), Winnie-the-Pooh (*The Untitled Book*). During a fairly reclusive life, Gorey read and reread his favorite authors, including Jane Austen, Murasaki Shikibu (author of *The Tale of Genji*), Anthony Trollope, Agatha Christie, E. F. Benson (the deliciously comic Lucia cycle), Ronald Firbank, and William Roughead. Nearly all these figures consequently inspired a book or two. As Gorey once said, he tended to regard his works "as Victorian novels all scrunched up."

In their tonal quality, Gorey's deadpan sentences owe much to the laconic campiness of Ronald Firbank and the affectless dialogue and imperturbable voice of Ivy Compton-Burnett. ("Harold Snedleigh was found beating a sick small animal to death with a rock when he was five years old.") His best captions possess a prissy, costive archness, at once ironic and affectionate. In *The Broken Spoke* he presents "cycling cards" from the turn of the last century, with preposterous period-style descriptions: "Innocence, on the Bicycle of Propriety, carrying the Urn of Reputation safely over the Abyss of Indiscretion."

Gorey himself shows admirable discretion in *The Curious Sofa*, his version of elegant French pornography and, to his mind, "the cleverest book I ever did." Sexual naughtiness of all sorts is conveyed solely through genteel euphemism: "Alice, quite exhausted, was helped to bed by Lady Celia's French maid, Lise, whom she found delightfully sympathetic." With similar disingenuousness, *The Gashlycrumb Tinies* presents a child's alphabet, each letter memorializing one little boy or girl after another: "A is for Amy who fell down the stairs"; "B is for Basil, assaulted by bears."

Some of Gorey's best prose can be savored in his very first master-piece, *The Unstrung Harp* (1953), a portrait of a writer working on a novel of the same name:

> Mr. Earbrass has been rashly skimming through the early chap-ters, which he has not looked at for months, and now sees TUH [*The Unstrung Harp*] for what it is. Dreadful, dreadful, DREADFUL. He must be mad to go on enduring the unex-quisite agony of writing when it all turns out drivel. Mad. Why didn't he become a spy? How does one become one? He will burn the MS. . . .

Later on, Earbrass attends an author's party:

> The talk deals with disappointing sales, inadequate publicity, worse than inadequate royalties, idiotic or criminal reviews, oth-ers' declining talent, and the unspeakable horror of the literary life.

Edward Gorey's work—much of it collected in *Amphigorey* and its companion volumes—looks back to the collage-novels of surreal-ist Max Ernst (*The Hundred Headless Woman*) and the whimsically captioned steel engravings of E. V. Lucas and George Morrow's proto-dadaist classic *What a Life!* In his mixture of words and pictures he also anticipates more contemporary phenomena such as Japanese manga comics, the cartoons of Garry Larson's "Far Side" and Garry Trudeau's "Doonesbury," the graphic novel, and many forms of com-puterized storytelling. Gorey, however, possesses a distinctive vision that is nobody's but his own. Through his genius and industry, he cre-ated a whole climate of the imagination—humorous and decorously macabre—that we now simply describe as Goreyesque.

Heroes of Their Time

Poets may sigh and preachers may exhort, but when the barbarians are at the gates or when the Dark Lord's armies are massed on the plain before Helm's Deep, the world still turns to warriors with a strong right arm. As the medievalist W. P. Ker once said, an epic is usually "the defense of a narrow place against odds."

What matters more than mere victory is to go down fighting. We remember the three hundred Spartans at Thermopylae because they died to the last man, steadfastly true to their code of honor. Little wonder, then, that our tales of Greek champions and northern dragon-slayers are nearly always suffused with melancholy and a sense of impending doom. No victories are final, and the enemy will soon be back. Moreover, the heroic world always seems on the wane, a mighty age of iron about to be succeeded by a diminished age of brass or tin. Yet somehow heroes—sometimes very unexpected heroes—still rise up to match our daydreams. The downtrodden will turn on their oppressors; the most wretched of the earth will refuse to give in or give up.

In this category the heroes range from a slayer of monsters to striking coal miners, from Persia's greatest champion to the dirt-poor families of Depression-era Alabama. These are men— and women—who have looked hard at life and found that there wasn't much to smile about, but still went out and faced their destinies with courage and determination.

BEOWULF (eighth century)

In a properly ordered world, all children would be regaled from an early age with fairy tales, Greek myths, Bible stories, the epics of Troy and Rome, the romances of Arthur, and the sagas of the north. Nearly all these poems and legends provide instances of the great medieval ideal: the hero who blends *sapientia* and *fortitudo,* wisdom and fortitude.

Perhaps no early epic warrior better exemplifies these paired virtues than Beowulf, who travels across the sea to combat Grendel, the nightmare monster that emerges from a pestilent pool to spread horror and violent death. Grendel is driven to murder for a surprisingly poetic reason: He can't bear the sound of the feasting and revelry at King Heorot's hall. Being a creature of darkness—a "shadow-walker"—he hates the world of light and all that it implies of humane order, civility, and goodness. As this suggests, this sole surviving Anglo-Saxon epic is a poem of contrasts—of youth and age, good and evil, the warmth and security of kingly halls and the cold, desolate wildness of the natural world outside.

The plot of *Beowulf* is surprisingly intricate, an interlacing of history and myth, Christian faith and pagan fatality. Though the surviving manuscript dates from the eighth century, the poem's action is set two hundred years earlier, during the chaotic period when Germanic tribes roamed northern Europe. Beowulf himself might even be based on an actual person, despite the folkloric name suggestive of brawny strength (Bee-wolf, i.e., Bear). His own lord, Hygelac, is actually mentioned in Gregory of Tours's *History of the Franks.*

In essence, we have two complementary themes: the portrait of a model hero in youth and age, coupled with a meditation on the sad destinies of nations. To repay an old debt incurred by his father, Beowulf journeys from Denmark to what is now southern Sweden to help the elderly king of the Geats. For twelve years Hrothgar and his thanes have suffered nightly depredations by the ravenous Grendel. This diabolic, humanoid beast—there are hints that Satan might be his father—boldly enters Heorot, the king's hall, and seizes sleeping warriors, whom he tears limb from limb and devours. No one seems able to stop this monstrous killing machine. Our young hero, however, posssesses the epic strength of thirty men, and he is eager to prove his prowess and valor. He doesn't have long to wait. *"Com on wanre niht/scrithan sceadugenga"*—through the black night came gliding the shadow-walker. There follows a thrilling scene of hand-to-hand combat, ending when Beowulf rips one of Grendel's arms from his shoulder, and the beast drags itself off to die in the outer dark.

Alas, on the evening following this bloody triumph, Grendel's vengeful and far more powerful mother attacks Heorot, compelling Beowulf to follow her spoor into a shadowy, unearthly realm. The Gothicky passage evoking the wasteland abutting the "mere" or lake inhabited by these devilish creatures is one of the most famous set pieces in Old English poetry. The poet depicts a realm of ghosts and demons, of windswept crags, dark cliffs, and bare trees hung with frost. The lake itself looks fetid and poisonous; at night unearthly fire burns on its surface. Animals, pursued by hunters, prefer to die at its edge rather than to save their lives by plunging into its dreaded waters. Yet Beowulf dives into the deadly lake and swims downward for nearly a day until he at last reaches an underground lair. There he is attacked by sea monsters, then by "Grendel's dam" herself, and his weapons fall away useless. The indomitable warrior, casting his eye about the monster's submerged plunder, haply spies an ancient sword, one forged during the days of the giants. He plunges it into the monster, then cuts off her head, even as her blood melts the iron of the blade.

Most readers will readily enjoy the first two-thirds of *Beowulf,* while welcoming editorial notes that explain the apparent "digressions" about the fate of various princes, doughty warriors, and disloyal liegemen. All this backstory helps to set the poem firmly in its bleak Teutonic landscape, where a man's family, tribe, and king define who he is and what is expected of him. That weighty burden of the heroic past, of history bearing down like a doom, grants to epic its grave and august power, whether we read of windy Troy or Middle Earth.

However, the last third of *Beowulf* can feel slightly thin, a bit of a letdown. After his triumphs as a youth, Beowulf eventually becomes king of the Danes, and fifty years pass. Then the land begins to be ravaged by a dragon, and the old warrior, like an aging gunfighter, straps on his sword one last time. He succeeds in killing this third monster but is himself mortally wounded, and his passing signals the twilight of the Danes. This elegiac close will recall the tone of other somberly majestic Old English poems, especially "The Wanderer," "The Seafarer," and "The Battle of Maldon": "Fate goes ever as fate must."

Most of us read *Beowulf* in translation, for its Old English is notoriously difficult even for graduate students in medieval studies. (The recent version by poet Seamus Heaney is quite thrilling, while that by Michael Alexander, in prose, achieves greater exactness and fidelity.) For a long time, many people dismissed *Beowulf* as more linguistic monument than living artwork. J. R. R. Tolkien, in his essay "The Monster and the Critics," properly chastises those who regard the poem as "small beer." If *Beowulf* is beer, he says combatively, it is in fact "a drink dark and bitter; a solemn funeral-ale with the taste of death."

Tolkien also stresses that the poem's somber power resides in the very compactness of its Anglo-Saxon diction: "Therein lies the unrecapturable magic of ancient English verse for those who have ears to hear: profound feeling, and poignant vision, filled with the beauty and mortality of the world, are aroused by brief phrases, light touches, short words resounding like harp-strings sharply plucked."

How else but in such bleakly beautiful poetry should we sing of warriors and heroes?

ABOLQASEM FERDOWSI (940?–1020)
Shahnameh: The Persian Book of Kings

The *Shahnameh* is the great epic of ancient Persia, opening with the creation of the universe and closing with the Arab conquest of the worn-out empire in the seventh century A.D. In its pages, the eleventh-century poet Ferdowsi chronicles the reigns of a hundred kings, the exploits of dozens of epic heroes, and the seemingly never-ending conflict between early Iran and its traditional enemy, the country here called Turan (roughly what is now eastern Iran and parts of Afghanistan). To imagine an equivalent to this violent and beautiful work, which is especially impressive in Dick Davis's recent translation, think of an amalgam of Homer's *Iliad* and the ferocious Old Testament book of Judges.

Even these grand comparisons don't do the poem justice. Embedded in the *Shahnameh* are love stories, like that of Zal and Rubadeh, which recall the heartsick yearnings of Provençal troubadours and their ladies; tragedies of mistaken identity, hubris, and incompatible moral obligations that might have attracted Sophocles; and meditations on the brevity of earthly existence that sound like Ecclesiastes: "Our lives pass from us like the wind." Though ostensibly historical, the poem brims with myths and legends, accounts of miraculous births and herculean labors, tales of fairies and demons and enchanted arrows and terrible curses, descriptions of richly caparisoned battle elephants, and giant birds straight out of the Arabian Nights. Little wonder that artists have often taken its stories as the inspiration for those manuscript illuminations we call Persian miniatures.

Many of the episodes of the *Shahnameh* clearly draw on the same teeming ocean of story that was known to Western poets and myth-makers. Consider old King Feraydun's Lear-like division of greater Persia into three realms, one for each of his sons, with bloody

centuries-long consequences; the awesome warrior Rostam's seven
great trials; the almost Biblical blinding of Kay Kavus's army by the
White Demon; a heroic father who unknowingly meets his own
valiant son on the field of battle (English majors will remember this
as the subject of Matthew Arnold's poem "Sohrab and Rustum"); Kay
Khosrow's Buddha-like renunciation of the throne and his Christ-like
ascension into heaven surrounded by his disciples. There's even that
misogynistic favorite about the high-ranking older woman (think of
Potiphar's wife or Racine's Phaedra) who lusts after her stepson:

> Now when the king's wife, Sudabeh, saw Seyavash, she grew
> strangely pensive and her heart beat faster; she began to waste
> away like ice before fire, worn thin as a silken thread. . . .

Like Racine, Ferdowsi makes us feel the aging Sudabeh's anguish:

> "But look at me now," she implores Seyavash. "What excuse can
> you have to reject my love, why do you turn away from my body
> and beauty? I have been your slave ever since I set eyes on you,
> weeping and longing for you; pain darkens all my days, I feel the
> sun itself is dimmed. Come, in secret, just once, make me happy
> again, give me back my youth for a moment. . . ."

The story of Seyavash provides a study in conflicting loyalties,
like so many of the chapters in the *Shahnameh*. The blood relations
between Iran and Turan are intricate, as many of the major characters
can trace their lineage back to Feraydun, and there is occasional in-
termarriage even between traditional enemies. In fact, the most common theme is that of fathers and sons—usually kings who don't want
to relinquish power and young men who want to prove they deserve
it. Aging Goshtasp can't bear to give up his kingship, even to his own
son, so he sends the brave young warrior on an impossible mission:

bring the proud and invincible Rostam back to the court in chains. There's no good reason for this order, as that hero has long been a champion of one unworthy Iranian sovereign after another. But Esfandyar owes loyal obedience to his father and king, even as he recognizes the injustice, indeed the senselessness, of the command. Worse yet, Rostam admires the young man and urges every possible escape clause, finally even agreeing to return to the Persian court with Esfandyar. But not in chains, for he has vowed never to be bound. In the end two admirable people, trapped by mutually opposing vows, must reluctantly meet in armed combat to the death.

The gigantic Rostam is a recurrent figure throughout the first half of the *Shahnameh.* He lives for five hundred years, swings his mace like mighty Thor, and is usually called upon when the situation grows truly desperate. When young, Rostam searched for a horse that could support his mammoth size and weight. He finally found Rakhsh, as famous in Persian lore as Bellerophon in Greek mythology. What, he asks, is the cost of this dragon-like animal? The herdsman replies, "If you are Rostam, then mount him and defend the land of Iran. The price of this horse is Iran itself, and mounted on his back you will be the world's savior."

There's much more to the *Shahnameh* than these few highlights. Because the poem's geography is largely Persia's eastern empire, Ferdowsi makes no mention of Darius or Xerxes, those enemies of the Greeks. Instead we learn about Bahram Gur, who enjoyed hunting with cheetahs, once killed a rhinoceros single-handed, and eventually defeated the armies of the emperor of China.

As most long poems gradually fall prey to a certain repetitiousness, the wise reader will parcel out the *Shahnameh* over time. The epic scale of the book should not, however, overshadow its memorable smaller moments, or even some of its single sentences. One beautiful woman's mouth is described as "small, like the contracted heart of a desperate man." A witch appears to Rostam, "full of scents and tints." A king's three daughters, "as lovely as the gardens of paradise, were brought before him, and he bestowed jewelry and crowns on them that were so heavy that they were a torment to wear."

Like Ovid's *Metamorphoses,* Horace's *Odes,* and one of Shakespeare's most famous sonnets (No. 55—"Not marble, nor the gilded monuments of princes/ Shall outlive this powerful rhyme"), this great epic ends with its author proclaiming that his poetry will bring him immortality:

> *I shall not die; these seeds I've sown will save*
> *My name and reputation from the grave,*
> *And men of sense and wisdom will proclaim,*
> *When I have gone, my praises and my fame.*

—————

THE ICELANDIC SAGAS (twelfth to fifteenth centuries)
Njal Saga; Laxdaela Saga; Grettir Saga; Egil Saga

Why aren't the Icelandic "family" sagas better known and more widely read? They are written in a clean, straightforward prose, without obvious poetic flourishes or tedious allegorizings. They sound so laconic and unemotional you might imagine they were set down by a thirteenth-century Hemingway. (We don't, in fact, know very much about their authors.) For the most part, the sagas describe events that took place between 700 and 1000 A.D. when Iceland finally converted to Christianity. Thematically they mix history and romance, with touches of folkore and myth, while structurally they nearly all deal with the bloody workings-out of insults or jealousies that lead to feuds that lead to quiet hatred, then to revenge and usually murder. After which the process continues, sometimes through the generations. The Icelanders may have given us the Althing—the earliest known "parliament"—but the law they truly believed in was the *Lex talionis,* the biblical eye for an eye. Think of the sagas as Mafia crime dramas, or spaghetti westerns on ice.

They usually open in the same understated fashion: "There was a man called Ulf" or Mord Fiddle or Ketil Flatnose. Soon we are told about his wife, children, and in-laws, and perhaps follow him for a time on his daily round of farming or sheep-herding. Sometimes the protagonist will go out viking—sailing around the coasts of Europe, looting and plundering. In the Vinland sagas, Erik the Red and his son Leif head westward and reach what we now call Newfoundland, and possibly even New England.

Although the heroes are typically great warriors, they are usually more than that: Egil Skallagrimson is also a major poet, Njal a sage lawgiver (with a bit of the shaman about him), and Kjartan Olafsson is said to have been "the most handsome man ever to have been born in Iceland." Women, too, often play a key role in these tragic dramas. In *Laxdaela Saga* the beautiful Gudrun is forced to wed her lover's best friend, with tragic consequences. In due course she marries three more times, and survives to an impressive old age, but when asked which of her four husbands she loved the best, Gudrun only says, "I was worst to the one I loved the most."

Nearly all these heroes eventually recognize that their lives are fated, and they must bend to their gray and somber destinies. Gunnar, in *Njal Saga,* knows that if he doesn't leave Iceland, he will be destroyed. While boarding his ship he stumbles, and as he rises he looks back at his homeland, which suddenly seems so lovely that Gunnar cannot bear to depart. He eventually marries Hallgerd, a woman of dangerous beauty, blessed with golden hair so long that it can veil her whole body. But Hallgerd is both impetuous and spiteful, and her enemies always end up dead. Eventually, Gunnar loses his temper over his wife's ill-bred behavior and strikes the she-devil. The golden-tressed Hallgerd does nothing, and time passes, then comes a day when Gunnar's adversaries lay siege to him in his house. Undaunted, he unleashes arrow after arrow, wounding and killing his foes—until a lucky sword blow slashes his bowstring. Gunnar turns to Hallgerd and says, "Let me have two locks of your hair, and help my mother plait them into a bowstring for me." Hallgerd asks, "Does anything depend on it?" Gunnar replies, "My life depends on it, for they will never overcome me as long as I can use my bow." "In that case," says Hallgerd, "I shall now remind you of the slap you once gave me. I do not care in the least whether you hold out a long time or not." Gunnar quietly answers, "To each his own way of earning fame," then adds, "You shall not be asked again." He strides out with his broadsword and holds his enemies at bay for a long time. "But in the end they killed him."

Tragic irony and gallows humor pervade these tales. In *Grettir Saga*, the hero battles and finally destroys a ghost-demon named Glam. In the full moonlight, however, the dying Glam spits out a terrible curse: From this moment on, despite all his strength and valor, Grettir will always be deathly afraid of the dark. While this sounds bad enough—imagine how dark it grows in Iceland—the hero, through the machinations of his enemies, next finds himself declared an outlaw. This means that anybody can kill him on sight without recrimination, and that no household may offer him hospitality. The fiercest warrior in Iceland must therefore dwell in a cave and face the dark alone, night after night, quaking with almost unendurable fear.

Njal Saga is the longest, and arguably the greatest, of these Icelandic classics. One of Njal's sons, the great swordsman Skarp-Hedin, smiles only when he is about to go into battle. At one point he realizes that his enemies are waiting to ambush him on a frozen river, so he sneaks upstream, puts on a pair of primitive ice-skates, and with a sword in each hand, skates into their midst. Two-thirds of the way through the story, Njal and his sons are surrounded by their enemies—120 altogether—and burned to death in their house. The sole survivor is Njal's foster son Kari. At first Kari works to gain retribution through the courts of the Althing. He turns to the shrewd Thorhall to plead his case, but the lawyer suffers from a terrible, debilitating boil on his leg, which forces him to conduct the prosecution from his tent, giving careful instructions to a proxy, who acts as his mouthpiece at the court. Each day as the trial proceeds, the boil grows more and more virulent and painful. Finally, just as the case is about to be won, the overconfident underling proceeds on his own, without consulting Thorhall, and ruins everything. All is lost:

> When Thorhall heard this he was so shocked that he could not speak a word. He sprang out of bed, snatched with both hands the spear that Skarp-Hedin had given him, and drove it deep into his own leg. The flesh and core of the boil clung to the blade as he gouged it out of his leg, and a torrent of blood and matter gushed across the floor like a stream. Then he strode from the booth without a limp.

A moment later he lunges his spear into one of the 120 so-called "Burners" and a great melee erupts.

Finding that the law has failed him, the implacable Kari chooses to pursue justice on his own. One by one, he tracks down and kills the men who destroyed the only real family he had ever known. Finally, only the leader Flosi is left. As Kari sails toward Flosi's home to complete the task that has consumed his life, his ship is wrecked on the rocks. Wet and freezing, with heavy snow falling and no other habitation nearby, the weary avenger drags himself to his enemy's house and claims the ancient right of hospitality.

Nearly all the sagas are now available in English. Start with the famous ones mentioned here—I've cited the Penguin translations by

Magnus Magnusson and Hermann Palsson—and if you like them as much as I think you will, go on to the others. Don't overlook the shorter works, such as the charming fairy tale of "Audun and the Bear," a particular favorite, naturally enough, of the poet W. H. Auden.

CHRISTOPHER MARLOWE (1564–1593)
Plays and poems

Biographical information about Shakespeare (1564–1616) is frustratingly sparse, and it is no more plentiful for his great contemporary Christopher Marlowe, stabbed to death at age twenty-nine in an argument over a bar bill. But where Shakespeare is everyone and no one, Marlowe has passed into history as the most glamorous figure of England's literary renaissance. Almost any of his melodramatic heroes—the wizard Dr. Faustus, the conqueror Tamburlaine, the homosexual Edward II, the duplicitous Barabas—might be played by their flamboyant, youthful creator.

In his own time, and ever since, Marlowe has been viewed as the epitome of the intellectual overreacher—"I count religion but a childish toy,/ And hold there is no sin but ignorance." So says Barabas in *The Jew of Malta,* voicing what seem to be Marlowe's own opinions. Born in Canterbury, the young man first soaked up learning as a poor scholarship student at Cambridge, then became a translator, poet, playwright, atheist, sodomite, streetfighter, counterfeiter, spy, and finally a man who knew too much for his own good. One afternoon Robert Poley, Ingram Frizer, and Nicholas Skerres—their very names are sinister—enticed him to the Widow Bull's in Deptford, where they ate and drank, then quarreled over "the reckoning." A struggle ensued, only to stop when Marlowe's own dagger, with his hand still around its hilt, was driven back through his right eye deep into his brain. "Cut is the branch that might have grown full straight," as the chorus concludes in *Dr. Faustus*. Was it a contract killing, as many scholars now believe? Whatever the truth, Christopher Marlowe's life was suddenly over; his legend had just begun.

From the very first, "Kind Kit" Marlowe inspired deep emotions: not only affection, from fellow writers like Thomas Nashe (who worked with him on *The Jew of Malta*) and Thomas Kyd (his sometime roommate and the likely author of an early play about Hamlet, as well as *The Spanish Tragedy*) but also envy, animosity, and hatred. Yet even when his enemies attacked this upstart, they somehow portrayed him as insidiously attractive, an Elizabethan Rimbaud or Jim Morrison. His former school chum Gabriel Harvey tut-tutted that Marlowe neither "feared God, nor dreaded Div'll,/ Nor ought admired, but his wondrous selfe." Thomas Warton asserted that the poet's translation of Ovid's *Amores* conveyed "the obscenities of the brothel in elegant language." (Quite true: In one love poem Marlowe boldly writes, with a soupçon of sadomasochism: "Lo, I confess, I am thy captive I,/ And hold my conquer'd hands for thee to tie"; another deals with sexual impotence.) It seems appropriate that this same genius should also have composed the most limpidly beautiful lyric of the age, "Come live with me, and be my love."

According to C. S. Lewis's memorable summation, Marlowe is "our great master of the material imagination; he writes best about flesh, gold, gems, stone, fire, clothes, water, snow, and air." His one long poem, "Hero and Leander," portrays a delicious holiday world, where beauty and sensuality are one, and many readers will recognize its most famous couplet: "Where both deliberate, the love is slight;/ Who ever lov'd, that lov'd not at first sight?" This "erotic epyllion" shimmers throughout with sensuous passages, such as the provocative description of Hero and Leander making love: "She trembling strove; this strife of hers . . . another world begat/ Of unknown joy." Marlowe is particularly good at depicting the power of youthful male beauty. Of Leander he concludes that "Jove might have sipp'd out nectar from his hand," while he later describes a beautiful shepherd boy who "of the cooling river durst not drink,/ Lest water-nymphs should pull him from the brink."

Something of this elegant love banter continues in the earliest of Marlowe's dramas, *The Tragedy of Dido*. Not as admired as his later tragedies, it is nonetheless a kind of stately opera in prose (and one that occasionally recalls Purcell's musical masterpiece *Dido and Aeneas*). Consider any of its heroine's last pleading speeches before Aeneas abandons her to sail for Rome. Dido's sentiments are universal, and echo modern country-and-western heartbreakers as much as Virgil:

> *Why look'st thou toward the sea? The time hath been*
> *When Dido's beauty chain'd thine eyes to her.*
> *Am I less fair than when thou saw'st me first?*
> *Oh, then, Aeneas, 'tis for grief of thee!*
> *Say thou wilt stay in Carthage with thy queen,*
> *And Dido's beauty will return again.*

Marlowe's most celebrated play is doubtless *Dr. Faustus,* the story of the scholar who sells his soul to the devil and then doesn't quite know what to do with the power and knowledge he acquires. Naturally, the demonic Mephistopheles diverts his victim with sexual romps:

> *Marriage is but a ceremonial toy;*
> *And if thou lovest me, think no more of it.*
> *I'll cull thee out the fairest courtesans,*
> *And bring them ev'ry morning to thy bed:*
> *She whom thine eye shall like, thy heart shall have,*
> *Were she as chaste as was Penelope,*
> *As wise as Sava, or as beautiful*
> *As was bright Lucifer before his fall.*

Note, however, the unexpected shift to male beauty in the last line, the same kind of slither that takes place in the latter part of the gorgeous soliloquy about Helen of Troy ("Was this the face that launched a thousand ships?"):

O, thou art fairer than the evening's air
Clad in the beauty of a thousand stars;
Brighter art thou than flaming Jupiter
When he appear'd to hapless Semele;
More lovely than the monarch of the sky
In wanton Arethusa's azured arms;
And none but thou shalt be my paramour.

Some have held that *Edward II*—about that king's passion for his minion Gaveston—is a better-made play than *Dr. Faustus;* certainly its scene of Edward's murder, hinting of violation with a red-hot poker, makes for horrifying and powerful theater. To my mind, *The Jew of Malta* might well be regarded as Marlowe's meditation on espionage, since Barabas practices all the skills of the spy and the double agent. It is also a drama that Shakespeare must have seen, for at one point the merchant exclaims: "But stay: What star shines yonder in the east?/ The loadstar of my life, if Abigail." In our own time, the play's most notorious exchange provided T. S. Eliot with an epigraph (for "Portrait of a Lady"): "Thou hast committed—/ Fornication; but that was in another country;/ And besides, the wench is dead."

Great as all these works are, for Elizabethans, Christopher Marlowe was above all the dramatist of *Tamburlaine,* the shepherd turned conqueror, the wind from the east, the Scourge of God:

I hold the Fates bound in iron chains,
And with my hand turn Fortune's wheel about
And sooner shall the sun fall from his sphere
Than Tamburlaine be slain or overcome.

This vast two-part historical extravaganza established blank verse—what Ben Jonson called "Marlowe's mighty line"—as a medium for drama, and related its hero's whirlwind career with subtlety and feeling. Tamburlaine may rant, but he can also express himself in exquisite poetry, as when the dread warrior rejects a last-minute plea for mercy:

> *I will not spare these proud Egyptians,*
> *Nor change my martial observations*
> *For all the wealth of Gihon's golden waves,*
> *Or for the love of Venus, would she leave*
> *The angry god of arms and lie with me.*
> *They have refused the offer of their lives,*
> *And know my customs are as peremptory*
> *As wrathful planets, death, or destiny.*

Christopher Marlowe's works—translations, poems, and plays—all fit into a single compact volume. Who knows what so gifted a poetic genius might have accomplished had he lived as long as Shakespeare? We must nonetheless be grateful for what he did leave us—"infinite riches in a little room."

ÉMILE ZOLA (1840–1902)
Germinal; other novels

For many years Émile Zola was regarded as a "nasty" writer. His Rougon-Macquart cycle dealt largely with a single extended family's history of violence, insanity, drunkenness, and promiscuity. Moreover, the most notable—and the best—of its twenty novels were set among uneducated, working-class people: Gervaise, the fated victim of *L'Assommoir* (The Dram Shop), slaves away as a laundress; her daughter, the actress-heroine of *Nana,* rises to dubious acclaim as a *grande hori-*

zonale, a high-class prostitute; in *Germinal* her son Etienne leads an abortive coal-miners' strike. Little wonder that Zola's language needed to be earthy, sometimes vulgar, and occasionally obscene. This is the world as it truly is, and this is the bawdy, gaudy language actually spoken by men and women.

In the Rougon-Macquart series, Zola aimed to examine every aspect of mid-nineteenth-century society, so the ferocious *La Bête Humaine* (The Human Beast) focuses on railway workers, *Au Bonheur des Dames* (Ladies' Delight) on a giant department store, and *La Terre* (The Earth) on peasants. Other installments of the cycle take up art; Paris's central market, Les Halles (now gone); a bourgeois rooming house; and the clergy. While all these novels are connected by the Rougon-Macquart family's proclivity for drink and self-destructive violence, they aren't merely programmatic workings-out of a primal fault or a genetic destiny (despite their author's apparently scientific "plan"). At least five or six of Zola's books are truly shattering literary experiences, great novel-tragedies or novel-epics. While André Gide long ago chose *Germinal* as one of the ten best novels in the world, a more contemporary English man of letters, A. N. Wilson, recently named *The Debacle*—about the Franco-Prussian conflict—the most devastating war novel ever written. The journalist and social novelist Tom Wolfe frequently refers to Zola as his "idol."

Like a good reporter, Zola constructs his books on hard facts, drawing on his own on-site observations but also on scientific dossiers, government data, and newspaper articles. When he sits down to write, however, he imbues all this no-nonsense material with a pervasive sense of the mythic and timeless. Orpheus descends into a coal mine's underworld at four A.M.; Circe enchants her bourgeois admirers at the Théâtre des Variétés.

In his masterpiece *Germinal,* Zola presents far more than an indictment of mining conditions in nineteenth-century France. The novel becomes an epic of the oppressed, a stirring dithyramb to the power of hope and renewal. Its descendants include André Malraux's *Man's Fate* and *Man's Hope,* John Steinbeck's *The Grapes of Wrath,* and Ralph Ellison's *Invisible Man.*

No writer—not even Tolstoy or Victor Hugo—can better Zola at portraying masses of people in celebration, panic, or revolt. Because his books focus on men and women driven to the point of breakdown, they often seem melodramatic—but thrillingly so. In *Germinal,* Zola gives us a pitiful madman who strangles an innocent girl, a little boy who murders a soldier, an enraged striker who publicly bares her huge bottom in obscene defiance, and, not least, a broken-down draft horse that spends nearly its entire life underground but, as it dies, remembers grass and sunshine. In these pages, starving women turn, in ritualistic maenad-like frenzy, on their oppressor; an honorable mine owner discovers his wife's treachery; an anarchist plots and strikes; a flood traps major characters deep in the bowels of the earth; and a mining engineer works tirelessly to rescue the man he hates. Finally, in a kind of industrial-age *Liebestod,* two people—long kept apart by fate and circumstance—finally consummate their love while surrounded by the dead and the dying.

While such events may seem trite or over-the-top, they are not so when viewed in context. Many of the incidents are adopted from the historical record. Besides, how else should one write of hunger and virtual slavery, of men, women, and children worn out by unbearable lives, if not with justifiable rage? But Zola can be more subtly artful, too. Note his atmospheric use of colors—the red and black associated with the workers, the blue linked to the bourgeoisie, the dull leaden sky above the mine, the anemic white of the beasts and workers who have dwelt too long underground. Throughout the book, moreover, Zola employs analogies and verbs associated with planting, growing, fecundity, harvesting. The workers may be cut down this time, but they will rise once more. There will be other springs, as illustrated in this translation by Leonard Tancock:

Deep down underfoot the picks were still obstinately hammering away. All his comrades were there, he could hear them following his every step . . . The April sun was now well up in the sky, shedding its glorious warming rays on the teeming earth. Life was springing from her fertile womb, buds were bursting into leaf and the fields were quickening with fresh green grass. Everywhere seeds were swelling and lengthening, cracking open the plain in their upward thrust for warmth and light. The sap was rising in abundance with whispering voices, the germs of life were opening with a kiss. On and on, ever more insistently, his comrades were tapping, tapping, as though they too were rising from the ground. On this youthful morning, in the fiery rays of the sun, the whole country was alive with this sound. Men were springing up, a black avenging host was slowly germinating in the furrows, thrusting upwards for the harvests of future ages. And very soon their germination would crack the earth asunder.

Please do not be put off from discovering Zola because you think he's didactic or heavy-handed or inartistic. I first read *Germinal* when I was living in Marseille in 1971, and in my Garnier-Flammarion paperback, I scribbled "a great, sad book." That comment seems clearly something of an understatement, but it is also exactly right.

ERNST JÜNGER (1895–1998)
Storm of Steel

On the day Germany declared war in 1914, nineteen-year-old Ernst Jünger enlisted. For the next four years he fought with an infantry company—the 73rd Hanoverians—and participated in some of the most famous and bloody battles of all time: the Somme, Cambrai,

Passchendaele. He was either shot or severely wounded by shrapnel a half-dozen times but always recovered to fight again. By the end of the war, Jünger had risen to the rank of captain and been awarded, among other honors, the Iron Cross, First Class. Finally, on September 22, 1918, the Kaiser bestowed on him the order of *pour le Mérite.* Despite its French name, this is Germany's highest recognition for valor, and Jünger was (and remains) the youngest man ever to receive it.

As it happens, though, Jünger was more than just a warrior. He was also sensitive to nature, enjoyed reading Ariosto and *Tristram Shandy* while on leave or in the hospital, and later became both an entomologist and a distinguished novelist. Yet throughout a very long life—he lived to the age of 102—he was always a strong nationalist, a man of the right. At first he seemingly welcomed Hitler—the Führer actually sent him an inscribed copy of *Mein Kampf*—but he never joined the National Socialist Party and his best-known novel, *On the Marble Cliffs,* is partly an allegorical warning against Nazism. Even so, during World War II, Jünger again served Germany, this time as a *de jure* cultural officer in Paris. His admired wartime journals are full of aphorisms, philosophical reflections, and details of luncheons with writers and artists (including Picasso). But always there are the meetings with generals, the news from the front, the sudden pistol shots in the Bois de Boulogne.

Still, Jünger's most lasting work will always be *Storm of Steel* (1920), the immensely powerful memoir, based on extensive diaries, of his four years of hard combat during World War I. Its most recent translator, Michael Hofmann, notes that this stark reportorial account of battle has been deeply admired by literary masters as different as Borges and Brecht, Alberto Moravia and André Gide. This last wrote that *Storm of Steel* "is without question the finest book on war that I know: utterly honest, truthful, in good faith." Hofmann himself likens the book to the *Iliad.* It is dedicated simply, even apolitically: "For the fallen."

Page after page depicts almost unimaginable horror:

The defile proved to be little more than a series of enormous craters full of pieces of uniform, weapons and dead bodies. . . . One company after another, pressed together in the drumfire, had been mown down, then the bodies had been buried under showers of earth sent up by shells, and then the relief company had taken their predecessors' place. And now it was our turn.

For the most part, Jünger simply records his war. He doesn't analyze the justice of the conflict or wonder about its outcome. He doesn't dwell on the sudden death of noble comrades, or the seemingly pointless waste of men's lives, or the futility of a lost cause. Instead, day by day, he performs his duty as a soldier, and he tells us, with clinical honesty, what he does and what he sees.

As *Storm of Steel* progresses, Jünger describes gas attacks, the eerie confusion of battle, the nightly drinking to bring on dreamless sleep. In particular he emphasizes the never-ending possibility of sudden unexpected death, whether from the unceasing artillery barrages or from bombs or the exploding shells that send deadly slivers of metal flying everywhere. The pounding of war, the possibility of being hit by flying steel, never lets up:

I think I have found a comparison that captures the situation in which I and all the other soldiers who took part in this war so often found ourselves: you must imagine you are securely tied to a post, being menaced by a man swinging a heavy hammer. Now the hammer has been taken back over his head, ready to be swung, now it's cleaving the air towards you, on the point of touching your skull, then it's struck the post, and the splinters are flying—that's what it's like to experience heavy shelling in an exposed position.

Ultimately, bravery has nothing to do with survival; it's purely a matter of luck, of chance. Most of the field operations end disastrously. At Regneville, Jünger leads a night-commando operation:

> I had got together some kit appropriate to the sort of work I meant to be doing: across my chest, two sandbags, each containing four stick-bombs, impact fuses on the left, delay on the right, in my right tunic pocket an 08 revolver on a long cord, in my right trouser pocket a little Mauser pistol, in my left tunic pocket five egg hand-grenades, in the left trouser pocket luminous compass and whistle, in my belt spring hooks for pulling out the pins, plus bowie knife and wire cutters.

Jünger uses up his Rambo-like armaments, but the mission proves an utter fiasco; the men wander through English trenches in darkness, lose their way, fight and die for nothing: Of the fourteen who had started out, only four return.

On page after page, Jünger sets down the death of his comrades. Friends bleed unstoppably when shrapnel slices through their carotid arteries, they are suddenly shot when standing sentry, earthworks or houses collapse and bury them alive. Little wonder that when Jünger fights, it is often in a berserk rage. Yet in general he shows no hatred of his enemies: "It was always my endeavour to view my opponent without animus, and to form an opinion of him as a man on the basis of the courage he showed." During the course of *Storm of Steel*, Jünger does kill many men—with rifle, pistol, stick-bomb, grenade—but he notes the cost. Once he shot a young British soldier, "little more than a boy":

> I forced myself to look closely at him. It wasn't a case of "you or me" any more. I often thought back on him; and more with the

passing of the years. The state, which relieves us of our responsibility, cannot take away our remorse; and we must exercise it. Sorrow, regret, pursued me deep into my dreams.

This is as close to introspection as Jünger manages in *Storm of Steel*, until the final chapters. There his tone finally grows weary, fatalistic: "The seasons followed one another, it was winter and then it was summer again, but it was still war." The purpose, he writes, "with which I had gone out to fight had been used up." And yet the conflict went on, until:

It was our last storm. How many times over the last few years we had advanced into the setting sun in a similar frame of mind! Les Eparges, Guillemont, St-Pierre-Vaast, Langemarck, Passchendaele, Moeuvres, Vraucourt, Mory! Another gory carnival beckoned.

One closes *Storm of Steel* with a heavy heart. So many human beings dead! And for what? These men were labeled "the Huns" by the West, vilified as evil and ruthless, yet they were, in normal life, schoolteachers, factory workers, and artists, as well as husbands, fathers, sons, and brothers. Each faithfully undertook his obligation as a soldier, and each died heroically or foolishly or unfairly. Jünger's great book matter-of-factly conveys the mysterious glamour of war, the exhilaration of its excess and intensity, and, not least, the undeniable glory of men bravely preparing for battle as for "some terrible silent ceremonial that portends human sacrifice."

JAMES AGEE (1909–1955)
Let Us Now Praise Famous Men; film criticism

James Agee's gifts always led him to exceed the boundaries in whatever form he was working. His most ambitious work, *Let Us Now Praise Famous Men,* started life as a magazine article that got out of hand. But Agee couldn't resist his passion, or his need to turn the prosaic into prose poetry. As a result, his nonfiction continues to feel vital today because it remains so nakedly vulnerable, so provisional, so utterly lacking in the subtle artistic poison of self-confident complacency. As critic Robert Phelps once observed, Agee was "a born sovereign prince of the English language," and he turned everything he wrote into art.

Like many of the world's most interesting books, *Let Us Now Praise Famous Men* has a lot wrong with it. Originally, *Fortune* magazine commissioned Agee and photographer Walker Evans to report on the conditions of cotton farmers in Depression-era Alabama, but killed the resulting article as unusable. Agee, however, couldn't forget the Rickettses, Woods, and Gudgers, his "Three Tenant Families." So he rewrote and further amplified his original essay, turning his one-time magazine piece into the great nonfiction epic of the American Depression.

Like Melville in *Moby-Dick,* Agee mixed together autobiography, reflections on art and society, lists and catalogs, bits of conversation, newspaper clippings, prayers, litanies, and the imagined thoughts of real people. He produced page after page of near-Homeric description of old shoes, denim overalls, and homemade clothing, sang about the haunting beauty of Louise Gudger's eyes, confessed his own sense of guilt and shame before the hopelessness of the lives around him, and pointed out the even greater degradations visited upon the Negro. In the end, his aim was nothing less than a celebration of human fraternity, like Beethoven's Ninth Symphony. But instead of composing an "ode to joy," this vibrant and anguished prose-epic would honor the wretched of the earth, opening with Walker Evans's stark, unflinching, and now very famous photographs.

The book's first intended publisher naturally wanted cuts; Agee naturally refused. He kept working on his text, never satisfied, even after Houghton Mifflin finally brought the great work out to insulting reviews and pitiful sales (six hundred copies the first year). Certainly, the book can be frustrating: Agee circles around his subject like a restless sheepdog, unable to settle. He keeps talking about what he's going to talk about, and the pages roll by until the reader eventually arrives at the very last sentence on the very last page, where our author announces that he is finally turning to the story "which I shall now try to give you." But the book is over, and we have already—in a collagist, temporally skewed way—had the story. The effect is almost Faulknerian.

Melville, Beethoven, Faulkner—these are the kinds of overreachers against whom Agee hopes to be measured. From out of his lengthy analyses of cotton-picking or the nail-by-nail description of a tenant house, emerge similes and paragraphs of breathtaking beauty and surprise.

The inside of an old trunk is "unexpectedly bright as if it were a box of tamed sunlight." A row of chairs is said to "sit in exact regiment of uneven heights with the charming sobriety of children pretending to be officers or judges." More elaborately, Agee tells us that a mirror is so tarnished that it gives to its "framings an almost incalculably ancient, sweet, frail, and piteous beauty, such as may be seen in tintypes of family groups among studio furnishings or heard in nearly exhausted jazz records made by very young, insane, devout men who were soon to destroy themselves, in New Orleans, in the early nineteen twenties." That unexpected adjective "devout" and the musical cadence of the syntax are characteristic of young Agee.

Similar restrained miniatures enhance nearly every page of *Let Us*

Now Praise Famous Men, yet Agee's natural bent is always toward glorious lyrical excess. Read slowly, for instance, his two-page list of what he saw pinned to the wall around the family fireplace of the desperately poor Ricketts family:

> Calendars of snowbound and staghunting scenes pressed into bas-relief out of white pulp and glittering with a sand of red and blue and green and gold tinsel, and delicately tinted; other calendars and farm magazine covers or advertisements of dog-love; the blessèd fireside coziness of the poor; indian virgins watching their breasts in pools or paddling up moonlit aisles of foliage; full-blown blondes in luminous frocks leaning back in swings, or taking coca-cola through straws, or beneath evening palmleaves, accepting cigarettes from young men in white monkey-coats, happy young housewives at resplendent stoves in sunloved kitchens, husbands in tuxedos showing guests an oil furnace, old ladies leaning back in rocking chairs, their hands relaxed in their needlework, their faces bemused in lamplight, happy or mischievous or dog-attended or praying little boys and girls, great rosy blue-eyed babies sucking their thumbs to the bone in clouds of pink or blue, closeups of young women bravely and purely facing the gravest problems of life in the shelter of lysol, portraits of cakes, roasts of beef, steaming turkeys, and decorated hams, little cards by duplicate and a series depicting incidents in the life of Jesus with appropriate verses beneath, rich landscapes with rapid tractors in the foreground, kittens snarled in yarn, or wearing glasses, or squinting above pink or blue bows. . . .

And on and on as Agee, without emotion, sets down these clichéd images of modern advertising, circa 1937—all of them stared at and dreamed over, day after day, by people who stitch their clothes together out of flour sacks.

After he published *Let Us Now Praise Famous Men* to resounding indifference, Agee drifted back to journalism, turning out book and film reviews, mainly for *Time* and the *Nation*. By common consent, the movie pieces are the best ever written by an American, with only one weakness: Agee was reviewing from 1943 to 1948, probably the dullest period in Hollywood screen history. But he did manage to welcome the great Italian neo-realist films (*Open City, Shoeshine*), to defend Charlie Chaplin's derided masterpiece *Monsieur Verdoux,* and to celebrate the greatness of the silent era.

Agee wrote that movies, like the photographs of his friend Walker Evans, succeeded by "picturing the way that places and things and people really look and act and inter-act, and making the information eloquent to the eye." That sounds almost theoretical, but Agee was nothing if not primarily impassioned; his pieces often sound as personal as love letters. He could encapsulate a film's plot or describe its stars with aphoristic economy: In *The Big Sleep,* for instance, Humphrey Bogart can "get into a minor twitch of the mouth the force of a slug from an automatic," while Lauren Bacall is "like an adolescent cougar."

In the classic American vein of artistic self-destruction, James Agee drove his body hard and his spirit harder, smoking, drinking, womanizing, and talking nonstop through the night; there were three rocky marriages, several children, and suicidal impulses. He felt everything intensely, drawing on an almost mystical religious sensibility as well as a deep regard for human beings in all their fallen glory. His childhood especially haunted him, and after his death—from a heart attack in a New York taxicab at the age of forty-five—some scraps of autobiographical fiction, largely about the events surrounding his father's funeral, were edited into *A Death in the Family* (1957). It received the Pulitzer Prize that properly should have gone to *Let Us Now Praise Famous Men.*

Love's Mysteries

John Donne wrote, "Love's mysteries in souls do grow/ But yet the body is his book." This intermingling of the spiritual and carnal generates that wonderful exhilaration and sense of renewal we associate with falling in love. Lust and adoration, yearning and satiety, fidelity and promiscuity, transcendence and bawdiness—all these polarities electrify our hearts and bodies, keeping us on edge, dizzily off-kilter. The enemy of love isn't hate but complacency and indifference.

The writers in this section of *Classics for Pleasure* traverse the whole spectrum of the erotic: passionate longing, seduction, courtship, renunciation, marriage, breakup, regret, nostalgia. This category might easily comprise half the books in the world's literature: What poet or novelist doesn't talk about love? But rather than write again about Gustave Flaubert's *Madame Bovary*, Ford Madox Ford's *The Good Soldier*, or Vladimir Nabokov's *Lolita*, I've suggested some less familiar yet equally rewarding masterpieces.

SAPPHO (fl. ca. 600 B.C.E.)
Poems and fragments

Sappho is the first great love poet of the Western world, and many would argue the greatest of all time, even though we merely possess fragments of her work and only occasionally a lyric in its entirety.

As a Greek poet, she is slightly preceded in time by the startling, confrontational Archilochos. His most famous line, in Richmond Lattimore's translation, is the epigram "The fox knows many tricks; the hedgehog only one. One good one." Yet this often rancorous soldier has also left us one of the most poignant expressions of erotic longing: "If it were only my fortune just to touch Neoboule's hand."

Such yearning, for the lost or out of reach, lies at the heart of Sappho's poetry. Here, love is sometimes a blessing but more often a fever, and Eros is always bittersweet. Sappho's accounts of lovesickness and jealousy, her portraits of young women in flower, her simplicity, directness, and physical ache—all these echo in us, even after two and a half millennia. Like an early Imagist, she delivers maximum emotion with minimum words.

She is reputedly impossible to translate well, and yet people keep trying. In our own time Richmond Lattimore, Mary Barnard, Kenneth Rexroth, Willis Barnstone, Guy Davenport, Jim Powell, and Anne Carson have all captured enough of Sappho to make her a living poet in English. Now and then, her verse can be almost vulgarly direct—"You make me hot" is the way Davenport renders one fragment—or as moving as three simple words and a comma: "If not, winter." This is Carson's translation of a stray line (also used as the title of her Sappho collection), and what more does one need to know about the longing for love? Some have claimed that this suggestive incompleteness grants the poetry a spurious richness—one of the fragments gives us only two words, "here" followed by a gap and then "again." One may easily imagine frenzied lovemaking in that empty space, but one might well be mistaken. By a sad necessity, the lost lines now enrich the poetry's erotic pathos.

Was this inhabitant of Lesbos a lesbian? Probably, though there is some argument about this, since she was married long enough to give birth to a cherished daughter, speaks admiringly of men's beauty, and reportedly threw herself into the sea out of despair over a fellow named Phaon. But then what does one make of a celebrated poem in which Sappho observes a beloved young woman, at what is probably a marriage feast, and suffers near emotional collapse? Her skin burns; she breaks into a sweat, turns pale, and feels as if she is about to die.

It may surprise modern readers to learn that the ancient Greeks recognized Sappho as the greatest of their lyric poets. She was even judged worthy of being considered a tenth muse, for no one could equal her in the matching of words to word-music. Here are a few lines, fifteen words in Kenneth Rexroth's translation:

The moon has set,
And the Pleiades. It is
Midnight. Time passes.
I sleep alone.

Sappho isn't the only female poet of antiquity, but there aren't, alas, many others, so we must be especially grateful for what survives. Something of her heartbreakingly pure voice comes through in any version of the original Greek: "I loved you once, Atthis, long ago."

ARTHURIAN ROMANCES (twelfth and thirteenth centuries)
Chrétien de Troyes, *Yvain*, or *The Knight with the Lion*
Gottfried von Strassburg, *Tristan*
Wolfram von Eschenbach, *Parzival*

Arthurian romances are fundamentally concerned with matters of conduct. At their best they are never mere tales of derring-do, the metallic clash of arms, and the perfunctory rescue of fair damsels. The greatest examples—and the three I've listed here are high points of medieval literature—focus on serious moral dilemmas, conflicting loyalties, the reformation of character, the allure of social status and the claims of the spiritual. These "romances" deal largely with love, in all its forms, from sexual passion and marital happiness to family loyalty and religious transcendence.

In *The Knight with the Lion*, Chrétien de Troyes transports the noble Yvain into the otherworldly forest of Broceliande, where he seeks a magic well, fights and kills its guardian, and then falls in love at first sight with Laudine, the dead man's wife. A serving maid convinces the grieving widow that her kingdom deserves a valiant warrior to defend it, and the only logical candidate is the knight who defeated her husband. So, hardly over her mourning, she weds Yvain, who two weeks later is convinced by Sir Gawain that a real knight should be off adventuring. Yvain promises to return to his new bride within the year but, caught up in the excitement of chivalric bloodletting, he forgets about the time. Laudine sends a message—essentially, "Don't bother to come home"—and Yvain promptly goes mad with remorse and ends up living like a wild man in the forest, eating roots and berries. After saving a lion from a huge snake, he is accompanied everywhere by the great, tawny beast, which often comes to his rescue during unequal combats. Once restored to his reason, Yvain spends the rest of the poem gradually working his way back into Laudine's good graces.

As this partial summary indicates, Chrétien's initial story suggests mythic origins straight out of J. G. Frazer's *The Golden Bough*: Whosoever kills the priest-king of the sacred site will immediately inherit his guardianship and his goddess-wife. The poet nonetheless directs our real attention to the dynamics of marriage and, in particular, to Yvain's psychological collapse. The man has failed to honor his obligations as a true lover and husband, mainly because he has been spending too much time at work, i.e., off jousting and brawling with his buddy Gawain. Without being overtly didactic, Chrétien shows us how the demoralized knight learns to make himself worthy of love after frivolously abandoning a wife who had accepted him against her natural inclinations. The poem tracks Yvain's progress through various kinds of delusion to clarity and self-understanding.

By contrast, Gottfried von Strassburg (who based his work on that of a poet named Thomas) provides the classic exposition of what is still our most influential romantic archetype: the fatal passion of Tristan and Isolde, a love more powerful than any social or religious prohibition, a love so strong that it defies death itself. Their story—among the most popular tales of the Middle Ages—underlies every romantic tragedy since, from Dante's Paolo and Francesca to Shakespeare's Romeo and Juliet to Vladimir Nabokov's Humbert Humbert and Lolita. When Isolde says to her beloved, "For you and I are always but one thing with no distinction," we can already hear the ringing declaration of Catherine Earnshaw in *Wuthering Heights*, "I *am* Heathcliff."

Many people know the rough outline of the story—Tristan is sent to bring Isolde from Ireland to wed King Mark, the two accidentally drink a potion that causes them to fall madly in love with each other, and they thwart every law of society and God to satisfy their all-consuming desire. In Gottfried's version, as in Wagner's opera, so intense is the lovers' passion that it grows increasingly mystical and their sufferings likened to those of religious martyrs. Indeed, a famous passage in Gottfried describes a grotto, called a shrine or temple of love, in which the couple are able to live for a time in harmony and bliss, acolytes of Eros.

Tristan raises many questions about which people still argue: Would you betray your country, your marriage vows, your honor, and your religion for love? Should you? Do Tristan and Isolde enjoy great sex simply because their passion is forbidden? (In their grotto, when they are free of social constraints, the pair start to grow a little bored with each other.) Is their mad infatuation just that—madness, not real, because it was initiated by a magic potion? Can physical passion elevate us to a truly spiritual realm? Must such erotic incandescence always lead to death?

Some of these themes are more deeply explored in Wolfram von Eschenbach's *Parzival,* arguably the greatest work of medieval German literature (with the possible exception of that somber and complex epic *The Nibelungenlied*). While *Yvain* describes love within the chivalric system, and *Tristan* depicts an ecstasy that overwhelms every constraint, *Parzival* shows us the claims not of passion but of compassion, by chronicling the spiritual rebirth of a hero who journeys from the rowdy secular court of Arthur to the hushed sodality of the Grail.

The action ranges across most of the known world, but its hero, Parzival, starts off as a country bumpkin who, when he first glimpses some knights, guesses they must be angels. We laugh—Wolfram displays a real taste for humor and wordplay—but isn't there a wisdom behind this ignorance, a suggestion that true knights should be angels, of a sort? Against his mother's wishes, young Parzival goes off to Arthur's court, where he commits a series of blunders, inadvertently injures an innocent person, and acts like an ill-bred clod. Eventually, however, he is instructed in proper knightly behavior, marries Conduiramurs (*conduire à amour,* "leads to love"), and decides he'd better go home to check on his aged mother. En route he stops at a castle, where he meets the wounded Fisher-King Anfortas and views a curious ritual involving a bleeding spear and a procession with some kind of sacred artifact. Because he once erred in churlishly thrusting himself forward, Parzival now chooses to remain silent.

In time, the young knight learns that he has made a huge mistake in not demonstrating more active sympathy for the suffering Anfortas. Meanwhile, Wolfram contrasts Parzival's spiritual journey upward with an account of his friend Gawain's more conventionally secular adventures, those typical of a famous knight and ladies' man. In due course, a miserable Parzival makes his way to a hermit, where he confesses his spiritual despair and learns that only humility and Christian charity will bring him relief, and even redemption. Now aware of the limits of courtly convention, Parzival vows to serve God rather than man, finally heals Anfortas, and accepts his calling as the new Grail King.

Whether from childhood reading, the movies, or the musical *Camelot,* many of us are familiar with the main stream of Arthurian legend with its focus on King Arthur, Lancelot, and Guinevere. But these allied masterworks of Chrétien, Gottfried, and Wolfram should be more widely appreciated. Here be wonders and marvels, but also much tenderness and suffering, and every variety of love.

<hr>

MARIE-MADELEINE DE LA FAYETTE (1634–1693)
The Princess of Clèves

The Princess of Clèves (1678) is sometimes called the first modern French novel. It certainly displays all the traits commonly associated with the French mind of the seventeenth century: austere diction, clarity of design, delicate psychological probing and portraiture, an intensely felt moral dilemma, and a stately decorousness that cannot quite disguise the most heart-rending passion. This short book is, in some ways, the novelistic equivalent of a tragedy by Racine, and the agonies felt by the princess are no less acute than those of Titus (in *Bérénice*) when, out of duty to Rome, he gives up the woman he loves.

At no court, La Fayette tells us in her novel's opening paragraphs, has there ever been gathered so many lovely women and handsome men as at that of Henri II. In this world, romantic intrigue has grown almost tiresome: most husbands take mistresses, queens dally with courtiers, and everyone looks the other way. Of those many courtiers, though, none is more dashing, more admired, or more promiscuous than the Duc de Nemours.

Into this erotic hothouse there one day arrives a young woman, reared according to the strictest religious principles, obedient to her mother, and as beautiful as she is pure. Before she knows it, however, this treasure has been married to the infatuated Monsieur de Clèves and taken his name. She respects and even admires her husband— but feels nothing more.

Almost from the moment the Princess de Clèves first glimpses the Duc de Nemours she finds herself suffering from a passion she has never known before. Yet what can she do except live with her secret? Though she finds it impossible to curtail her feelings, she can certainly control them, and determines to betray no sign of her inner agitation or tender regard. After all, she is a married woman and the duke a notorious gallant, albeit a gentleman of perfect refinement and, it would seem, the most sincere devotion.

Time passes, but the princess can neither suppress her emotional turmoil nor forget its source. "Do I wish to begin a love-affair?" she asks herself, in John D. Lyons's translation. "Do I wish to fail in my duty to Monsieur de Clèves? Do I wish to expose myself to the cruel repentance and mortal anguish that are inseparable from love? I am overwhelmed by an affection which carries me away in spite of myself; all my resolutions are vain; I thought yesterday what I think to-day, and I act to-day in direct contradiction to my resolutions of yesterday."

Inevitably, Monsieur de Clèves learns that his wife suffers from love—albeit an unexpressed love—for another man.

The princess naturally does all she can to repair this damage to her marriage, but her husband's injured ego and resulting coldness further cut her off from the most basic domestic happiness. Moreover, she still cannot shake off the remembrance of the gracious and amiable Monsieur de Nemours, who seems to have genuinely fallen in love with her.

Much else happens in this short novel—an incriminating letter, court gossip, an affair made public, a sudden death, and, finally, a quietly shattering conclusion. Modern readers may be surprised, even horrified, by the final pages. Yet *The Princess of Clèves* is a work of the most finely considered literary art, dominated by its leading character's severe emotional reserve, her scrupulous honesty, and an inner torment that is all the more lacerating for being set in an elegant balletlike world of the most complete immorality. Little wonder that Madame de La Fayette's masterpiece has been admired by writers as worldly as La Rochefoucauld (who probably advised her on its composition), as passionate as Stendhal, and as witty as Nancy Mitford.

—➤●◄—

SÖREN KIERKEGAARD (1813–1855)
Diary of a Seducer

In *Either/Or* (1843) and *Stages on Life's Way* (1845), the Danish philosopher Sören Kierkegaard examines three forms of love—esthetic, ethical, and religious, this last being the one to which he urges us to aspire. One might crudely summarize these as lust, marriage, and spirituality. Under the "esthetic" category, Kierkegaard describes a sensual approach to life in which one values pleasure, amusement, and the moment above all else. He portrays the positive aspect of this *carpe diem* lifestyle in an extended meditation on the figure of Don Juan, who represents pure libido, acting without calculation or meanness, full of joy and exuberance. Not surprisingly, many of the Don's former mistresses are always happy to see him again.

But there is a darker side to the "esthetic" approach to love—that of the intellectual seducer, the advocate of an ultra-refined erotic gamesmanship. To better describe what he means, Kierkegaard transcribes the diary of such a seducer by the name of Johannes. These pages form the climax of part one of *Either/Or,* and have always been that long book's most famous—even notorious—section, frequently published on its own as a kind of short novel.

In his diary Johannes tells us that he thinks of each of his seductions as a "case study." He observes a young woman's personality and behavior, then gradually creates conditions that will lead her to alter the way she acts and feels. Carefully reading her psychological state at every moment, he contrives to keep his victim anxious and off-kilter. Johannes never hurries his intended along "the way assigned to her"; as an esthete and connoisseur, he savors "slow draughts." Looked at from a theological viewpoint, he is like the Serpent with Eve: The young woman must finally choose to sin of her own free will.

Why is Johannes a seducer? To a large extent, seduction serves as his way of combating boredom. Anyone who pursues an esthetic life is always fleeing ennui and searching for the "interesting"—a word that recurs throughout the diary. Unlike Don Juan, that pure, almost naïve sensualist, Johannes lives in his head. He views the world as a great improvisatory theater, one in which he will adopt whatever persona seems most amusing or useful. Language is his chief instrument; he tellingly observes, in Gerd Gillhoff's translation, that Ulysses wasn't handsome but that his eloquence "caused the goddesses of the sea to be tormented with love for him." His own aim is chillingly perverse: "When one can bring it about that a girl sees in the abandonment of her self the sole purpose of her freedom, that she feels her whole happiness depends on this abandonment, that she does not shrink from obtaining it by begging and yet is free, then and only then is there enjoyment."

Such a statement makes clear how much *Diary of a Seducer* touches upon one of the most common male sexual fantasies: The woman must not merely surrender her virtue, she must actively desire her own corruption. Valmont, in Choderlos de Laclos's *Les Liaisons dangereuses*—the most coldly brilliant novel of amorality and sexual calculation ever written—manipulates the highly religious Madame de Tourvel into willingly, eagerly offering herself to him. Dracula's female victims first fear, then hunger for the poisoned kiss of the vampire. The protagonist of Pauline Réage's *Story of O* learns that to please her lover she must freely give up every shred of her own identity. In all these instances, and many others, a sophisticated "old practitioner" (Johannes' term) transforms an innocent young woman into his plaything by awakening hitherto unacknowledged desires. It's hardly surprising that a Copenhagen newspaper once ran a caricature in which the author of *Either/Or* sits astride the shoulders of a fashionably dressed beauty. The caption? "Kierkegaard training a woman."

Part of the hypnotic power of *Diary of a Seducer* derives from its repeated emphasis on the transgressive. For instance, Johannes periodically underscores his preference for innocent and "natural" young girls: There is simply not as much piquancy in the embrace of an experienced, sophisticated woman. In the case of Cordelia, the unfortunate "case study" of the diary, Johannes raises such a tumult of passion—"a mental concupiscence that sees me everywhere"—that the girl will actually reject the constraints of an engagement and abandon the prospect of a good marriage.

Afterward, in his most devilish move, the capstone of his campaign by indirection, "from a distance," Johannes deliberately starts to behave with coldness and disinterest. By this time, he knows that the still virginal Cordelia will turn to the sexual energies he has awakened to do all she can to win him back. She will become the temptress; she will become the seducer. Finally, abandoned in every sense, the unhappy Cordelia will sink into spiritual bondage:

> You have become everything to me. I would stake all my bliss on becoming your slave . . . I will wait, wait until you grow weary of loving others; then shall your love for me rise up from its grave, then will I love as always, thank you as always, as before, Johannes, as before.

Nothing graphic occurs in *Diary of a Seducer* and yet if read slowly, with care, the book is a deeply unsettling study in sexual politics, an outline of how power, freedom, and identity may interact. It is also, in its way, a warning to all those who live for pleasure alone. Johannes regularly plunges into the social whirl, indulges in erotic daydreams and wish-fulfillments, savors pleasing memories, and keeps himself relentlessly focused on his fleeting enjoyments. Should he ever succumb to boredom for more than a moment, he knows it is only a short step to "dread," Kierkegaard's name for the spiritual angst that comes upon us when we realize how empty and meaningless our lives are without God. But what of poor Cordelia? What fate awaits her? However you look at *Diary of a Seducer,* this insidious *récit,* this philosophical "thought-experiment," will leave you disoriented and stricken.

GEORGE MEREDITH (1828–1909)
Modern Love

George Meredith is best known for his novels—*The Egoist, The Ordeal of Richard Feverel*—and as the author of an important essay on comedy. But he was also a poet, one championed in particular by the historian George Macaulay Trevelyan, who committed reams of Meredith's verse to memory. Many readers have been content with a few of his short poems, above all "Lucifer by Starlight" with its ringing last line: "the army of unalterable law." But Meredith also wrote one uneven but anguished series of poems that deserves more attention: the fifty "sonnets" (they have sixteen rather than fourteen lines) collectively titled *Modern Love* (1862). These trace, in agonizing detail, the breakup of a marriage.

Meredith opens with the couple in bed—"By this he knew she wept with waking eyes." The husband listens to his wife's sobs as the two lie there, staring into the darkness without speaking, "looking through their dead black years." The next morning, "each sucked a secret, and each wore a mask." The man still adores his wife, but she no longer loves him, and he has become "a shuddering heap of pain":

Lord God, who mad'st the thing so fair,
See that I am drawn to her even now!
It cannot be such harm on her cool brow
To put a kiss? Yet if I meet him there!
But she is mine! Ah, no! I know too well
I claim a star whose light is overcast:
I claim a phantom-woman in the Past.
The hour has struck, though I heard not the bell!

Despite all, the man strives to carry on as if nothing is wrong, though he is unable to be truly affectionate, constantly "convulsed at a checked impulse of the heart." She still feels love, too, but it has "changed its aim"—to the other man in her life. Nonetheless, the wedded pair maintain the public charade.

Are we simply to blame this faithless woman, then? "Yet it was plain she struggled." Throughout the poem, Meredith switches back and forth between omniscience and the voices of the husband and wife. "Where came the cleft between us? whose the fault?" Sometimes it is hard to know who is talking, which all the better reflects the odd mirroring of the couple's emotions: "Used! Used!" Over time the husband grows more and more angry, even as his physical desire persists— "Had he not teeth to rend, and hunger too?/ But still he spared her."

In time, the husband chafes at his sentence: "Shall I, unsustained,/ Drag on Love's nerveless body thro' all time?" Even memories of the past have come to be poisoned by jealousy and uncertainty, and, after all, everyone knows that nothing lasts forever: "'I play for Seasons; not Eternities!'/ Says Nature, laughing on her way." But his wife's beauty is unfaded, and the husband hotly remembers the pleasure of sex with her: "Love's great bliss,/ When the renewed for ever of a kiss/ Whirls life within the shower of loosened hair!"

One night the husband, confronting his partner-in-suffering as she lies in bed, brandishes pages of her old love letters to him, pages filled with frank avowals of desire and passion:

> *. . . She trembles through;*
> *A woman's tremble—the whole instrument—*
> *I show another letter lately sent.*
> *The words are very like: the name is new.*

"The name is new." Tears follow, and even a temporary reconciliation, as the pair still keep up appearances ("At dinner, she is hostess, I am host"). No one suspects their agony. But the pressure is wearing out the poor husband, and he yearns for "the May-fly pleasures of a mind at ease." Instead he finds a forgotten lock of hair in a drawer, still scented with perfume, and he aches over what is lost. Yet about the infidelity, as about the marriage itself, "She will not speak. I will not ask." When the two visit a country house and are given a double bed in the attic, the man sleeps on the floor.

Finally, having been told that "distraction is the panacea," the husband finds himself another woman—one filled with common sense, who seems to care for him: "I am approved./ It is not half so nice as being loved,/ And yet I do prefer it." His wife, her lip quivering, even claims that "she's glad/ I'm happy."

Yet somehow the couple go on a while longer with "this wedded lie." The mistress, after meeting the wife, wonders if her lover really cares for her. Maybe his avowals are false. He protests: "You know me that I never can renew/ The bond that woman broke. . . . She killed a thing, and now it's dead." His new lady relents. Later that evening the man wanders near a shadowy brook, "half waking, half in dream," feeling in harmony with the stars, and suddenly glimpses a couple in the moonlight: "What two come here to mar this heavenly tune?/ A man is one: the woman bears my name,/ And honour. Their hands touch!" Even though he is happy with his new mistress, seeing his wife with this other man destroys him: "Can I love one,/ And yet be jealous of another?. . . . The dread that my old love may be alive/ Has seized my nursling new love by the throat." Suddenly his beautiful wife looks more alluring than ever: "How many a thing which we cast to the ground,/ When others pick it up becomes a gem!"

So he follows her, catches her wrists, and one of the two—Meredith doesn't make it clear which—says, "You love . . . ? love . . . ? love . . . ? all on an indrawn breath." The next day they walk together, almost as they did in older, happier times:

'Tis morning: but no morning can restore
What we have forfeited. I see no sin:
The wrong is mixed. In tragic life, God wot,
No villain need be! Passions spin the plot;
We are betrayed by what is false within.

But even such weary understanding quickly breaks down. The husband plucks a flower, smells it, and reawakens "the time when in her eyes I stood alive." When she asks for the flower, he lets it drop to the ground. Then, as the husband moves off, the wife stops and crushes the blossom under her heel, after which Meredith delivers his final bitter judgment, in the voice of either: "These are the summer days, and these our walks."

At last, the couple "parley" seriously, and the break is made. Together on the seashore, they pause for a moment to watch the swallows gathering in the sky and to remember the lost joy they once felt for each other:

> *Love, that had robbed us of immortal things,*
> *This little moment mercifully gave,*
> *Where I have seen across the twilight wave*
> *The swan sail with her young beneath her wings.*

Those last two lines, arriving when they do, and spoken with such heartache, seem to me as beautiful as anything in Yeats.

The torment and the marriage over, Meredith sums up his "piteous" story:

> *Lovers beneath the singing sky of May,*
> *They wandered once; clear as the dew on flowers:*
> *But they fed not on the advancing hours:*
> *Their hearts held cravings for the buried day.*
> *Then each applied to each that fatal knife,*
> *Deep questioning, which probes to endless dole.*
> *Ah, what a dusty answer gets the soul*
> *When hot for certainties in this our life!*

Despite its fustian moments and overuse of exclamation points, *Modern Love* is greatly moving. We know that Meredith's own marriage—to Thomas Love Peacock's daughter—broke up, yet his poem is so filled with "tragic hints" that it transcends the particular, for don't people in such circumstances try hard to do their best, to make the right decisions, to carry on? As Meredith says, usually "the wrong is mixed"—even if "passions spin the plot." Alas, once trust is gone, so, too, are those "May-fly pleasures of a mind at ease." And then comes the time of "endless dole." It's enough to make one weep.

—➤◦◄—

C. P. CAVAFY (1863–1933)
Collected Poems

Constantine Cavafy, said E. M. Forster in 1923, could sometimes be glimpsed standing in the streets of Alexandria, Egypt, "at a slight angle to the universe." Since then, the literary world's axis has shifted, and Cavafy now seems a central pillar of twentieth-century poetry. The title of one of his poems, "Waiting for the Barbarians," has practically become a catchphrase, while "The God Abandons Antony" has long been an anthem of stoic hedonism. Here is Aliki and Willis Barnstone's version:

When suddenly at the midnight hour
you hear the invisible troupe passing by
with sublime music, with voices—
don't futilely mourn your luck giving out, your work
collapsing, the designs of your life
that have all proved to be illusions.
As if long prepared, as if full of courage,
say good-bye to her, the Alexandria who is leaving.
Above all don't fool yourself, don't say it was
a dream, how your ears tricked you.
Don't stoop to such empty hopes.
As if long prepared, as if full of courage,
as is right for you who are worthy of such a city,
go stand tall by the window
and listen with feeling, but not
with the pleas and whining of a coward,
hear the voices—your last pleasure—
the exquisite instruments of that secret troupe,
and say good-bye to her, the Alexandria you are losing.

What makes Cavafy so distinctive, so memorable, a poet is what W. H. Auden called his tone of voice. To some he may sound merely decadent, a celebrant of furtive homosexual encounters, or a nostalgicist for the Hellenistic culture of the Asian shore, but to the sympathetic his voice is knowing, accepting, kindly, infused with the wisdom of the retired epicurean. In "Ithaka," for instance, the Odysseus-like reader is urged to enjoy life's journey to the fullest, to "wish that the way be long" and that reaching home should come only after one has accumulated much knowledge, experience, and treasure.

By instinct, Cavafy is primarily an elegist, capable of recalling with equal emotion the touch of a hand and the fall of an empire, of memorializing both the carnal favorites of ancient Antioch and the perfect limbs of the dirty young blacksmith down the street. To this Greek living in Egypt amid Arabs and British colonials, the world appears as a palimpsest: When Cavafy looks at Alexandria he glimpses, beneath the blandness of a modern urban wasteland, the playground of youthful gods. That imagined city, a city of sybarites, teaches one to enjoy the sensual pleasures of this world, to live without self-delusion or self-pity, to meet all experience with irony and aesthetic appreciation, to admire the fleeting beauty of youth and the permanent beauty of art. Little wonder that Lawrence Durrell (in *Justine*) called Alexandria "the great winepress of love."

There are many translators of Cavafy's poems, most notably Rae Dalven, Theoharis C. Theoharis, Edmund Keeley and Philip Sherrard, and Aliki Barnstone. Though the Keeley/Sherrard version has long been viewed as standard, all these editions possess their merits and are worth acquiring: It's nearly always rewarding to read several translations when one doesn't know a poem's original language. Moreover, the Cavafy canon isn't fully settled, and the various collections in English tend to differ somewhat in their contents: The poet never formally published his work and disliked the fixity of hard covers. Though Cavafy did bring out a couple of booklets (the first in

1904, in an edition of only one hundred copies), he much preferred to gather his loose-leafed poems into folders that he would simply give to his friends and admirers.

His mature poems hardly seem like poetry at all. (The novelist Marguerite Yourcenar once likened them to aides-memoires, or "reading notes.") Cavafy prefers nouns and avoids epithets, uses rhyme sparingly if at all, offers lots of historical or physical detail, and typically casts a poem as a dramatic monologue. Even his titles are oddly prosaic, though touched with a kind of shabby grandeur: "A Byzantine nobleman in exile composing verses" or "The melancholy of Iason Kleandros, poet in Kommagini, 595 C.E." In fact, Cavafy gains most of his power, as the Greek poet George Seferis insists, when we view his work as "one and the same poem" and "read him with the feeling of the continuous presence of his work as a whole. This unity is his grace." Everything he writes—even the historical poems—sounds like a fragment from a great confession, melancholy, witty, refined, sexy:

> *When I entered the house of pleasure,*
> *I did not stay in the front rooms where they celebrated*
> *Conventional lovemaking...*
> *I went to the secret rooms*
> *And I touched and lay down on their beds....*

Memory and reverie, then, followed by the re-creation of the voluptuous past, are the central elements of Cavafy's technique (just as they are in Proust). Only art can preserve, even enhance, the vanished moments of ardor and fleeting encounters with youthful bodies. The resulting poems burn with passionate immediacy. "The artisan of words," said Cavafy, "has the duty to combine what is beautiful with what is alive."

For all his apparent paganism, Cavafy remained an orthodox Christian. He was reportedly timid, somewhat vain, and fond of drink. As a boy, he spent a half-dozen years in England with his then wealthy family (they lost most of their money after the father's death) and learned French and English well enough to work as a copyist and translator in Alexandria's Irrigation Department. Until he was thirty-six, the poet lived with his mother and had to sneak away for his trysts; later he took an apartment with his brother on the Rue Lepsius: "Where could I live better? Below, the brothel caters for the flesh. And there is the church which forgives sin. And there is the hospital where we die." During the final days of his battle with cancer of the throat, he would read only detective novels, preferably those by Georges Simenon.

In the years since his death in 1933, Constantine Cavafy has come to be honored as the finest Greek poet of the last century. In critical esteem, his reputation in America rivals that of Rilke or Neruda. Certainly, his voice remains one of the most seductive in all modern literature.

⸺⸙⸺

GEORGETTE HEYER (1902–1974)
The Grand Sophy; Venetia; Friday's Child; Cotillion; A Civil Contract

The cover illustrations of Georgette Heyer's books, whether for her original hardcovers or for subsequent paperbacks, typically show slender young women in long gowns, often holding a parasol or fur muff, with stately Georgian architecture in the background. Occasionally, a spruce and well-turned-out young man with Byronic good looks lingers nearby. There's no question about the nature of these novels—they are love stories, marketed for female readers. Indeed, the name Georgette Heyer is virtually synonymous with the literary genre usually called "Regency romance."

Certainly many of her books are set during this period, the early years of the nineteenth century. What truly matters, though, is that Georgette Heyer remains as witty as any writer of the past century, as accomplished as P. G. Wodehouse in working out complex plots, and as accurate as a professional historian in getting her background details right. Her characters wear the correct clothes, use the appropriate slang, visit the properly fashionable coffeehouses, and move smoothly in the society of the time. In short, Heyer composes superb historical novels, laced with comedy, intrigue, delightful characters, and yes, romance. In truth, the contemporary author whose work Heyer's most resembles is Patrick O'Brian, the highly esteemed creator of the Jack Aubrey/Stephen Maturin naval adventures. Both look to Jane Austen as their model and inspiration.

A novel such as *The Grand Sophy*, for instance, one of the most admired of Heyer's Regencies, pays obvious homage to the strong-willed characters and spirited cross-talk of *Pride and Prejudice*. The Rivenhall family is beset with woes and gloom: The feckless father has gambled away much of the family fortune, daughter Cecilia has spurned an excellent suitor and fallen in love with a dreamy poet, and younger son Hubert has run up vast debts while at Oxford. Worst of all, elder son Charles has unexpectedly inherited a goodly sum from a rich uncle and so taken over the household finances. He has turned himself into a stern, moralistic kill-joy, and even contracted an engagement with the ever-so-proper Eugenia Wraxton, blessed with "a naturally joyless nature" and "reared on bleak principles." Together, Charles and Eugenia cast a pall over the entire family.

Then, one afternoon, a coach pulls up to the front portico:

Miss Stanton-Lacy's arrival was certainly impressive. Four steaming horses drew her chaise, two outriders accompanied it, and behind it rode a middle-aged groom, leading a splendid horse.

The steps of the chaise were let down, the door opened, and out leaped an Italian greyhound, to be followed later by a gaunt-looking female, holding a dressing bag, three parasols, and a bird cage. Lastly, Miss Stanton-Lacy herself descended, thanking the footman for his proffered help, but requesting him instead to hold her poor little Jacko. Her poor poor little Jacko was seen to be a monkey in a scarlet coat . . .

And so arrives, like a *dea ex machina,* Sophia Stanton-Lacy, age twenty, the cousin of the young Rivenhalls, daughter of the rakish European diplomat Sir Horace Stanton-Lacy, and herself an utterly irresistible force of nature. Sir Horace has gone off to Brazil on some hush-hush business and left his little girl in the care of the Rivenhalls, hoping that with their help she might find a suitable husband. But Sophy—rather too tall and nowhere near as beautiful as the fair Cecilia—has been reared with considerable laxity. She rides the magnificent stallion Salamanca like a hussar, drives a phaeton as well as any man, carries a silver-handled pistol, and is the toast—the Grand Sophy—of the army and the diplomatic corps. Not that Miss Stanton-Lacy is fast or vulgar, for she can conduct herself perfectly at balls and dinner parties, but she is fearless, independent, and mischievous. As Sir Vincent Talgarth says, when he and some of his fellow army officers recognize the young woman while riding in the park: "Dear Sophy, I am tolerably certain that you cannot have been in London above many days. Not the smallest rumor of any volcanic disturbance has come to my ears, and you know how quick I am to get abreast of the news!"

When Sir Vincent learns that Sophy is staying with the Rivenhalls, he adds, "My heart goes out to the family. Do they tread blindly toward their doom, Sophy, or did they willingly receive a firebrand into their midst?" For along with her other qualities, the brilliant Sophy loves to scheme, and quickly decides that she is going to save her unhappy cousins from themselves, whether they like it or not. One Rivenhall, at least, certainly doesn't like it:

"Let me tell you, my dear Cousin," says the cross and sorely vexed Charles Rivenhall, "that I should be better pleased if you would refrain from meddling in the affairs of my family!"

"Now that," Sophie answers, "I am very glad to know because if ever I should desire to please you I shall know just how to set about it. I daresay I shan't, but one likes to be prepared for any event, however unlikely."

By now, it's obvious that the two cousins are meant for each other, like those other famously quarrelsome couples Elizabeth Bennet and Mr. Darcy or Beatrice and Benedick. Still, the Grand Sophy will need to exert all her powers to properly mix and match up more than a half-dozen assorted lovers. Is there any doubt that she can do it?

Under his amazed and horrified gaze, large tears slowly welled over her eyelids and rolled down her cheeks. She did not sniff or gulp, or even sob; merely she allowed her tears to gather and fall.

"Sophy!" ejaculated Mr. Rivenhall, visibly shaken . . . "Pray do not! I did not mean—I had no intention—You know how it is with me! I say more than I mean, when—Sophy, for God's sake do not cry!"

"Oh, do not stop me!" begged Sophy. "Sir Horace says it is my *only* accomplishment!"

Mr. Rivenhall glared at her. *"What?"*

"Very few persons are able to do it," Sophy assured him. "I discovered it by the veriest accident when I was only seven years old. Sir Horace said I should cultivate it, for I should find it most useful."

Not all of Heyer's work—there are some forty romance novels, the first having appeared in 1921—is quite this madcap. In the much-admired *Venetia* (1958), for example, a young woman resigned to spinsterhood encounters a notorious rake, and both gradually work their way toward a kind of mutual redemption. Many fans regard *A Civil Contract* (1961) as her finest achievement—in it, the plain but rich Jenny agrees to marry the man she loves (who needs her money), even though he is still infatuated with the beautiful Julia. But marriage, Jenny recognizes, isn't so much a matter of infatuation as of comfort and companionship. This clear-eyed realism lies behind all of Heyer's work, no matter how giddy the goings-on beforehand.

No romantic herself, Heyer believed in self-control, order, and discipline. She approached her writing as a professional, worked hard on her Regency novels (and her excellent mysteries), hated the taxman, and lived quietly as the wife of a successful lawyer. Her astute and witty books should be more widely appreciated—by men as well as women.

ANNA AKHMATOVA (1889–1966)
Selected poetry

Virginia Woolf famously remarked that the world changed in or around 1910. In Russia, the tall and slender, beautiful, but somewhat imperious Anna Akhmatova was the leading lady of that change, the finest love-poet of her generation. She could be stunningly direct and sensual, startlingly bold: "Don't you love me or want to look at me?/ O, you are so handsome, damn you." "I've put on my tightest skirt/ To look even more svelte." "But raising his dry hand/ He lightly brushed the flowers:/ 'Tell me, how do men kiss you, Tell me how you kiss.'" "With a hand almost not trembling/ Once again he touched my knees."

Alexander Blok (1880–1921), the leading poet of the previous generation, said of this early poetry that Akhmatova "writes verse as if she is standing in front of a man." And not, it would seem, just standing. Sometimes her poems hint at a taste for masochism. Certainly, the artistic crowd at the legendary St. Petersburg cabaret The Stray Dog could rival even contemporary Bloomsbury in its sexual freedoms.

"We're all drunkards, here, and harlots," Akhmatova once proclaimed, just as she later announced that "the institution of divorce was the best thing mankind ever invented." Open marriages, gay couples, bisexuals, strings of lovers, ménages à trois—Akhmatova and her friends tried them all. "Forgive me," she coolly wrote to one lover, "for so often mistaking/ other people for you." In "Evening" (1912), "Rosary" (1914), and "White Flock" (1917), the poet transmuted both her serious affairs and passing fancies into lyrics of permanent beauty. She called herself "the naughtiest girl of Pushkin's town."

The young Anna (née Gorenko) was a privileged tomboy who grew into a free-spirited schoolgirl (losing her virginity at sixteen) and then an even more free-spirited woman. In 1910 she married the poet Nikolay Gumilyov (1886-1921), keeping her pen name of Anna Akhmatova. The marriage wasn't a happy one, and both soon started having affairs on the side. Even on her honeymoon in Paris, the young bride met a then unknown painter named Modigliani, with whom she would walk in the Luxembourg Gardens, for whom she would buy roses, and for whom she would pose in the nude.

While Gumilyov was away for six months trekking through Abyssinia, his new wife started to work seriously at her poems. When Akhmatova showed her notebooks to her husband, Gumilyov was so impressed that he immediately found them a publisher. Soon husband and wife, in company with their friend Osip Mandelstam (1891–1938), were promulgating a new poetry of clarity, sharpness, and simplicity, which they labeled Acmeism. Along the way, Anna gave birth to her son Lev in 1912, left him in the care of his grand-mother, fell in love with a painter, amicably divorced, married an As-syriologist (who introduced her ex-husband's translation of *Gilgamesh*), carried on several affairs, and lived with a composer *and* an actress. Through it all, she wrote, wrote, wrote, even as World War I, the Oc-tober Revolution, and the Russian Civil War were gradually destroy-ing the fabric of society and civility. In 1921 Gumilyov was shot as a traitor. By the late 1920s the economy was in ruins and millions of people were starving.

During the next forty years, during which Stalin refused to allow her to publish any of her own work, Akhmatova earned a little money from the perfunctory translation of anything from Rubens's letters to Korean poetry. But she also kept writing. Her book-length elegy for the 1930s, *Requiem* (not published until 1988), was memorized by friends to preserve it. The poem builds to the famous lines: "That was when the ones who smiled/ Were the dead, glad to be at rest."

For many, *Requiem* represents the Akhmatova that we know best—the voice of suffering Russia, the vilified poet who stood three hundredth in line "in bitter cold . . . under that blind red wall" to ob-tain news of her imprisoned son, who burned her manuscripts lest they incriminate friends or family, and who was there on the evening when the secret police first arrested Mandelstam. Through luck and charity she herself managed to survive near starvation, bouts of tuber-culosis, heart ailments, and the loss of almost everything that matters in a human life: "So much to do today:/ kill memory, kill pain,/ turn heart into a stone,/ and yet prepare to live again."

At the end of the 1930s, Akhmatova enjoyed a brief respite from critical neglect, learned that Mandelstam had died (a correspondent cautiously wrote, "Our friend Nadya is widowed") and then chose to remain in Leningrad when the Germans invaded Russia. For some mysterious reason, she was among those the government airlifted out to Tashkent, where she spent the war years. In that central Asian city she drank heavily, wrote about those who suffered during the purges, composed a play (which she destroyed out of fear), and eventually began *Poem Without a Hero,* a phantasmagorical dream-vision about 1913 and a world that had vanished forever, except in her memory: "Bonfires warmed the Christmas holidays,/ And carriages slid off the bridges. . . ."

In the mid-1940s the Russian-born philosopher Isaiah Berlin, "the guest from the future," managed to call on her, and the two spent a night discussing art, poetry, and exiled acquaintances. Unfortunately, Stalin decided that this "half-nun, half-harlot" was now consorting with English spies, and over the next decade she was again blacklisted. Only in the late 1950s, after Khrushchev attacked the excesses of the Stalin era, did Akhmatova find her writings rediscovered and openly honored.

Like Rilke, Akhmatova attracts translators, and there are many fine editions of her selected poetry. Still, these only supplement *The Complete Poems of Anna Akhmatova,* translated by Judith Hemschemeyer—handsomely laid out, prefaced by important memoirs (by Anatoly Naiman and Isaiah Berlin), replete with photographs and illustrations. Poet and Russian scholar Elaine Feinstein has written the most recent biography of this fascinating woman and artist.

Anna Akhmatova was eventually awarded a government pension and even a little dacha in the country, where she passed sedentary days with a stream of visitors, eager to see the living legend. A late fragment from these years reads "Pray, at night, that you won't/ Awake to sudden fame."

DAPHNE DU MAURIER (1907–1989)
Rebecca

"Last night I dreamt I went to Manderley again." With these unforgettable words the reader is launched into one of the most powerful visions of . . . what? Daphne du Maurier's *Rebecca* is a far more complex work of art than commonly believed, being one of the half-dozen greatest romance novels of the century and a subtle undercutting of the whole romance genre. It is, simultaneously, a devastating examination of the sexual politics of marriage, a haunting study of jealousy and psychological obsession, and a classic of suspense.

Structurally, *Rebecca* offers a tour de force of narrative control and point of view worthy of Henry James. The entire story comes to us filtered through the mind of the unnamed first-person narrator, a naïve young woman who falls in love with the melancholy and aristocratic Maxim de Winter, a man at least twenty years her senior. To the world the master of Manderley seems quite the Byronic figure, broken-hearted by the drowning death of his beloved wife Rebecca. Yet, de Winter rather brusquely proposes to the infatuated narrator, even though she hardly seems his type—too young, too innocent, and very different from her forceful and glamorous predecessor.

Once the newly married couple returns to Manderley, a magnificent house and estate on the coast of Cornwall, du Maurier starts to darken the narrative. The new Mrs. de Winter feels herself overwhelmed by Manderley's traditions, staff, and forbidding housekeeper, Mrs. Danvers. More and more, she grows convinced that everyone is comparing her unfavorably to Rebecca, whose spirit seems to haunt the halls, the garden paths, and, especially, the little cabin down by the cove. Does Maxim truly love her? He grows moody, introspective, as if he were thinking constantly of his lost love.

But nothing is quite what we have been led to imagine.

On the surface, *Rebecca* adopts, and slightly modernizes, most of the elements of *Jane Eyre, Wuthering Heights,* and what used to be called shopgirl romance—the Gothicky manor house, the darkly handsome hero with a secret sorrow, the wild landscape, a heroine who feels out of place, an atmosphere of impending doom, a riddle that must be solved before any happiness is possible. This is a reliable formula, one still used today in the more traditional Harlequin paperbacks. But the narrator of *Rebecca* isn't the sparky, intrepid heroine we might find in one of Georgette Heyer's witty Regency novels; she is soft, impressionable, and repeatedly humiliated by the imperious and even brutal Maxim, who for much of the novel, regards her as a child and treats her as he would a pet dog. And she accepts everything for "love," even condoning a terrible crime. *Rebecca* says less about love than about the snares of passion, the ache of jealousy, and the shifting balance of power between a husband and wife.

It is, in fact, a novel built around dreams, fantasies, and delusions. Is this marriage a fairy tale or a nightmare? It takes a long time before the scales fall from the second Mrs. de Winter's eyes.

At the novel's conclusion, we are left with normal, ordinary life. Or are we? Even after the drama is played out, both de Winters find themselves surrendering to memories, alive to what was rather than what is. Perhaps Rebecca does triumph after all. The novel, after all, bears her name.

Indeed, from a contemporary viewpoint, the first Mrs. de Winter is a good deal more admirable and interesting than her mousey successor: The vibrant Rebecca sets up with Maxim what is essentially a marital contract and insists that she be allowed to live her own life. (Fans of Congreve's *Way of the World* will recall a famous scene in which Millamant insists on a similar agreement before she weds.) Rebecca is tough and self-confident, goes after what she wants with determination, establishes and furnishes "a room of her own," and accepts bad news with stoic equanimity. Mrs. Danvers says that Rebecca is at heart a man, and we can read this as code for a woman who refuses to confine herself to the strictures and proprieties then dictated by society.

Compared to Rebecca, the unnamed narrator has no substance, no real identity—first she is Mrs. Van Hopper's companion, then she is Maxim's wife. But what does it mean to identify oneself in this subservient way? At one point, the phone at Manderley rings and a voice asks for Mrs. de Winter; the narrator answers that she is dead, when, of course, she herself is now Mrs. de Winter. Yet which of the two wives is truly most alive?

In her many novels and stories, Daphne du Maurier often explored the unsettling aspects of marriage and sexuality—spiritual domination, regret, jealousy, even incest and lesbianism. We now know that she could, and did, fall in love with both men and women, and combined in herself elements of both Rebecca and the novel's narrator. Her view of life was often grim, so it's hardly a surprise that she also created one of the darkest fables of our time, the famous story of what happens when nature murderously turns on man: *The Birds*.

Words from the Wise

O nce we would have called the writers in this category "moralists." They address what philosophy students often call the Big Questions: How should a human being live in the world? How does one deal with pain and suffering? Over the centuries thinkers have offered a handful of suggestions. This world is a testing-place for heaven, and we endure its tribulations in anticipation of a reward after death. The world is all there is and only stoic indifference can help us survive its ceaseless heart-breaks and setbacks. The world and God are the same and we must simply accept what comes to us, surrendering ourselves to the natural order of things. To be happy means to be good. To be happy means to keep busy. To be happy means to stop think-ing about being happy.

As usual with questions of ethics and belief, there are no def-inite answers, or at least none that will satisfy everyone. But sometimes we can't help but ponder the meaning and direction of our lives, and the writers in this category offer insight, sugges-tions, and solace. That's why "wisdom literature" is another name for these guides to that hectic intersection of philosophy, reli-gion, and practical life.

LAO-TSE (ca. 570 B.C.)
Tao Tê Ching

Apart from the Bible and the Indian *Bhagavad Gita,* the *Tao Tê Ching* is the most translated book in the world. There are, it's said, more than a thousand commentaries and at least one hundred English versions. Tao (pronounced "dow") means "way," as in a path, road, or direction; Tê (pronounced "duh") refers to individual power, virtue, integrity, and spirit; Ching (pronounced "jeang") is the Chinese word for a classic. Thus the book's title has sometimes been rendered "The Book of the Way and Its Power" or "The Way of Life" or "The Classic Book of Integrity and the Way." It is a short text of roughly five thousand characters, of both poetry and prose, but each line, each page is astonishingly suggestive, like the surviving fragments of the pre-Socratic philosophers. Lin Yutang, once a well-known interpreter of Asian culture to the West, maintained that "if there is one book in the whole of Oriental literature which should be read above all others, it is, in my opinion, Latzu's *Book of Tao* . . . It is one of the profoundest books in the world's philosophy . . . profound and clear, mystic and practical."

Few would argue about Lao-tse's importance or profundity, especially since Taoism pervades Chinese life to this day and is a crucial element of what we call Zen Buddhism. But the *Tao Tê Ching* is a poetic text, both tantalizing and hortatory, and not in any obvious way practical, even though much of it has been regarded as a guide to good government (advocating, as it does, a libertarian noninterference in the lives of citizens and a general return to simplicity). Scholars now regard the book as a collection of sayings from a long oral tradition, perhaps edited by the semilegendary Old Master (which is what Lao-tse means). Ordinary readers, though, revere the *Tao Tê Ching* as a kind of breviary or prayer book, to which one can turn for advice, insight, and relief from the madding crowd: "The person of superor integrity/ does not insist upon integrity; For this reason, he has integrity." (trans., Victor Mair); "Knowing all and believing that one knows nothing is true knowledge (of a superior kind). Knowing nothing and believing that one knows everything is the common evil of humans." (trans., Derek Bryce and Leon Wieger). "Great eloquence seems tongue-tied." (trans., D. C. Lau).

All in all, Lao-tse's pages provide a spiritually refreshing alternative to the gung-ho, can-do spirit of the West: Instead of self-promotion, showiness, aggression, and calculation, we are asked to practice modesty and stillness and spontaneity, to trust in the natural rhythms of life, to live harmoniously with our self and the universe, to go with the flow: "Really, only by not pursuing life/ can one live a worthy life." (trans., Sam Hamill). The *Tao Tê Ching* asks us to say no to cleverness, in all its forms, and to choose instead what Laurence Binyon has beautifully called "the authority of the heart."

At the center of the book is the plea for non-action (*wu-wei*), for permitting things to take their own course. Lao-tse's is a mystical volume in that it argues for acquiescence and spiritual receptivity, and its greatest symbols are strikingly "feminine": water, softness, valleys, the infant, the uncarved stone. Periodically we are counseled to relax the body, free ourselves from categorical thinking, calm the mind and spirit. In particular, the Tao asks us to recognize the value of emptiness and nothingness: A pot is useful because its surrounding clay encloses nothing; "We put thirty spokes together and call it a wheel;/ But it is in the space where there is nothing that the usefulness of the wheel depends." (trans., Arthur Waley). Much of the Taoist spirit can be found in the philosophy behind yoga.

Pure Taoism doesn't ask for ritual observances, nor does it regard the world as a realm of suffering and pain, a wheel from which we must free ourselves. Our goal on earth is to fulfill our being (our *tê*), to enjoy life in as immediate and authentic a way as we can for as long as we can, to satisfy our desires without becoming attached to them, and when we die, to calmly accept that the time has come for us to be even more closely united with the Tao. Those who follow the Way eventually become the Way.

Yet all too often as we age we grow harder, stiffer, and more un-yielding, forgetting that, like an infant, we should remain pliantly open to experience. The *Tao Tê Ching* counsels us to keep ourselves receptive, tender, patient, and tolerant. Only by turning away from the quest for wealth and honors, by rejecting the rat race, can we live a worthy life. No wonder Thoreau admired Lao-tse.

As there are many translations of the *Tao Tê Ching*, readers should sample several, if only to gain a fuller sense of the original's richness. The more modern editions follow the text of the Ma-Wang-Tui man-uscipts, which were discovered only in 1973 and provide the earliest extant version of the book, as well as a dramatically new ordering of its eighty-one "chapters." Still, the *Tao Tê Ching* isn't a work one reads for the plot, but for its serenity and suggestiveness. After all, is there any other Asian masterpiece so beloved by those who live in the heart-sick and troubled West? Its pages tell us that our deepest self is fun-damentally good, and that our lives can be happy if we will only follow our true nature, an inner way that is also the greater Way.

HERACLITUS (fl. ca. 500 B.C.)
Philosophical fragments

Among the Greek philosophers before Socrates, probably none has been so attractive to general readers as Heraclitus. This is so, in large part, because his thought has come down to us in brief, pungent, and endlessly tantalizing fragments that resemble aphorisms or even Zen koans. In antiquity he was already referred to as "the obscure" or "the dark." Nonetheless, some of his most famous sayings have passed into common parlance: "Character is fate." "One cannot step into the same river twice." "The waking have one common world, but the sleeping turn aside each into a world of his own."

At the heart of Heraclitus's thought lies the notion that life and the cosmos are constantly in flux, yet behind this unending change and decay lies an essential unity. Day fades into night and night grows back into day; "the way up and the way down are one and the same"; "the beginning is the end." The apparent strife between opposites hides a more fundamental attunement. Without work, we could have no leisure; without hunger, no satisfaction. Stasis leads to weariness, and real rest comes only from change.

Wisdom, to Heraclitus, lies in the ability to perceive the inner unity, the organizing principle or logos, behind all things. To represent that unity, he usually resorts to the symbol of fire—a flame, after all, remains the same yet is never still. It has also been conjectured that the beginning of St. John's Gospel, "In the beginning was the word" [in Greek, *logos*], may reflect Heraclitean influence. Other writers who pay homage, directly or indirectly, to the philosopher include poets like Gerard Manley Hopkins ("That Nature is a Heraclitean Fire and of the Comfort of the Resurrection") and T. S. Eliot.

The succinct elegance of Heraclitus's expression has led the scholar Albrecht Dihle to call him the "first great prose stylist of the Greek language." For we moderns, the fact that his work exists only in fragments, unlike, say, that of Plato, imbues it with an attractive quicksilver edginess; the oracular assertions rise from the page like philosophical sound bites. As James Hillman has said, for Heraclitus "the world is only revealed in quick glances. There can be no completion . . . No sooner known and explained, the event has changed. Therefore, 'the known way is an impasse.'"

Legend has it that Heraclitus was heir to the throne of Ephesus, but gave it up to become a philosopher. It remains astonishing, even

unnerving, to realize that he was a virtual contemporary of Gautama
Buddha, Lao-tse, and Confucius, while Persia's Zoroaster and the Hebrew author of Ecclesiastes lived during that same century. What was
it about the time around 500 B.C. that led to such a blossoming of
philosophical and religious thought?

⟶•◦•⟵

CICERO (106–43 B.C.)
On Duties; Discussions at Tusculum; The Dream of Scipio;
the letters to Atticus

Up until the nineteenth century, Cicero was probably the most influential cultural and philosophical figure of Roman antiquity. His
admirers ranged from St. Jerome, who once dreamt that he was more
of a Ciceronian than a Christian, to Erasmus, who dubbed the pagan
writer St. Cicero. Petrarch established him as a model for the Renaissance humanist, while eighteenth-century thinkers as eminent as
Voltaire, Kant, Schiller, John Adams, and David Hume turned to
him as a moralist and guide to life. During the Renaissance and the
seventeenth century Cicero's orations provided textbook examples of
stately, majestic prose, not only for those who worked in Latin but
also for many writing in the European vernacular languages, such as
Thomas Browne and Bossuet. Edward Gibbon's elegantly balanced
sentences also bear the mark of his study of the antique Roman's
diction.

In modern times, however, Cicero has frequently come to be
viewed as little more than a second-rate littérateur. As a thinker, he
borrows most of his ideas from the Greeks; as a politician, he sometimes seems less a beacon of stern and noble virtue than a flexible
trimmer (or perhaps we should say a true politician). His once admired speeches now sound over-elaborate and even pompous.

Yet several of his works still reward a reader's attention, starting with one he never intended to be part of his published oeuvre. His biographer and translator D. R. Shackleton Bailey has written that "no other Greek or Roman has projected himself into posterity like Cicero" and that he does this through his correspondence. His more than nine hundred letters to his lifelong friend Atticus, his brother Quintus Cicero, and others show us the private life of a leisured, shrewd, and cultivated Roman politician and gentleman. It was Cicero who suggested that the acme of modest human happiness would be a library in a garden.

His philosophical writings, being brief and elegant, remain attractive. *The Dream of Scipio*—sometimes judged a work of proto–science fiction—provides a vision of the fundamental nature of things that influenced mankind's conception of the universe for centuries: The military tribunal Scipio Africanus dreams that he floats up through the cosmos and describes what he learns from this out-of-body experience. He sees the earth at the center of the universe, hears the enchanting music of the spheres, reveals that above the moon everything is timeless and eternal, while below it is mortal and finite. He even asserts that we all carry our real selves—a spirit—within our corporeal frame. Scipio travels so high up that our world and the affairs of men, the desire for fame and the pursuit of power, look trifling and inconsequential, indeed mundane; after all, what do such things matter *sub specie aeternitatis?*

At the very least, *De Officiis* (translated as On Duties, or On Moral Obligation) and *Tusculanae Disputatione* (Discussions at Tusculum, or Tusculum Disputations) remain highly readable summaries of ancient thinking about ethics, wisdom, the conduct of life, and the nature of happiness. The *Discussions at Tusculum* takes the form of a country-house conversation among friends; *On Duties* is a letter from Cicero to his son. According to historian Michael Grant, the latter has "exercised more influence on the thought and standards of the western world than any other secular work ever written." In it and the Tusculum dialogues we learn of the crucial value of self-control and manly indifference to life's vicissitudes, the importance of turning the other cheek, the value of friends and the duties of a citizen, the importance of enjoying the beauty of this world, and the pleasures of art and literature. Along with the poet Horace, Cicero is the classic exemplar and proponent of *humanitas*—of tolerance and civility, instinct guided by reason, moderation, and decorum.

He is more than merely a genial host or guide to etiquette. Cicero asks us to look hard at our daily behavior and to live up to our best principles (something he himself didn't always do). What could be a more modern ethical issue than this one (in Michael Grant's translation)?

> Imagine yourself doing something in order to acquire excessive wealth or power, or tyranny, or sensual satisfaction. Suppose that no one were going to discover, or even suspect, what you had done: on the contrary, that neither gods nor men would ever have an inkling. Would you do it?

Well, would you?

—————

ERASMUS (1466?–1536)
The Praise of Folly

Erasmus was the world's first public intellectual. Before him, men of learning had been philosophers and theologians, courtiers, and poets, but Erasmus was all of these, and more. He published editions of the classics and the Greek New Testament, set down witty dialogues about social issues of the day (the *Colloquies*); compiled a guide to government (*The Education of a Christian Prince*); produced a collection of ancient proverbs and maxims (*Adagia*) that made classical learning available to ordinary people, especially when coupled with his extensive essay-like commentaries; and conducted so vast a correspondence that its modern editor, P. S. Allen, dubbed him "the Master of those who talk." Over the years Erasmus argued religion with Martin Luther, named Sir Thomas More his closest friend, and was revered by Rabelais. The artists Holbein and Dürer depicted the renowned scholar at work in his cap and fur-lined robes. Kings, emperors, and popes competed for his presence at their courts.

Recent scholarship has shown that Erasmus carefully cultivated his image as a polymath, the Renaissance heir to St. Jerome. Yet this greatest of all early-modern humanists also possessed a genuine gift for friendship, and probably knew more people of every class and walk of life than anyone of his time. He wasn't merely scholarly; he was lively and intellectually playful, both kindly and witty. (The similarly high-spirited Lucian was his favorite Greek author.) He tended to write in a hurry, and possessed a real *cacoethes scribendi,* a compulsion to scribble. However, all Erasmus's writing and all his learning supported his unswerving devotion to Christianity. Unlike some believers, he never felt that one had to choose between the ideals of antiquity and the teachings of Christ (indeed, he once beseeched the aid of St. Socrates). While certain reformers might believe in redemption through revelation, Erasmus argued more practically for better education as the path to a good and holy life in this world, and to future happiness in the next.

For much of his own good and holy life, Erasmus was quite simply the most famous man in Europe, but he worked hard to achieve that eminence. He was born out of wedlock (in the Netherlands) and his father might have been a priest. (Older readers may recall the once-famous fictional retelling of his parents' love affair, Charles Reade's *The Cloister and the Hearth.*) Largely educated in a monastery, Erasmus ultimately took holy orders, though he never cared for monkish routine. His was a restless spirit, and he passed much of his career as a scholar-gypsy. He traveled to Paris to learn Greek, then to England, where he was welcomed by its greatest humanists—the circle of Thomas More and John Colet—and then to Italy, where he owlishly spent his time in libraries and among scholars. (It is astonishing to realize that in the fall of 1506, while Erasmus was visiting Florence, he could have met Leonardo, Michelangelo, Raphael, and Machiavelli.)

As a thinker and Christian apologist, Erasmus promulgated learning, tolerance, and moderation, while also representing the leading edge on all the important intellectual developments of his time. Alas, in his final years he found himself trapped between his sympathies for Luther and his commitment to the church. Both eventually turned on him as a wishy-washy Laodicean, "neither hot nor cold," and dismissed his humanistic middle way in favor of the twin zealotries of the Reformation and Counter Reformation.

At least Erasmus was spared the next century's religious wars. For if there was one thing he hated it was fanaticism, especially when it took the form of martial violence. War, he said, is delightful only to those who have no experience of it. Erasmus despised nationalistic feeling, urged countries to be content with their present borders, and argued for orderly government, checks upon rulers, and arbitration to settle differences. He implored the moral forces of the world—religion, education, philosophy—to help eradicate organized bloodshed, believing that war only brought the breakdown of all civilized values to both sides of any conflict. "The most disadvantageous peace," Erasmus frankly maintained, "is better than the most just war."

Scholars revere this iconic Renaissance man as the cold-climate counterpart to Petrarch or Leonardo. But Erasmus truly lives for most readers in one work alone, a *jeu d'esprit* scribbled in a week (though later polished and expanded). Returning in 1509 from his single visit to Italy, where he'd been shocked by papal worldliness and pomp,

Erasmus traveled to England, where he stayed with his friend Thomas More. Soon after he arrived, the disheartened humanist fell ill (possibly with a kidney stone), and so whiled away his time in bed by composing a little satire in Latin, the title of which punned (in Greek) on his host's name: *Moriae Encomium—The Praise of Folly.* A bit slapdash and disorganized, the result was eventually published and became an international bestseller, with forty editions appearing in Erasmus's lifetime alone.

What makes *The Praise of Folly* somewhat enigmatic is its yoking together of a number of incongruous aspects of "folly." Initially, Folly—dressed as a medieval jester—presents herself as the spirit of youth, energy, sex, and pleasure, as well as of silliness, self-love, and irrationality. In fact, Folly suggests that she's the intuitive and passional side of life, far more fundamental to our well-being than propriety or reason. Throughout, Folly boldly sings her own praises as she presents seemingly logical arguments to prove that she is at the root of courage, industry, and even prudence.

But gradually Erasmus slides into more pointed satire—against scholastic learning, scientific investigation, religious hypocrisy, and fanaticism, against sophists and lawyers and all those who are smug, greedy, and self-satisfied. To counter these he presents another form of Folly, a kind of holy simple-mindedness. Christ endured the "folly" of the Cross and reminded his followers to imitate "children, lilies, mustard-seed, and humble sparrows, all foolish, senseless things, which live their lives by natural instinct alone, free from care or purpose." Gradually, Folly becomes the "natural," in all its senses, standing in opposition to the mind-forged manacles of societal norms and expectations. Eventually, this sort of folly then modulates into mystical distraction and ecstasy. Just as Plato asserted that the madness of physical lovers, during which the spirit seems to leave the body, is the highest form of ordinary happiness, so Christianity offers a similar joyful dream state, when the soul temporarily unites itself with God.

The Praise of Folly is a tissue of paradoxes, sometimes high-spirited or tongue-in-cheek, at other times bitter and deadly serious. But the book always remains lively, a showpiece of linguistic and philosophic virtuosity. Most editions supply notes to explain the references, but anyone can pick up a paperback and read it for pleasure. Indeed, one imagines that Shakespeare did just that, for he seems to have remembered the following address of Folly—in Betty Radice's translation—when he set down Jaques' "All the world's a stage" speech in *As You Like It:*

> Now, what else is the whole life of man but a sort of play? Actors come on wearing their different masks and all play their parts until the producer orders them off the stage, and he can often tell the same man to appear in different costume, so that now he plays a king in purples and now a humble slave in rags. It's all a sort of pretence, but it's the only way to act out this farce.

The Praise of Folly doesn't settle easily into the mind. Instead, like More's *Utopia* or Denis Diderot's *Rameau's Nephew,* the book's virtuosic liveliness allows it to escape any ready-made interpretation or categorization. About all one can do with certainty is enjoy its wit, ponder its paradoxes, and remember that sometimes, at least, 'tis wise to be foolish.

THE ENGLISH RELIGIOUS TRADITION

In English there are five main sources for religious eloquence: the King James version of the Bible; *The Book of Common Prayer; The Pilgrim's Progress* by John Bunyan; the hymns of writers like Isaac Watts, Charles Wesley, and others; and the classical traditions of preaching and homily. What links them all is a Shaker plainness and cleanness of diction, just barely covering profound spiritual conviction and emotion. This is, in short, the speech of men and women doing the Lord's work, honoring him and praising him with ceremony, reverence, and humility.

Take this passage from the Gospel of Luke:

> And it came to pass in those days, that there went out a decree from Caesar Augustus, that all the world should be taxed. . . . And Joseph also went up from Galilee, out of the city of Nazareth, into Judea, unto the city of David, which is called Bethlehem (because he was of the house and lineage of David), to be taxed with Mary his espoused wife, being great with child. And so it was, that, while they were there, the days were accomplished that she should be delivered. And she brought forth her firstborn son, and wrapped him in swaddling clothes, and laid him in a manger; because there was no room for them in the inn.

Toward the end of December, year after year, these words are spoken aloud from pulpits and altars, and, for most listeners, they never fail to deliver a shivery thrill of pleasure. Why is this? The plain sentences don't possess any narrative excitement, as we all know the story already, indeed we probably know it far better than any other in all the world. But the language—like that of so many other passages from the Bible—keeps us spellbound with its deeply felt nobility and seriousness.

The solemn harmonies of such prose are largely ignored in these days of text-messaging and political newspeak. Nonetheless, sometimes only the full organ roll of liturgical English can match the sacredness of weddings, funerals, and religious holy days. For instance, what soul doesn't feel, as well as hear, the sorrowful music in the sixteenth-century *Book of Common Prayer*'s "Order for the Burial of the Dead"?

> Man that is born of a woman hath but a short time to live, and is full of misery. He cometh up and is cut down like a flower; he flieth as it were a shadow, and never continueth in one stay. In the midst of life we be in death.

These magnificently somber phrases eventually build to one of the great climaxes in English literature:

> Behold, I show you a mystery. We shall not all sleep, but we shall all be changed, and that in a moment, in the twinkling of an eye by the last trump. For the trump shall blow, and the dead shall rise incorruptible, and we shall be changed. . . . Death where is thy sting? Hell where is thy victory?

To some readers, those last plaintive questions may be better known from the final pages of *The Pilgrim's Progress,* when Mr. Valiant-for-Truth enters the river of death and pronounces the same words (though he substitutes "Grave" for "Hell"). As wonderful as they are, these phrases merely cap a farewell speech that would be right at home in Middle Earth. This battle-worn soldier of Christ announces:

> I am going to my fathers, and though with great difficulty I am got hither, yet now I do not repent me of all the trouble I have been at to arrive where I am. My sword, I give to him that shall succeed me in my pilgrimage, and my courage and skill, to him that can get it. My marks and scars I carry with me, to be a witness for me that I have fought his battles who now will be my rewarder.

Bunyan then concludes with positively Handelian grandeur: "So he passed over, and all the trumpets sounded for him on the other side."

Theologically, the graceful moderation of the established Church of England was anathema to the ardently Puritan Bunyan. But, apart from the Old and New Testaments, no religious texts have more influenced the English-speaking imagination than *The Book of Common Prayer* and *The Pilgrim's Progress*. The simple beauty of the Prayer Book's prose, especially in its collects (generally thought to have been composed by Archbishop Thomas Cranmer), displays perfect pitch for sound and rhythmical balance:

Almighty and most merciful Father, we have erred and strayed from thy ways, like lost sheep. We have followed too much the devices and desires of our own hearts. We have offended against thy holy laws. We have left undone those things which we ought to have done, and we have done those things which we ought not to have done, and there is no health in us.

Bunyan, in his turn, wrote what George Bernard Shaw thought was the most perfect English, at once clear and forceful. Certainly his phrases and dramatis personae have passed into common parlance: "Fly from the wrath to come." "I have laid my hand to the plough." "The Giant Despair." "The Slough of Despond." "The Delectable Mountains." "Vanity-Fair." In addition to the allegorical figures (Christian, Mr. Worldly-Wiseman), Bunyan also uses such surprisingly modern phrases as "Were you doers, or talkers only?"

And he ends Part One with a chilling sentence. Ignorance has arrived at the Celestial City and knocks on the door. So very close to his heavenly goal, he nonetheless lacks the proper "certificate" and is suddenly, unexpectedly, damned, bound hand and foot, and thrust by angels through a door in the side of a hill. Writes Bunyan: "Then I saw that there was a way to Hell, even from the Gates of Heaven, as well as from the City of Destruction." On which harrowing note he brings his original vision to a close: "So I awoke, and behold, it was a Dream."

Such declamatory moments remind us that Bunyan passed much of his life, when not in prison for his religious beliefs, preaching in the open air. In our era of so much bland speech-making, we sometimes forget about the sheer power of oratory. Great preachers even now preserve its tradition, one in which human elocution alone, backed by passionate conviction and a desire to save souls, can bring people to tears, to their knees, or to their feet. Think, for a supreme example, of Martin Luther King, Jr.

The almost legendary eighteenth-century preacher George Whitefield was so magnificent a speaker that the atheist philosopher David Hume declared that he would travel twenty miles on foot to hear him. At one time every high-school student read, with growing terror, the rolling periodic sentences of Jonathan Edwards's sermon "Sinners in the Hands of an Angry God." After describing the horrors of the pit, Edwards dramatically reminds us of the sharp precariousness of life:

> The bow of God's wrath is bent, and the arrow made ready on the string, and justice bends the arrow at your heart, and strains the bow, and it is nothing but the mere pleasure of God, and that of an angry God, without any promise or obligation at all, that keeps the arrow one moment from being made drunk with your blood.

Our preachers grow most eloquent when describing hell fire. But our hymns and carols sing of God's mercy and loving kindness. Here the diction tends to be simple and profoundly moving, a truly populist poetry, as in this passage by Isaac Watts. We can hardly murmur the words without the memory of many voices sounding forth on Sunday morning:

> *O God, our Help in ages past,*
> *Our Hope for years to come,*
> *Our Shelter from the stormy blast,*
> *And our eternal Home.*

From H. F. Lyte's "Abide with me" and William Blake's "Jerusalem" to "We Shall Overcome," these are the songs that see us through the hardest times. Like the Bible, *The Book of Common Prayer,* and *Pilgrim's Progress,* like the resounding voices of great preachers, they ask us to think about our lives and how we conduct them. It is right and good that we should do this. They feed what Philip Larkin once called the hunger to be more serious that lies within each of us—even the agnostic and the atheist.

———❧———

BENEDICT DE SPINOZA (1632–1677)
Ethics; Theological-Political Treatise

He's been called "Satan incarnate" and "the most impious atheist who ever lived upon the face of the earth." But he is also revered as arguably the greatest philosopher since Plato, the political theorist who first enunciated the general principles for a secular democratic society, and in many ways a modern saint. Baruch, later Benedict, de Spinoza devoted his entire adult life to thinking about the biggest questions of all: the nature of God and the universe, the function of religion, man's elusive quest for happiness, the ideals of government, and how we should conduct our lives. His own was one of absolute simplicity—a rented room, a little gruel for supper, and an occasional pipe of tobacco, most of it paid for by his small earnings as a lens-maker. Yet as the poet Heinrich Heine said, "All our modern philosophers . . . see through the glasses which Baruch Spinoza ground."

As with Shakespeare, we know very little about his early life, and nowhere near enough about his maturity. So his biographers have perforce closely examined the world in which he grew up, that of Jews who fled the Inquisition in Spain for the relative tolerance of the seventeenth-century Netherlands. As a youth, Spinoza was taught the legalistic traditions of Talmudic scholarship but also introduced to the seductive mysticism of the Kaballah. His teachers clearly expected great things from him. Nonetheless, by his early twenties the young scholar began to voice opinions judged heretical, refused to keep quiet, and was finally, dramatically, excommunicated, the rite of *cherem* cutting him off entirely from his friends, family, and community.

For the rest of his life, Spinoza lived as a Dutch citizen and a philosopher. As he himself says in one of his early treatises ("On the Improvement of the Understanding"):

> After experience had taught me that all the usual surroundings of social life are vain and futile; seeing that none of the objects of my fears contained in themselves anything either good or bad, except in so far as the mind is affected by them, I finally resolved to inquire . . . whether, in fact, there might be anything of which the discovery and attainment would enable me to enjoy continuous, supreme, and unending happiness.

What a dreamer! And yet in his *Ethics* (posthumously published in 1677) Spinoza aims to discover a way of life that would provide just such "continuous, supreme, and unending happiness." Alas, many people have been put off this inquiry because it is organized like Euclid's *Elements*. The thought progresses through axioms, propositions, definitions, proofs, demonstrations, and corollaries. While studying the *Ethics* one frequently longs for the engaging style of Descartes or the baroque grandeur of Hobbes (two near contemporaries from whom Spinoza learned). Yet it pays to persevere. The appendices to the five "books" and the frequent mini-essays called "scholia" provide short, even lively, summaries of the arguments built on this "cumbersome, geometric order," as the author himself once called it.

Still, Spinoza recognizes that he needs all this cool, austere reasoning. People, he demonstrates, are constantly being led astray by the randomness of their sensual experience, by their imaginations and passions. Only mathematics provides a model for conclusions that cannot be refuted, that are either right or wrong; thus, "I will write about human beings as though I were concerned with lines and planes and solids." So the *Ethics* is systematically divided into five sections: Book One treats the existence of God and his properties; Book Two describes the nature of the mind; Book Three charts man's psychological and emotional life; Book Four analyzes our self-destructive passions; and Book Five shows how we can control our passions and achieve "blessedness."

Of Spinoza's starting point, his metaphysical description of the nature of things, nineteenth-century scholar Ernest Renan once asserted that "the truest vision ever had of God came, perhaps, here." Spinoza's vision is one of fundamental unity. God didn't at some point long ago decide to create the universe, the earth, and human beings. Such an act would imply duality between creator and created, which would suggest that God had at one time been incomplete or less than perfect. No, everything that exists is part of the single substance of God, perceived as an aspect of his two attributes, Extension (basically the physical world) and Thought (mental processes). As these are themselves part of a single substance, there is no division between mind and body, as had been promulgated (or worried about) by philosophers from Plato to Descartes. God, in fact, is nature, or as Spinoza writes, *Deus Sive Natura,* "God, or Nature."

Because everything is inherent in God eternally, speculation about teleology is pointless; there are no goals or ends for man or the universe. We aren't in any way "special." From this rather bleak beginning, the philosopher goes on to lay out his *Ethics* proper. Human psychology, he determines, is based entirely on self-interest and self-preservation, while being largely subject to ever-changing combinations of desire, pleasure, and pain. Such domination by the changeable senses and the outside world inevitably results in emotional turmoil: "Like waves on the sea, driven by contrary winds, we toss about, not knowing our outcome and our fate." To overcome this "human bondage" to ephemeral passions, we should learn to moderate our desires, live according to reason, and ultimately aspire to an intellectual love of God. This acceptance of the universe as it is will create an inner peace of mind or blessedness during life, and permit a kind of impersonal immortality after our deaths.

Some of Spinoza's prescription for a satisfying life may sound familiar. The ancient Greeks advocated *ataraxia,* or stoic indifference to the world's ills. St. Augustine confessed that our hearts are restless until they rest in God. Buddhists believe that we must free ourselves from the wheel of desire to find spiritual beatitude. But, unlike these austere systems, Spinoza's doesn't reject the body or the delights of the world: "It is the part of a wise man, I say, to refresh and restore himself in moderation with pleasant food and drink, with scents, with the beauty of green plants, with decoration, music, sports, the theater and other things of this kind, which anyone can use without injury to another. For the human body is composed of a great many parts of different natures, which constantly require new and varied nourishment." We should strive to be cheerful, too—"Why is it more proper to relieve our hunger and thirst than to rid ourselves of melancholy?" More than occasionally, Spinoza's *Ethics* sounds like a European version of Lao-tse's *Tao Tê Ching.*

While the *Ethics* describes man as he is fundamentally, in a state of nature, the *Theological-Political Treatise* (1670) is an impassioned attack on superstition and a defense of tolerance and democratic principles. Spinoza was among the first to show that Holy Scripture is "faulty, mutilated, corrupted, and inconsistent," and that it has been used by organized religion to instill not virtue but obedience. All those "ceremonial rites," he says, "serve only to control people's behavior and preserve a particular society." Politicians, moreover, regularly turn to organized religion to control and manipulate:

> The greatest secret of monarchic rule . . . is to keep men deceived, and to cloak in the specious name of religion the fear by which they must be checked, so that they will fight for slavery as they would for salvation, and will think it not shameful, but a most honorable achievement, to give their life and blood that one man may have a ground for boasting.

All too often, Spinoza points out further, people "pay homage to the Books of the Bible, rather than to the Word of God." In fact, the only real message of any true scripture is simply to know and love God and to love one's neighbor as oneself. As a result, "in judging whether or not a person's faith is pious, we must look only to his works. If they are good, his faith is as it should be."

Unfortunately, so long as men are swayed by passions, we require the state to insure our security. Spinoza imagines a kind of social contract, à la Hobbes, as the start of government, but proves that a democratic republic best maintains the rights of all its citizens. In particular, he argues for free speech and utter openness in government in his never-completed *Political Treatise:*

> Better that right counsels be known to enemies than that the evil secrets of tyrants should be concealed from the citizens. They who can treat secretly of the affairs of a nation have it absolutely

under their authority; and as they plot against the enemy in time
of war, so do they against the citizens in time of peace.

He does point out that democracies all too often raise mediocrities to
power.

There's much more beauty and truth to Spinoza than is clumsily
adumbrated here. While his writing requires focus and concerted attention, it rewards the effort:

> He who rightly knows that all things follow from the necessity
> of the divine nature, and happen according to the eternal laws
> and rules of Nature, will surely find nothing worthy of hate,
> mockery, or disdain . . . Instead he will strive, as far as human
> virtue allows, to act well, as they say, and rejoice.

SAMUEL JOHNSON (1709–1784)
"The Vanity of Human Wishes"; *Rasselas;* Essays from the *Rambler*
and the *Idler; Lives of the Poets*

Not enough people read Samuel Johnson. Boswell's famous biography is so entertaining that its depiction of the witty and commonsen-
sical "Great Cham" of literature has simply overshadowed Johnson's
own writing. Yet Boswell tends to emphasize the clubman, the coffee-
house arbiter of taste, the public figure, rather than the deeply humane critic and moral essayist. For Johnson was no mere talking
head. Throughout his life he was prey to an intense melancholy, regularly feared for his sanity, and thought often about death. In his writing he reflects constantly on how we live and how we should live.

In his somber poem "The Vanity of Human Wishes" (1749),
Johnson surveys the disappointments that await each of us: "Life pro-

tracted is protracted woe." Fortunes rise and fall. Children are ungrateful (he speaks of "the daughter's petulance, the son's expense").
Heartbreak, crippling illness, and the decrepitude of age break us
down, for "as year chases year, decay pursues decay." Even the learned
find no serenity: "There mark what ills the scholar's life assail,/ Toil,
envy, want, the patron, and the jail." And so, Johnson despondently
wonders, "Must helpless man, in ignorance sedate/ Roll darkling
down the torrent of his fate?"

To this down-to-earth mind the only abiding refuge was, in fact,
belief in God and an eternal reward in the afterlife. Yet Johnson was
no religious fuddy-duddy but, in his no-nonsense way, a man of the
world, of this world. His strong mind always engaged with the reality of lived experience. Time after time, he reminds us of the "treachery of the human heart," of how we move restlessly from want to
want, prey to the snares of self-delusion. And he does so not from a
position of superior wisdom, but as one of us, a fellow sufferer. Despite a prose that is sometimes rather florid for modern taste, his
Rambler and *Idler* essays flash with truths we recognize:

> He that compares what he has done with what he has left un-
> done will feel the effect which must always follow the compari-
> son of imagination with reality; he will look with contempt on
> his own unimportance, and wonder to what purpose he came
> into the world; he will repine that he shall leave behind him no
> evidence of his having been, that he has added nothing to the
> system of life, but has glided from youth to age among the
> crowd, without any effort for distinction.

Who hasn't felt this sense of waste and disappointment, of dreams un-
fulfilled or unfollowed? Which of us once past bright-eyed youth is
pleased with what he or she has become?

Johnson notes that our minds seldom focus enough on the present, and "recollection and anticipation fill up almost all our moments." Moreover, "the desires of man encrease with acquisitions; every step which he advances brings something within his view, which he did not see before, and which, as soon as he sees it, he begins to want. Where necessity ends curiosity begins, and no sooner are we supplied with every thing that nature can demand, than we sit down to contrive artificial appetites." The true wisdom of life is to do the task before us, to enjoy the company of our friends and families, and to labor for our own happiness by promoting the happiness of others. As for achievement itself:

> All the performances of human art, at which we look with praise or wonder, are instances of the resistless force of perseverance: it is by this that the quarry becomes a pyramid, and the distant countries united with canals.

Still, in the end, only "a little more than nothing is as much as can be expected."

Much of Johnson's thought about life's realities is distilled in his philosophical romance *Rasselas* (1759). Here the princely hero and his sister Nekayah flee the luxury and boredom of a secluded "Happy Valley" and travel into the world to discover the secret of a fulfilling life. They undergo many adventures and vicissitudes in their search before they are "convinced that happiness is never to be found," though each of us "believes it possessed by others, to keep alive the hope of obtaining it ourself." During their quest they do learn many harsh truths. An emperor proves no wiser than his subjects. The wealthy tremble with fear at the possible loss of their riches. Powerful viceroys are suddenly turned out by their even more powerful sovereigns. Hermits yearn for the world they long ago abandoned. Scholars lose their reason. "Marriage has many pains, but celibacy has no pleasures." Old age brings infirmity and regrets. In short, human life "is every where a state in which much is to be endured, and little to be enjoyed." Yet somehow, lest we dry up within, we must commit ourselves to the world.

Despite illness and neurotic tics, and lacking the advantage of good looks, connections or wealth—"Slow rises worth, by poverty depressed"—Johnson eventually made himself into the greatest all-around man of letters of his time. He compiled the first true English dictionary. He annotated the works of Shakespeare more brilliantly than any single editor before or since. His literary commentary—embodied in the short biographies of the *Lives of the Poets* (1781)—established him as the finest of all practical critics. Yes, we should always read Boswell's sparkling *Life of Johnson,* but we honor Samuel Johnson even better by reading his own works as well. Perhaps all his poems, essays, stories, travel journals, and short biographies may be most aptly viewed as nothing less than moral wisdom, providing both humane counsel and much-needed consolation.

Everyday Magic

At the end of the novel *Little, Big,* John Crowley wistfully describes the closing of the portals between our world and Faery: "The world we know now, is as it is and not different; if there was ever a time when there were passages, doors, the borders open and many crossing, that time is not now. The world is older than it was. Even the weather isn't as we remember it clearly once being; never lately does there come a summer day such as we remember, never clouds as white as that, never grass as odorous or shade as deep and full of promise as we remember they can be, as once upon a time they were."

Yes, the magic has gone away: We are grownups now, hardheaded realists, practical people. And yet some part of us still yearns for the Other World, that wondrous realm of *A Midsummer Night's Dream* and of Keats's fairy lands forlorn. Many of our poems, folk tales, and children's classics summon us to rediscover those lost worlds, that secret garden. In the books in this category a troubled knight wanders into a castle of heart's desire, a sensitive young man discovers Atlantis in the middle of the bustling city of Dresden, a grouchy sand fairy may grant you a wish, and an old Punch-and-Judy puppeteer will show you a box of delights. Everything finally depends on how you see the world around you, as a certain Miss M. can assure us. In these books we step through the looking-glass, we open the door into summer.

SIR GAWAIN AND THE GREEN KNIGHT
(fourteenth century)

Ask readers to choose the most delightful work of medieval literature, and odds are that *Sir Gawain and the Green Knight* would head
the list. It conveys a wonderful Mozartean lightness and wit, an air of
make-believe and festivity, tinged with real darkness. It's a perfect
adult Christmas story. Just listen:

On New Year's Day all the court of King Arthur gather together
for a holiday feast. The ladies look particularly lovely, the knights steal
kisses, and all's right with the world. But the king wishes to be told
or shown some marvel before he will sit down to eat. Almost immediately, a noise outside the hall is followed by the entrance of a magnificent knight "the whole of him bright green." Taller by a head than
any man there, he swaggers into the party and issues, almost playfully,
a challenge. He defies any of these supposedly brave warriors to give
him a stroke from his huge ax, with the proviso that a year and a day
later he must be allowed to deliver a similar stroke in return. Gawain
agrees, and swiftly brings the ax down through the Green Knight's
neck, slicing through the white flesh as if it were grease. Like a loose
soccer ball, the severed head rolls among the lords and ladies. But
suddenly the bloody torso strides forward and picks up its green head,
which opens a pair of red eyes and speaks: Remember, Gawain, to
meet me in a year and a day at the Green Chapel.

In a strikingly beautiful passage, the author—whose identity is
unknown—describes the changing of the seasons: the shining rain of
spring, the soft winds of summer, the dust rising from the fields at
harvest time, and the gradual return of winter. On All Saint's Day—
November 1—Gawain sets off to locate the Green Chapel and fulfill
his pledge. But what had once seemed, during a moment of high spirits, just a strange game is now a serious matter of life and death.

Searching for this mysterious Green Chapel, of which no one seems to have heard, Gawain undergoes adventures with dragons, trolls, and other wild beasts, and all the while the winter days grow darker, colder, and increasingly desolate. Finally, on Christmas Eve, Gawain prays that he might discover a warm shelter for the night, and immediately glimpses a castle, covered with turrets, so perfect it might have been cut out of paper.

Once he is admitted, the knight encounters the castle's broad-shouldered, red-bearded lord; the man's wife, who seems more beautiful than Guinevere; and a hideous bent-backed old woman. With seemingly unfeigned courtesy, they all invite him to stay for the Christmas season, and the next day sweetly passes in courtly conversation and games and feasting. In the evening Gawain explains that, for reasons he doesn't care to go into, he must journey on in his search for the Green Chapel. His jovial host laughingly replies that his new guest is in luck. This very chapel is so close by that the celebrated knight should feel free to spend the next three days at the castle, taking his ease. That settled, the lord of the manor asks Gawain to enter into the spirit of the festive season by playing a little trading game: Each morning he himself will go out hunting while Gawain rests up and does as he pleases, and in the evening the two will exchange whatever they have acquired during the day.

The next dawn the host assembles his knights and they all hurry out to hunt deer while Gawain slumbers in a warm bed, snugly surrounded by curtains. Suddenly he detects the sound of his door quietly opening, peeks out, and glimpses the host's wife softly entering his room. He pretends to be asleep as she makes her way to his bed and sits down beside him. Gawain asks to be allowed to dress, but the lady laughingly tells him that he shouldn't bother to get up, as she has a much better plan in mind. Isn't he after all known far and wide as the greatest lover among the knights of the Round Table? And aren't the two of them alone together, and her husband far away hunting, and the door shut and locked? Surely, she adds, they could make good use of this time. Leaning over him, she confesses that he can do anything he wants with her, making her meaning unmistakable by saying, "You are welcome to my body."

To reveal any more would spoil the story for new readers of this delicious, very adult medieval romance. But think how Gawain must feel: He knows that in three days he will be facing a murderous ax-stroke and, unlike the Green Knight, he cannot simply put his head back on. Meanwhile, this seductive woman beside him is so alive, so willing, so eager. Should he not enjoy the little time left to him? But what of his obligations as a guest, his honor as a knight, his hope of heaven? What should he do?

Throughout *Sir Gawain and the Green Knight* the author addresses serious questions of courtesy, reputation, and moral conduct, but he also suffuses his poem with irony, constantly plays with the gulf between appearance and reality, and keeps everyone guessing until the very end. Even then he leaves open the deepest meaning of his story. Suffice it to say that Gawain eventually does make his way to the sinister Green Chapel, an evil-looking mound in a water-splashed glen, where one could easily picture "the devil saying his matins." As he stands there on the appointed day, the knight hears a loud noise echoing along the cliffs nearby, the whirring sound that someone would make if he were sharpening a scythe on a grindstone. But it is not a scythe. And Gawain strides forth to meet his destiny.

Unlike Chaucer, whose English is recognizably our own, the Gawain-poet writes in a northern dialect that somewhat resembles the language of *Beowulf.* What's more, he employs the Old English alliterative line, which suggests that even in Norman Britain some of the old poetic ways were still kept alive. The standard scholarly edition of the poem was first prepared by none other than the young J. R. R. Tolkien (with E. V. Gordon, later revised by Norman Davis). Today there are several excellent translations—by the poet W. S. Merwin, among others—as well as a good deal of academic commentary: *Sir Gawain* is, after all, a mysterious and endlessly rewarding masterpiece. So, too, is the same poet's lovely elegy titled *Pearl*, in which he laments the death of his daughter and is granted a vision of heaven. *Purity* and *Patience*, his other known works, are even more religious in character and, though masterly in their way, lack the touchingly human drama of *Sir Gawain and the Green Knight*.

⟫⊶⟪

THE CLASSIC FAIRY TALES

What are fairy tales? To many adults, they are simply bedtime stories, prose lullabies that begin "Once upon a time" and conclude with that most unlikely of all statements about the human condition, "And they lived happily ever after." No doubt it is that promised end of pure, unclouded bliss that causes us to regard them as mere children's fantasies. Life, we know, isn't like that.

Or is it? Like ancient myths and Jungian archetypes, fairy tales describe the main currents of existence; they reveal our secret desires and give us ways to understand the world and our place in it. Our love stories still follow the plots of "Cinderella," "Sleeping Beauty," and "The Frog Prince"; our adventure novels and movies still conform to the inexhaustible model of "The Brave Little Tailor." And how many marriages are variants on "Beauty and the Beast"? In some cases, the Beast must either be outwardly civilized or his inner goodness finally appreciated; in others, Beauty herself must cast off the reserve of the maidenly and discover the sensual Beast within her own breast.

Certainly in our own homes we continue to work through the age-old patterns of these family romances, these core samplings of our psyches. Anyone with same-sex siblings understands "Cinderella" or the three brothers in "The Water of Life," just as all parents occasionally wish they could be rid of Hansel and Gretel, even if the kids are now named Jason and Jennifer. In an age of divorce, Snow White still knows the hatred and envy of the trophy second wife. Perrault's Donkey-Skin continues to fend off incestuous advances; "Little Red Riding Hood" can readily be interpreted as a tale of pedophilia; and Bluebeard is any husband with a secret, hidden life that could expose the lie that is his marriage.

To generalize broadly, most fairy tales are either about the tensions of home life or about social injustices and inequities. Children learn to be independent, while parents are taught to let them go out into the world. The most problematic forces in these narratives tend to be forceful, often uppity, women—witches, fairy godmothers, adventurous girls, greedy wives, and mothers whose love for their children transcends death itself. Here, sisterhood is powerful and sometimes deadly. As in real life, judging by appearances is almost always a big mistake. Entertained by the marvels and wonders, we quietly learn that compassion, high spirits, kindness to people and animals, intelligence, and sincere feeling will bring us our dreams.

Say fairy tale, though, and most people will think of the brothers Jacob and Wilhelm Grimm. These Germanic philologists gathered the oral tales of the *Volk,* the peasantry, and aimed to be true to what they heard. Surprisingly, perhaps, their stories don't always end happily, but they do end justly. In that most wonderful of all their Märchen, "The Fisherman and His Wife," the spiritually dissatisfied wife wishes herself emperor and then pope, only to go too far, so that, like Adam and Eve, she tries to become like God. She and her poor husband consequently end up back where they started, in a hovel. Most of these tales are, to use an old pun, terribly grim in their content—child abuse, sadism, dismemberment, cannibalism—but even the chilling "Juniper Tree" will conclude with the defeat of evil and the triumph of good. Largely because they are distanced from us through a kind of textual dreaminess—"In the old days, when wishes still came true . . ."—the macabre horrors can seem as formulaic and unreal as the talking animals, little more than symbolic steps in the protagonist's maturation.

This isn't true for the more literary tales of Hans Christian Andersen. These can be downright sentimental and religiose, but their heroes and heroines tend to be distinctive, real personalities, even those that are inanimate objects like a candle or a broken bottle. Little Hans Andersen must have been asleep when his nurse finished her bedtime stories with "And they lived happily ever after." By the close of some of the more famous of Andersen's tales, the characters are lucky to be alive, let alone happy. Think of the pre-Disney Little Mermaid, or the Little Match Girl who freezes to death: Life is violent, unhappy, and often pretty well hopeless. Flesh out "The Steadfast Tin Soldier" by updating the beloved ballerina into a dollar-a-dance blonde, and you've got the makings of a lean, noirish tale by James M. Cain: "Her name was Stella, and I was just a one-legged ex-GI. But on Christmas Eve she looked like the stuff that dreams are made of." As much as any noir author, Andersen shows us a brutal universe where love leads to unhappiness or even a fiery *Liebestod:* The tin soldier and the paper ballerina burn up together in the stove.

Though Grimm and Andersen are the marquee names in fairy tales, readers should also look for the elegant French narratives of Charles Perrault (who gave us, among others, "Puss in Boots" and "Beauty and the Beast") and the Countess d'Aulnoy, if only for her unforgettable and erotically charged "The Yellow Dwarf" (a favorite of Charles Dickens). In our time writers and artists as various as Angela Carter ("The Company of Wolves"), Tanith Lee ("Red as Blood"), Stephen Sondheim ("Into the Woods"), and Sarah Moon (a shocking but award-winning suite of photographs about Little Red Riding Hood preyed upon by a sexual predator) have reworked the classic fairy tales. These simple-seeming stories remain immensely powerful, even as they are beautiful, wise, and thought-provoking. They deserve reading in themselves, not only as bedtime stories for sleepy offspring.

———»·•·«———

E. T. A. HOFFMANN (1776–1822)
Short stories

The celebrated "tales of Hoffmann" mix together, in varying combinations, the occult, the nightmarish, and the whimsical. Some of the best, like "The Golden Pot," are literary fairy tales, a popular genre among German Romantics; others are profoundly disturbing accounts of madness and psychological breakdown, most famously "The Sandman." One, "Mademoiselle de Scudery," is arguably the first modern detective story, revealing a serial murderer with a peculiar psychological twist. No matter how dreamy, scientific, or grotesque his subject matter, Hoffmann tends to adopt a somewhat jaunty and often satirical tone, which only adds to the reader's disorientation.

Hoffmann's influence suffuses much of nineteenth-century art and fiction. Hawthorne ("Rappaccini's Daughter"), Gogol ("The Nose"), and Dostoevsky ("The Double") exhibit his unsettling mix of the real and the imagined. Drawing on three of the stories, Jacques Offenbach produced his popular opera *The Tales of Hoffmann,* while Tchaikovsky later turned one of the fairy tales into his ballet *The Nutcracker.* Freud uses "The Sandman" as the test case in his celebrated essay "The Uncanny," showing that a particular form of dread is created when the familiar suddenly appears strange (he later links this reaction to the return of a repressed childhood trauma). More recently, twentieth-century "magic realism" sometimes seems just another name for the Hoffmannesque, while Robertson Davies's entertaining novels, with their focus on artists, magicians, and the supernatural, clearly reflect their author's admiration for the German storyteller. So, too, does the literary fantasy of Angela Carter and Steven Millhauser.

Hoffmann's central importance to storytelling lies in his blurring of the prosaic and the poetic, the real and the supernatural, the human and the mechanical, the bustling world outside and the psychological confusions within. Myths and fairy tales had long presented impossible events or occurrences, but these nearly always took place in the past, or in a distant Other World, or in a patently unreal universe of "once upon a time." While Hoffmann almost certainly knew his contemporary Ludwig Tieck's story "The Elves," in which a fairy realm exists, invisibly, next door to an ordinary German village, that fantasy classic still carries the aura of a classic folk tale. Hoffmann modernized magic. Mesmerism, clockwork toys, "nervous" conditions, the psychology of artists and musicians, alienation, the nature of dreams, somnambulism, prenatal influence, magnetism—all these were hot topics in his day. Hoffmann thus invested the unexplainable with a touch of science, as well as the added chill of the near and contemporary. That innovation provided the essential foundation of the modern horror tale.

Though the actual prose is brisk and clear, Hoffmann's writing nearly always creates a sense of boundaries breaking down, of spiritual vertigo. In his novel *The Devil's Elixir*, the protagonist seems to exchange personalities with a dead man. Does he? How much is real, how much imagined? Clockwork figures also fascinated Hoffmann, and his essayistic tale "Automata" includes a long conversation about the uneasiness people feel at any parroting of human forms. Of course, the lifelike doll Olympia, with which Nathanael falls in love in "The Sandman," provides the most famous and unnerving case, the whole story suggesting that human beings themselves may be only marionettes, manipulated by forces beyond their control. (This theme finds its obsessive modern exponent in the work of science-fiction writer Philip K. Dick.) As Balzac shrewdly observed, E. T. A. Hoffmann is "the poet of what doesn't appear, and yet has life."

Other elements that Hoffmann invested with uncanny power include windows, mirrors, lenses, eyes, and music. Nearly all of these are used to reinforce the suspicion that the universe offers far more than we can ordinarily see; that artists, occult scientists, and madmen may gain access to another dimension, that of the imagination. The bumbling Anselmus of "The Golden Pot"—an allegory about the making of a poet—finds himself torn between his longing for a bizarre realm of salamanders, blue-eyed serpent-maidens, and elemental spirits and his ordinary life in a practical Dresden full of court councillors and pretty girls. This marvel-filled story—described by literary scholar E. F. Bleiler as the greatest fantasy of the nineteenth century—insists, like so many Romantic poems, that one must rediscover a childlike poetic spirit in order to recognize the wonders all around us. But these wonders aren't always wholly benevolent, and Hoffmann includes a terrifying witch, a midnight invocation of satanic powers, a magic mirror, good and evil shape-shifters, and an angst-ridden moment when Anselmus finds his soul trapped inside a glass bottle. There's even a postmodern twist to the last chapter, when the author receives a letter from one of his characters.

"The Golden Pot" deliberately plays with the suspicion that we may inhabit a domain of mere appearance while the true realm of the spirit is ignored or dismissed as fanciful. Yet should our allegiance be to our dreams and the night-side or to the "real world" and its tangible rewards? It's a hard call. For where Anselmus's "madness" in "The Golden Pot" leads him to happiness and fulfillment, Nathanael's in "The Sandman" results in a far darker destiny. Similarly, the young hero of "The Mines of Falun" finds himself increasingly in thrall to the underground and its irresistible queen. Are all of them simply deluded? Or does each, in his own way, truly see into the secret heart of things?

Hoffmann's own life alternated between the opposing poles of the practical and the visionary. He was gifted as a painter and caricaturist, his opera *Undine* is still performed (and his music once elicited a letter from Beethoven), he generally passed his evenings by drinking to exaltation, and he turned out two novels and fifty stories in a dozen years. But he also worked conscientiously in various government posts, including that of a judge. In the end, though, he seems to have scorned all that we mean by the bourgeois, the comfortable ruts of ordinary existence; hence the satire in his stories of bureaucratic officialdom. Indeed, Hoffmann's brief life (he died at forty-six) and innovative fiction helped establish the figure of the artist *maudit,* in search of ecstasy and transcendence, at odds with a society that frequently dismisses him as insane. Baudelaire is as much Hoffmann's heir as Edgar Allan Poe.

PROSPER MÉRIMÉE (1803–1870)
Short stories

Prosper Mérimée's sentences may be dry, precise, and almost clinical at times, yet the very coolness of his narrative voice only renders more vivid the passion and murderousness described in his most famous stories. A friend of Stendhal and a proponent of "local color"—in this case, the customs of earthy, passionate people—Mérimée transformed the anecdote and nineteenth-century *conte* into the modern short story. V. S. Pritchett argues that he is, in fact, "the supreme 'pure' storyteller," unsurpassed in the "technical beauty" of his writing and "the ice-clear prose of his narrative."

Many of Mérimée's stories are world-famous, even if their author's name isn't. "Carmen," for instance, served as the basis for Bizet's ever-popular opera about a French soldier's infatuation with a

Gypsy slattern. Mérimée's original is just as heartbreaking in its evocation of erotic anguish and dark fatality. The nineteenth-century critic Walter Pater once called "Mateo Falcone," in which the son of a Corsican bandit betrays a trust, the cruelest story in the world. *"La Double Méprise"* (A Slight Misunderstanding) relates how a Don Juan manages, in the course of a few hours, to seduce a virtuous young wife he has just met. *The Chronicle of the Reign of Charles IX*—set during France's religious wars—is a major historical novel.

But these are only a few of the peaks in Mérimée's varied oeuvre, which includes plays, travel journals, and wonderful letters, as well as tales of witchcraft ("The Spanish Witches"), snake-worship ("Djoumane"), were-bears ("Lokis"), slave rebellions, and biblical vengeance. In a general sense, his overarching theme is the power of the repressed: That which we refuse to honor or acknowledge—dark forces within ourselves, our lot in life, our primitive duty—will ultimately irrupt with overwhelming and destructive violence. Many readers consider "Colomba," the savage story of a vendetta, as the author's best work, but Mérimée himself always preferred "The Venus of Ille." With the possible exception of Maupassant's "The Horla," it is the most famous French supernatural tale of the nineteenth century, neatly blending the comic, satiric, and horrifying.

In this story, while traveling around France in his official capacity as a government inspector, Mérimée visits the city of Ille, where a bumbling antiquary named Peyhorade has recently unearthed an ancient statue of Venus. Representing a chilly idealized beauty, this statue polarizes all who look upon it, some feeling attraction, others repulsion. Odd things happen in its vicinity: one evening, for instance, Mérimée observes a local prankster who throws a rock at the statue but is immediately struck by what seems to be a ricochet. The next day Mérimée and Peyhorade notice that the statue shows a white mark not only where it was struck at its breast but also on the fingers of its hand.

By now, the reader recognizes that the statue must, in some sense, be alive. But why? Mérimée uses the Venus of Ille to remind us that love is not to be toyed with: On the statue's base are carved the words *Cave amantem*—lovers beware. As it happens, Peyhorade's callow son is to be married to a splendid, vibrant young woman whom he clearly fails to appreciate. Alphonse is a clod, interested in nothing but sports and money. To him venality is, so to speak, more important than venery, and he fails to properly revere the power of eros. Though Mérimée regrets the obvious misalliance, he nonetheless agrees to remain for the marriage. Yet so boorish is Alphonse that on the wedding day itself he joins in a game of pelota and, having nowhere to put his bride-to-be's ring, slips it onto the finger of Venus. He then forgets it and must later use another at the ceremony. However, at the wedding supper that evening, a pale Alphonse privately tells Mérimée that when he tried to retrieve the original ring he felt the statue's finger bend around it. Mérimée scoffs, telling the young man that he has simply had too much to drink.

That night . . . but why say more? Even when you know how matters are likely to turn out, Mérimée sweeps you along with his storytelling. The bathos and rhetorical excess so common to nineteenth-century fiction is utterly alien to his personality. If reading the Victorians may be likened to devouring a rich Christmas feast, reading Mérimée is like sipping a dry martini—cold, bracing, and delicious. Be warned however: His characters may be primitive or exotic people, but that only means that they are stripped of the meretricious veneer of so much polite society. As a result, they reveal our most primal fears and secret desires with heartless and dreadful clarity.

FRANCES HODGSON BURNETT (1849–1924)
The Secret Garden

There are few novels for children equal to *The Secret Garden* (1911). Frances Hodgson Burnett's biographer Ann Thwaite says it "was one of the three or four most important books of my own childhood, in that it was read and re-read, and the atmosphere of it became part of my own life." She goes on to say that countless people share the view expressed by the critic Marghanita Laski: "It is the most satisfying children's book I know."

But a good children's book should be a good book for any reader, of any age. During Burnett's lifetime, grownups read her novels with avidity (just as they now devour J. K. Rowling's Harry Potter adventures). For example, the English prime minister William Gladstone loved *Little Lord Fauntleroy,* and asked to meet its author. I myself discovered *The Secret Garden* as an adult, and to me it is a deeply moving testimony to the power of nature to heal and renew broken souls. At times the story does grow improbable (not one but two odd and spoiled children!) and toward the end is a little sentimental, but we are meant to cry in this world as well as laugh and think.

The novel opens with a brilliant, even shocking, hook, one that draws in any reader, of whatever age:

> When Mary Lennox was sent to Misselthwaite Manor to live with her uncle everybody said she was the most disagreeable-looking child ever seen. It was true, too. She had a little thin face and a little thin body, thin light hair and a sour expression. . . . When she was a sickly, fretful, ugly little baby she was kept out of the way, and when she became a sickly, fretful, toddling thing she was kept out of the way also. . . . By the time she was six years old she was as tyrannical and selfish a little pig as ever lived.

When her parents unexpectedly die from cholera, ten-year-old Mary is sent from India to live with her Uncle Archibald in his vast manor house in England. Once there, she learns that her uncle is a recluse with a hunch back who doesn't wish to see her. This is strange enough, but she soon discovers that there are far greater riddles at Misselthwaite Manor. Where, for instance, is the garden established by Uncle Archibald's young wife, now dead these ten years? And where is the key to its hidden door? And what are those piercing cries Mary sometimes hears in the evening? During the first third of the novel, a reader may wonder if this might not turn into a Gothic thriller or Victorian melodrama.

For Burnett certainly knows how to keep up suspense—or to create a *coup de théâtre*. One afternoon a half-tamed robin hops about on a pile of fresh earth, next to a hole dug by a mole. Mary takes a closer look at the hole:

> As she looked she saw something almost buried in the newly-turned soil. It was something like a ring of rusty iron or brass and when the robin flew up into a tree nearby she put out her hand and picked the ring up. It was more than a ring, however; it was an old key which looked as if it had been buried a long time.

As the months pass at Misselthwaite Manor, Mary Lennox grows kinder, fatter, and happier. She comes to like the maid, Martha; the old gardener, Ben Weatherstaff; and, most of all, Dickon, Martha's twelve-year-old brother. Burnett depicts the boy as a spirit of the wild, a young Pan: "As she came closer to him she noticed that there was a clean fresh scent of heather and grass and leaves about him, almost as if he were made of them." Dickon can tame wild beasts and understands the ways of vegetables and flowers. Together, Mary and Dickon—and a third character, whom I won't identify for those new to the story—make the neglected secret garden bloom again. By so doing, they bring new life into the dead world of Misselthwaite Manor. As Burnett writes, "Mistress Mary always felt that however many years she lived she would never forget that first morning when her garden began to grow." Certainly, no reader ever forgets.

Frances Hodgson Burnett's other books include the great Victorian bestseller *Little Lord Fauntleroy* and the touching *A Little Princess* (originally titled, in a shorter version, *Sara Crewe*). *The Secret Garden* itself has never been out of print. Over the past century, this masterpiece has served as a template for innumerable children's novels—its greatest successor is Philippa Pearce's deeply moving *Tom's Midnight Garden*—and has even been alluded to by T. S. Eliot, in his opening to "Burnt Norton," where he speaks of the "the door into the rose garden" and a magical-seeming bird. For many readers, Burnett's classic remains not only a mythic story—with its telling symbolism of walled garden, peaceable kingdom, death, and rebirth—but also one of the best of all comfort books, a work to which one can return time and again for solace and renewal.

—————⊷•⊶—————

E. NESBIT (1858–1924)
Five Children and It

JOHN MASEFIELD (1878–1967)
The Box of Delights

Noel Coward—consummate wit, arch-sophisticate, showman—insisted that E. Nesbit "of all the writers I have ever read, has given me over the years the most complete satisfaction. Her writing is so light and unforced, her humour is so sure and her narrative quality so strong that the stories, which I know backwards, rivet me as much now as they did when I was a little boy. Even more so in one way because I can enjoy her actual talent and her extraordinary power of describing hot summer days in England in the beginning years of the century."

Besides being a superbly evocative storyteller, Nesbit is one of the first modern writers for children to avoid both didacticism and the killing tone of grown-up condescension. Her books matter-of-factly describe the fantastic interrupting quite ordinary daily life. Almost single-handedly, she created the ever-popular children's genre sometimes called "everyday magic," and her descendants include Edward Eager, Joan Aiken, Daniel Pinkwater, Roald Dahl, Diana Wynne Jones, and Madeline L'Engle.

In *Five Children and It*, two boys, two girls and their baby brother are spending a long summer in a rather drab country house, located between a chalk quarry and a gravel pit. They are privileged, but not rich. During this holiday the children are left largely to their own devices, and one sky-blue afternoon they decide to dig a hole to Australia.

As they scramble about in the gravel pit, Anthea unearths something very strange: "Its eyes were on long horns like a snail's eyes, and it could move them in and out like telescopes; it had ears like a bat's ears, and its tubby body was shaped like a spider's and covered with thick soft fur; its legs and arms were furry too, and it had hands and feet like a monkey's." The Psammead, or sand fairy, may resemble the prototype for one of Maurice Sendak's Wild Things, but like a genie it can, with certain provisions and caveats, grant wishes. The chief of these limitations is that the wish ends with sunset, and things revert to what they were. The grouchy Psammead eventually agrees to grant one wish a day to the children.

The rest of the book, a series of linked episodes, relates what happens when the siblings gradually learn the truth of the grown-up maxim "Be careful what you wish for; you might get it." After they acquire a vast heap of gold, no shopkeeper will accept the unfamiliar coins. After they ask to be made "as beautiful as the day," they feel like strangers to one another. In fact, "their faces were so radiantly beautiful as to be quite irritating to look at." And after they quite inadvertently wish that everyone would love the baby as much as they do, the little "Lamb" is first kidnapped by a Lady Chittenden, then fought over by a caravan of Gypsies.

Several of the wishes draw on the children's reading—tales of medieval knights or Red Indians—and the siblings naturally try to act like bookish heroes, with courage and dispatch. Some adventures prove more frightening or emotionally complicated than expected, though nothing very terrible ever quite happens to anyone, apart from a few missed dinners and several tongue-lashings from the housekeeper, Martha. These are cozy summer-afternoon adventures, laced with lighthearted comedy and told in an ingratiatingly colloquial manner.

Little wonder, then, that E. Nesbit proved so popular. For many years—from the realistic *The Story of the Treasure-Seekers* (1899) and *The Railway Children* (1906) through the fantastic *Story of the Amulet* (1906) and *Wet Magic* (1913)—she demonstrated, again and again, that the only truly important narrative gift is the ability to keep readers enthralled. Like no other children's writer of her time, she possessed the wand of the enchanter.

Despite *The Phoenix and the Carpet* (which is set at Christmas), Nesbit's novels are largely associated with the empty, lazy days of June through August. By contrast, John Masefield's *The Box of Delights* (1935) ranks high among the great paeans to winter. Though little known in the United States, the book is a much-loved yuletide favorite in Britain. It's a follow-up to *The Midnight Folk* (1927), but you don't need to know that warm-weather book to enjoy its far better, snow-filled sequel.

A day or two before Christmas, English schoolboy Kay Harker, who must be about twelve or thirteen, is traveling by train back to his home just outside the cathedral town of Tatchester. An orphan, he lives in a big house called Seekings with his guardian, the beautiful Caroline Louisa. This year the four Jones children will be visiting, and so the holidays should be especially festive, despite the threat of heavy snow. But as Kay approaches home, strange things begin to happen.

On the platform at Musborough Junction, where he must change trains, an old Punch-and-Judy showman helps the boy locate his mysteriously lost ticket. Back in his compartment, Kay finds himself in the company of two distinctly sinister men in clerical garb, who address each other first as Tristan and Lancelot, then as Gawaine and Dagonet, and who warn him about playing card games with strangers. They nonetheless trick him out of half a crown, and probably steal his purse as well. Feeling more than somewhat discombobulated, Kay descends at Tatchester, and there finds the Punch-and-Judy man again. This time the wandering puppeteer asks the boy to perform a small service for him:

Master Harker, there is something that no other soul can do for me but you alone. As you go down toward Seekings, if you would stop at Bob's shop, as it were to buy muffins now. . . . Near the door you will see a woman plaided from the cold, wearing a ring of a very strange shape, Master Harker, being like my ring here, of the longways cross of gold and garnets. And she has bright eyes, Master Harker, as bright as mine, which is what few have. If you will step into Bob's shop to buy muffins now, saying nothing, not even to your good friend, and say to this Lady 'The Wolves are Running' then she will know and Others will know; and none will get bit.

Kay agrees and thereafter begins to glimpse, in the distant fields and at misty crossroads, what look like large Alsatian dogs "trying to catch a difficult scent." In due course, the Punch-and-Judy man visits Seekings. Very dark powers, he explains, are after him. The enemy is closing in on Seekings itself, and indeed shadowy shapes do seem to be darting through the snowy darkness. Hoping to throw his pursuers off the scent, the old man asks Kay to take and safeguard a little box.

I won't tell any more of the story, except to say that that box possesses three magical powers, one of which allows its possessor to transport himself to wherever he wishes. Before Masefield's grand finale—at Tatchester Cathedral's one thousandth Christmas Eve service—there will be kidnappings and escapes, a visit to ancient Troy, a voyage with pirates, and marooning on a desert island. At stake is not only the ability to travel through time but also the Elixir of Life.

Every chapter in this wintry book is marvelous, but the real delight derives from Masefield's style and the idiosyncratic, colorful speech of his various characters. Here is the witch Sylvia Pouncer describing a distasteful former pupil: "He is a child for whom I had the utmost detestation and contempt; a thoroughly morbid, dreamy, idle muff with a low instinct for the turf, which will be his undoing in later life." And here's the gun-toting tomboy Maria Jones: "School! They know better than to try that game on me. I've been expelled from three and the headmistresses still swoon when they hear my name breathed. I'm Maria Jones, I am: somewhat talked of in school circles, if you take the trouble to enquire."

Masefield is just as delicious in capturing a country policeman's never-ending flow of trite catchphrases or the tone of a small-town newspaper: The dean of Tatchester, we are solemnly told by the latter, "is the well-known author of 'Possible Oriental Influences on Ancient Philosophies' as well as the famous handbook: 'Cheerfulness: The Christian's Duty.'" Even Masefield's background details charm; for instance, "the Shrine of the great Saint Cosric, Saxon King and Martyr, who had worked such famous miracles in the cure of Leprosy, and Broken Hearts."

E. Nesbit's books were first published in that golden late Victorian summer before the Great War, and they are generally as sunny and high-spirited as the holidays they describe. Masefield's *The Box of Delights*, however, appeared in 1935—and J. R. R. Tolkien's *The Hobbit* came out in 1937 and T. H. White's *The Sword in the Stone* in 1938. For all their considerable wit, these later children's classics are touched with wistfulness, that pervasive sense of the belated common to so much twentieth-century fantasy: The old gods are departing and, like childhood, the days of wonder will soon be over.

WALTER DE LA MARE (1873–1956)
Memoirs of a Midget; other works

Except for "The Listeners" and the poems of *Peacock Pie* ("'I'm tired—oh, tired of books,' said Jack,/ 'I long for meadows green'"), most of Walter de la Mare's work has been forgotten by the general public. In the mid-1920s, though, he was frequently regarded as one of the three or four finest living English writers, admired by such eminences as T. S. Eliot (who wrote a poem in his honor for his eightieth birthday). Now he seems—if only to those who've never read his work—solely a period author, "stuck fast in yesterday," with, say, Arnold Bennett, Ellen Glasgow, and James Branch Cabell.

But like these others, de la Mare is far more original and appealing than commonly believed. For instance, fans of the English ghost story rank his uncanny tales among the best ever written. "Seaton's Aunt"—about a psychic vampire—is probably the most famous, but he wrote several other anthology standards, all evocatively titled, including "All Hallows," "The Riddle," and "Crewe," not to mention the full-length novel of possession *The Return*.

In much of his fiction, de la Mare pushes hard up against the dreamlike, often surrendering to a lyrical, even long-winded, chromaticism and sometimes leaving the reader fuzzily confused. He reminds one of German Romantics like Novalis, hymning the night while their soul yearns after something it cannot name. "The protagonist of a typical de la Mare story," the critic John Clute has aptly written, "will discover that his life is a journey in which signposts point always to boundaries lying at the edge of his perception and beyond which may lie death, or a world of the imagination, or the fields of his true home. But whatever lies beyond the borderline, he will long for it." Not too suprisingly, de la Mare's modern admirers have tended themselves to be explorers of the liminal, writers who pitch their stories on a similar boundary between the real and the imagined—that master of spiritual disquiet Robert Aickman, for instance, or the great English practitioner of magic realism Angela Carter, whose phantasmagoric *Nights at the Circus* clearly takes some of its inspiration from de la Mare's masterpiece, *Memoirs of a Midget*.

First published in 1921, this long novel offers the partial autobiography of Miss M.—no full name is ever given—who, at least physically, never grows up. Most of the book takes place during her twentieth year, when Miss M. appears to be no more than two feet tall and sometimes even smaller—she can be easily carried by a servant and children sometimes mistake her for a doll; at one point she worries that a ripe pear falling from a tree might crush her. She is an only child, doted upon by her parents, and relatively at ease with her small stature, except when threatened by strangers or thwarted by adult-sized doors, utensils, or porch steps. But the novel isn't about disability; it's a study of character and social mores, and of how people confront the unyielding world.

In recent years we've enjoyed bestsellers narrated by heroes with Tourette's syndrome and autism, so readers should quickly adjust to de la Mare's unexpected heroine. It's also useful to remember that the 1920s were, in Britain, a period when writers dabbled with fantasy and unusual perspectives. Aldous Huxley's *Crome Yellow* (also pub-

lished in 1921) contains a chapter—originally a short story, "Sir Her-
cules"—about the disastrous effect of a full-sized and loutish son on
refined and cultivated midget parents. David Garnett's *Lady into Fox*
(1922) describes a man's attempt to carry on with his marriage after
his wife is transformed into a literal vixen, a theme reprised, with a
twist, by John Collier in his sardonic masterpiece *His Monkey Wife*
(1930). In Miss M.'s memoir, de la Mare even alludes to Sir Oran
Haut-Ton, the orangutan elected to Parliament in *Melincourt* by
Thomas Love Peacock, whose complete works were republished in
the 1920s. This, too, was the decade when Ronald Firbank produced
his comic tragedies of campy saints (*The Flower Beneath the Foot*) and
even campier clerics (*Concerning the Eccentricities of Cardinal Pirelli*).
In effect, the age was in rebellion against the Biedermeier realism of
the Edwardians.

Yet for all its strangeness of perspective, *Memoirs of a Midget* may
be regarded as one of the best novels that Henry James never wrote.
Its narrative voice is often severe, formal, elliptical, and diffuse, so
much so that the book might well have been called "What Miss M.
Knew." A reader who fails to pay attention will overlook, for a long
while, that Mrs. Bowater is not Fanny's real mother; that Mr. Anon is
a hunchback; that Fanny herself probably needs money for an abortion; that the Reverend Mr. Crimble is going insane; and that Miss
M. thinks a bit too well of herself.

It is also, as in so much James, a book containing a considerable
amount of death, violence, madness, and grotesquerie. "The world,"
writes Miss M., "wields a sharp pin, and is pitiless to bubbles." This
harshness of life appears early on, even in Miss M.'s most pampered
days:

As one morning I brushed past a bush of lad's love (or maiden's
ruin, as some call it), its fragrance sweeping me from top to toe,
I stumbled on the carcass of a young mole. Curiosity vanquished

the first gulp of horror. Holding my breath, with a stick I slowly edged it up in the dust and surveyed the white heaving nest of maggots in its belly with a peculiar and absorbed recognition. "Ah ha!" a voice cried within me, "so this is what is in wait; this is how things are."

But then Miss M. often meditates on life and death: "It's only when the poor fish—sturgeon or stickleback—struggles, that he really knows he's in the net." Because of her size, she is forced to think about life's limits all the time.

However, all isn't gloom in this odd and mysterious book. Seeing Miss M., a small boy on a train asks, "Mamma, is that alive?" The mother, embarrassed, tries to divert his attention, while her little son insists, "But she is, mamma. It moved. I saw that move." Finally, he descends to pleading, "I want that, mamma . . . I want that dear little lady. Give that teeny tiny lady a biscuit." As Miss M. comments, it was "the only time in my life I actually saw a fellow creature fall in love."

After the death of her parents, Miss M. goes to live with a Mrs. Bowater in a small town. At her new lodgings she eventually meets Fanny Bowater, at home from her job teaching in a provincial school. Fanny is beautiful, outspoken, and wonderfully alive—she's everyone's favorite character, an unscrupulous Elizabeth Bennet ("Socialism, my dear, is all a question of shoes")—and Miss M. falls desperately in love with her. Note that Miss M. is not a child; she's twenty, and Fanny is roughly the same age, and a pitiless heartbreaker to boot. Miss Bowater toys with Miss M., whose passions are awakened to such a pitch that today's readers may be astonished at the frank avowals not of girlish friendship but of passionate longing. But what do you expect from two young women who read *Wuthering Heights* together?

In the end, Miss M. learns that "people actually suffered and endured the horrible things written about in cheap, common books." As she says of one beloved, "We were never again to be alone together, except in remembrance."

This semi-forgotten classic was once regarded by more than one critic as, in Edward Wagenknecht's words, "the most distinguished novel that has come out of England in our time." Perhaps *Memoirs of a Midget* is too odd for such a blanket encomium, but in its sheer originality and uniqueness it is unforgettable. It lingers in the memory like a ghostly visitation or a dream.

Lives of Consequence

Both saints and sinners lead lives of consequence. Heroes of antiquity, Renaissance overreachers, scandalous courtiers, hard-working professionals, fiery polemicists, famous poets, and even a few magicians—these make up only a partial census of the people you'll meet in the following pages. All of them are worth knowing.

We rightly expect modern biographies to be thorough, accurate, and balanced. But in the great biographical classics of the past we revel in the idiosyncratic and partisan. Plutarch inspires us both by his tales of nobility and self-sacrifice and by his warnings against vanity and self-indulgence. When John Aubrey scribbles about the notable figures of his time, he might be the seventeenth-century equivalent of a Hollywood gossip columnist. Frederick Douglass's account of his years as a slave upsets and angers us, just as Henry James's letters reveal, again and again, a magnificently generous and melancholy heart.

When we are young, our favorite literary genres tend to be fiction and poetry. Why? Because these deal with that vexing matter of love, which seriously troubles most of us between, roughly, the ages of fifteen and fifty-five. In our middle years, though, we start to think more and more about the meaning of life—of our own lives, of any person's life. In such moods, we turn increasingly to biography and its cousins history and philosophy, seeking insight. The books here offer that, as well as plenty of entertainment—no matter what your age.

———≫•0•≪———

PLUTARCH (fl. ca. 66)
Parallel Lives of the Greeks and Romans

Plutarch's *Lives* can make a strong claim to be the most entertaining book in all antiquity. This assemblage—indeed, small library—of forty-six short biographies of the most notable Greeks and Romans offers lively anecdotes, condensed history, reflections on virtue and right conduct, and much of what we half-know about the legendary Theseus and Romulus, the notorious and sexy Alcibiades, and the orators Demosthenes and Cicero. There are also many pages devoted to such inspiring, if now less familiar, figures as Cato, Lucullus, Aristides, and Themistocles. For centuries Plutarch graced every gentleman's library as a bible of moral lessons and noble examples.

The Greek biographer opens his *Lives* with this leisurely, inviting sentence, promising to resist the siren call of make-believe and myth:

> As geographers . . . crowd into the edges of their maps parts of the world which they do not know about, adding notes in the margin to the effect, that beyond this lies nothing but sandy deserts full of wild beasts, unapproachable bogs, Scythian ice, or a frozen sea, so . . . I might say . . . Beyond this [book] there is nothing but prodigies and fictions, the only inhabitants are the poets and inventors of fables.

Despite this implicit contract to be faithful to the historical record and refuse the enticements of fanciful speculation, Plutarch lards his biographies with plenty of semi-mythical stories. For instance, in tracing the lineage of Lycurgus, the stern lawgiver of Sparta, he pauses for this little case study in self-control:

There goes a story of this king Sous, that, being besieged by the Clitorians in a dry and stony place so that he could come at no water, he was at last constrained to agree with them upon these terms, that he would restore to them all his conquests, provided that himself and all his men should drink of the nearest spring. After the usual oaths and ratifications, he called his soldiers together, and offered to him that would forbear drinking, his kingdom for a reward; and when not a man of them was able to forbear, in short, when they had all drunk their fill, at last comes king Sous himself to the spring, and, having sprinkled his face only, without swallowing one drop, marches off in the face of his enemies, refusing to yield up his conquests, because himself and all his men had not, according to the articles, drunk of water.

Given such an iron-willed ancestor, it's not surprising that Lycurgus transforms Sparta (or Lacedaemon) into what Plutarch labels "a complete philosophic state," based largely on unwavering devotion to duty and firm self-discipline—in short, on the principles of the armed camp. Other peoples might raise an army; the Spartans *were* an army. People there returned home from late-night events without using torches, so as to accustom themselves to moving in the dark; the young of both sexes marched naked in processions to overcome all softness and "womanishness"; the city itself stood always on the alert, and the education of its citizens was "one continued exercise of a ready and perfect obedience." However, when the Spartans "were in the field, their exercises were generally more moderate, their fare not so hard, nor so strict a hand held over them by their officers, so that they were the only people in the world to whom war gave repose." At times while reading this account of Sparta's ways, one can't help but think, with a shudder, of the Third Reich or Mao's China at least as often as Plato's ideal Republic and Thomas More's Utopia.

When Lycurgus felt that Sparta was finally organized just as he wished it to be, he thought hard about how to preserve his laws unchanged, even after his death. Finally, he "called an extraordinary assembly of all the people, and told them that he had now thought everything reasonably well established, both for the happiness and the virtues of the state; but that there was one thing still behind, of the greatest importance, which he thought not fit to impart until he had consulted the oracle." He must have paused here, waiting for perfect silence: "In the mean time, his desire was that they would observe the laws without the least alteration until his return."

Lycurgus, of course, never intended to come back from his journey to the oracle. Plutarch ends his account of the lawgiver by adding that one legend insists that at his death, wherever it occurred, Lycurgus ordered that his body be burnt and his ashes scattered to the sea, "for fear lest, if his relics should be transported to Lacedaemon, the people might pretend to be released from their oaths and make innovations in the government." Clearly, this was a man who planned for every contingency.

Nearly any page of Plutarch offers such stories and observations, and some of the best crop up in the lives of the more obscure Greeks and Romans. There are occasional longueurs, yes, and the little interchapters comparing "parallel" Greeks and Roman notables can be a bit forced. Many readers may also prefer the more modern English of, say, Rex Warner to the older Dryden/Clough translation cited here, which nonetheless possesses a distinct period charm. In whatever edition you read it, though, Plutarch's *Lives* is as much a work of wisdom literature as it is of history and biography.

—⇒•0•⇐—

GIROLAMO CARDANO (1501–1576)
The Book of My Life

Among the most entertaining autobiographers in the world is the cranky Renaissance mathematician, doctor, and astrologer Girolamo Cardano, once reputed to possess the greatest mind since Aristotle. Instead of relating his life in a chronological fashion, Cardano divides *De Vita Propria Liber* (The Book of My Life, 1557) into categories; in Jean Stoner's translation, chapters bear titles such as "Stature and appearance," "Those things in which I take pleasure," "Things in which I feel I have failed," and "Testimony of illustrious men concerning me."

It's hard to convey the winsome charm of this book. As Jacob Burkhardt wrote, in *The Civilization of the Renaissance in Italy,* whoever opens *The Book of My Life* "will not lay it down till the last page." Throughout, Cardano presents his past and present factually, almost matter-of-factually, in a scientific spirit that spares himself nothing, while revealing a winning, if dour, personality. To cite one example:

> Although various abortive medicines—as I have heard—were tried in vain, I was normally born on the 24th day of September in the year 1501 . . . I was not maimed, save in the genitals, so that from my twenty-first to my thirty-first year I was unable to lie with women, and many a time I lamented my fate, envying every other man his own good fortune.

His father, Cardano informs us, often turned for help to a "demon which he openly confessed attended him as a familiar spirit." He later tells us that he, too, has been accompanied throughout life by a similar guardian. Absurd? Crazy? Perhaps. Yet the belief in such good and evil spirits was hardly exceptional at the time. Only a few years previous, in 1471, Pope Paul II slept with a young man and was, reportedly, strangled in the act by demons. Or remember Dr. Faustus, modeled after the roughly contemporary Georg Helmsttetter of Heidelberg, and his diabolical familiar, Mephistopheles.

Throughout *The Book of My Life* this crotchety Italian magus—it's tempting to picture him as resembling Merlyn from *The Sword in the Stone*—likes to regale us with homely Wordsworthian details about his day-to-day activities. Cardano grumpily complains about becoming "the owner of all sorts of little animals that get attached to me: kids, lambs, hares, rabbits, and storks. They litter up the whole house." He tells us that he has lots of trouble finding well-fitting shoes. He admits to cheating at cards and claims that he devoted himself to so much serious study—his writings run to seven thousand folio pages—"as a counterpoise to an insane love for my children." He regularly attends public anatomy lessons, consults the stars, and casts horoscopes.

In fact, Cardano spent much of his life practicing astrology and even visited the celebrated Elizabethan wizard Dr. John Dee. Among Cardano's many books—he lists them in one chapter of this autobiography—are such wonderfully tantalizing works as *The Secrets of Eternity* (alas, never completed), as well as a standard text on games of chance, a commentary on Ptolemy, and a study of teeth. Not surprisingly, the highly opinionated Italian polymath could be extremely provoking to rival scholars. We are told by his biographer, Anthony Grafton, that in 1557 the textual scholar "Julius Caesar Scaliger . . . devoted more than nine hundred quarto pages to refuting one of Cardano's books, *On Subtlety*." This savage attack, adds Grafton, may be "the only book review ever known to undergo transformation into a textbook."

So great was Cardano's faith in astrology that it has been said he was led to commit suicide so that he might die on the very day predicted by his horoscope. This may seem far-fetched, but these things were taken seriously and believed in by even the most hard-headed.

The immensely wealthy merchant banker Anton Fugger used to keep an eye on his partners in distant cities by employing a magician to observe them in a crystal ball.

As well as the usual setbacks and successes, Cardano suffered one terrible personal tragedy: A beloved son, convinced of his wife's infidelity, poisoned her, and was found guilty of the crime and beheaded. Cardano was shattered, yet is bitterly realistic as he addresses his readers: "I am by no means unaware that these afflictions may seem meaningless to future generations, and more especially to strangers; but there is nothing, as I have said, in this mortal life except inanity, emptiness, and dream-shadows." He eventually recovered his natural vitality and ended his life a relatively happy man, proud of his fame and honors. What's more, as he is pleased to let us know, as an old man he still had fifteen teeth left in his mouth.

JOHN AUBREY (1626–1697)
Brief Lives

John Aubrey's *Brief Lives* (mainly written 1679–80) offers some of the best gossip in English literature. Aubrey himself never published his scandalous revelations in a book. He merely compiled notes for the crabby Anthony Wood's study of Oxford worthies, *Athenae Oxonienses;* collected material for a projected "Lives of our English Mathematical Writers"; and roughed out a short biography of a friend, the philosopher Thomas Hobbes. These were later given a little order and a name—*Brief Lives*—by modern editors, some of whom also incorporated material from Aubrey's writings about folklore, English antiquities and archeology, supernatural beliefs, and the county of Wiltshire.

Aubrey himself referred to his biographical dossiers as "minutes," that is, a series of notes, jotted down "tumultuarily." Yet, like a good reporter or Hollywood columnist, his minutes are factual, anecdotal, sometimes shocking, often based on eyewitness accounts, and in every way minutely detailed. Because Aubrey never got around to refashioning his scribblings into polished, orotund prose, they possess astonishing vitality, reflecting the hustle and helter-skelter of life in the seventeenth century. For John Aubrey either knew, or knew about, all the most interesting people of the day—poets and scientists, philosophers and statesmen, courtesans and crackpots.

What do we learn from these "brief lives"? Striking factoids, first of all: Syphilis was so revolting in its symptoms that lepers refused to live near its victims. Aubrey tells us that "The divine art of printing and Gunpowder" were thought to have frightened away all the Robin Goodfellows and fairies in England. Well, perhaps not all of them, for in "anno 1670, not far from Cyrencester, was an Apparition: Being demanded, whether a good Spirit, or a bad? Returned no answer, but disappeared with a curious Perfume and most melodious Twang. Mr. W. Lilly believes it was a Farie."

Aubrey's pages are packed with such curious anecdotes, as well as accounts of sexual misbehavior and literary trivia, pungently set down. Thomas Allen was thought to be so great a magician that his servant claimed to meet "Spirits coming up his staires like Bees." Francis Bacon, we learn, possessed "an eye like a viper." Upon being asked to show his mathematical instruments, Descartes reached into a little drawer and pulled out "a paire of Compasses with one of the Legges broken; and then, for his Ruler, he used a sheet of paper folded double." James Harrington fancied that "his Perspiration turned to Flies, and sometimes to Bees." After Dr. William Harvey published his epoch-making book on the circulation of the blood, his medical practice fell off dramatically because his patients were convinced that he'd lost his mind.

Many of Aubrey's best stories are what one might politely call scabrous. The playwrighting team of Beaumont and Fletcher liked to share the same woman. Sir William Davenant claimed to be the bastard son of Shakespeare. Not only was Mary Herbert, the Countess of Pembroke, a fine chemist and the leading patron of the arts of her time, she was also "very salacious, and she had a Contrivance that in the Spring of the yeare, when the Stallions were to leape the Mares, they were to be brought before such a part of the house, where she had a vidette (a hole to peepe out at) to looke on them and please herselfe with their sport; and then she would act the like sport herselfe with her stallions" i.e., her lovers. As for that well-mannered courtier Sir Walter Raleigh, Aubrey tells us that he "loved a wench well; and one time getting up one of the Mayds of Honour up against a tree in a Wood ('Twas his first Lady) who seemed at first boarding to be something fearful of her Honour, and modest, she cryed, sweet Sir Walter, what doe you me ask? Will you undoe me? Nay, sweet Sir Walter! Sweet Sir Walter! Sir Walter! At last, as the danger and the pleasure at the same time grew higher, she cryed in the extasey, Swisser Swatter Swisser Swatter."

Perhaps we should despise Raleigh for what must be judged as little more than rape, although such an utterly believable story gives a little hot blood to someone who can otherwise be merely a dry name in a textbook. Aubrey manages this repeatedly. Did you know that the racy poet Sir John Suckling was not only "the greatest gallant of his time, and the greatest gamester" but that he also invented Cribbage? "He played at Cards rarely well, and did use to practise by himself a-bed, and there studied how the best way of managing cards could be." My own favorite Aubrey anecdote is even more winsome, and concerns two minor versifiers of the time: When George Withers was in danger of being hanged, Sir John Denham pleaded for his life, saying to the king that so long as Withers lived he himself "should not be the worst poet in England."

Anthony Wood once described Aubrey as "a shiftless person, roving and maggotty-headed, and sometimes little better than crazed."

He sounds, in fact, like the classic absent-minded antiquary. Yet in his youth Aubrey carried on love affairs, suffered bankruptcy, and spent years dodging his creditors and sponging off aristocratic friends. He also practiced astrology and believed in physiognomy (the pseudo-science that claims a man's face and head reveal his character), enjoyed spending time in coffeehouses, and attended meetings of the Royal Society. (Samuel Pepys was another member, though he never mentions Aubrey in his diary and appears only twice, very briefly, in Aubrey's pages.) Moreover, even if he was "maggotty-headed" (whimsical and obsessive), this polymath must still be counted a pioneer in such fields as paleography, oral history, folklore, and archeology (he was the first writer to describe the stone circles at Avebury). Intellectually restless, Aubrey's mind could never settle on any one project for very long and he seems to have been incapable of actually finishing anything. How can you fail to like a man so exuberantly and charmingly feckless?

Throughout the manuscript of *Brief Lives* one finds the phrase *"Quaere de hoc"*—"Make enquiries about this." This personal "note to self" might well be Aubrey's watchword, for he was certainly curious, in every sense. In his pages the gods of Renaissance poetry, philosophy, and science reveal themselves as sweet and silly human beings much like ourselves. As a consequence, we only love them more.

ALEXANDER POPE (1688–1744)
Selected poems

An early review of Alexander Pope's celebrated "Essay on Criticism" referred to its author this way: "As there is no Creature so venomous, there is nothing so stupid and impotent as a hunch-backed Toad." The viciousness of this description is shocking given that Pope, a victim of Pott's disease (tuberculosis of the bone), suffered incredibly from physical debility—not only was he just four and a half feet tall, he was also afflicted with a twisted back and constant headaches, violent pain in his joints, shortness of breath, fevers, and an extreme sensitivity to cold. So great was his anguish that he would stoically refer to "this long disease, my life."

And yet Pope is arguably what the novelist Thackeray called him in a lecture: "the greatest literary artist that England has seen." He is, moreover, probably the most quoted writer in English after Shakespeare (unless that honor belongs to Lewis Carroll). Consider some of his famous lines: "A little learning is a dangerous thing . . . The proper study of Mankind is Man . . . To err is human, to forgive divine . . . I am his Highness' dog at Kew/ Pray tell me, sir, whose dog are you? . . . Blessed is the man who expects nothing, for he shall never be disappointed. . . . 'Tis with our Judgments as our Watches, none/ Go just alike, yet each believes his own."

For many readers introduced to Pope in high school English classes, the poet's heroic couplets are remembered for their wit, their classical learning, and their relentless focus on satirizing his now-forgotten literary enemies. This is the "Wasp of Twickenham" (the poet's home), whose verses resemble, in Lytton Strachey's description, "nothing so much as spoonfuls of boiling oil ladled out . . . upon such of the passers-by whom the wretch had a grudge against." Pope, then, is either commonly recalled as this "fiendish monkey" or as the author of the anthology favorite "The Rape of the Lock," which, for all its beauties and such delicious phrases as "the cosmetic powers," has long seemed to me an exceptionally campy work, an epic in drag.

Yet Pope is a magnificent poet, who can be as sensuous as Keats— "Die of a rose in aromatick pain"—or as wistful as Horace: "Years foll'wing Years, steal something every day./ At last they steal us from our selves away." More surprisingly, he can be as delicate and lovely as A. E. Housman. Take the lines from "Elegy for an Unfortunate Lady" that describe the unknown resting place of a "beck'ning ghost" in a moonlit glade. No marble marks the lady's grave because she has killed herself for love:

> *Yet shall thy grave with rising flow'rs be drest,*
> *And the green turf lie lightly on thy breast:*
> *There shall the morn her earliest tears bestow,*
> *There the first roses of the year shall blow;*
> *While Angels with their silver wings o'ershade*
> *The ground, now sacred by thy reliques made.*

Pope can even be erotic, as in the heartbreaking "Eloisa to Abelard." Years have passed since the doomed love affair of the famous couple, and Eloisa has become a nun. But her ardor for her lost Abelard burns even in the convent: "Ah wretch!" she calls herself, "Believed the spouse of God in vain/ Confess'd within the slave of love and man." Each night brings dreams of Abelard and "raptures, of unholy joy." She tries to think of heaven, but discovers a heart "so touch'd, so pierced, so lost as mine" unequal to the task:

> *Love finds an altar for forbidden fires,*
> *I ought to grieve, but cannot what I ought,*
> *I mourn the lover, not lament the fault;*
> *I view my crime, but kindle at the view,*
> *Repent old pleasures, and solicit new.*

Pope himself triumphed over many obstacles—a wrecked body, a persecuted faith (Catholicism), a formal education that ceased at about the age of twelve. Nonetheless, his friends came to include many of the most eminent scholars, noblemen, and writers of the day, among them the dramatist William Congreve and the satirical genius Jonathan Swift (who once wrote, "In Pope, I cannot read a Line,/ But with a Sigh, I wish it mine"). He was the first poet in history to make a living without a patron, for his books became bestsellers. He translated the *Iliad* from the Greek, to great acclaim (even if the classicist

Richard Bentley did remark, "a pretty poem, Mr. Pope, though you must not call it Homer"). With his earnings from this, Pope established the villa at Twickenham, whose garden and grotto became contemporary tourist attractions, harbingers of a new romanticism in landscape design.

It has been a long while since Pope's poetry was dismissed as "a classic of our prose," but there is an oblique truth to that old put-down: He can be sententious, or obscure in his contemporary references. For the most part, however, he remains effortlessly, wonderfully readable. Listen, in the opening of the "Epistle to Dr. Arbuthnot," to the harried voice of the famous literary man beset by would-be authors and fans: "Shut, shut the door, good John! Fatigu'd I said,/ Tye up the knocker, say I'm sick, I'm dead." Even *The Dunciad*—aptly described as a series of versified political cartoons—concludes with a magnificently oratorical vision of the triumph of Dullness:

> *Lo, thy dread Empre, Chaos! Is restor'd*
> *Light dies before thy uncreating word;*
> *Thy hand, great Anarch! Lets the curtain fall;*
> *And Universal Darkness buries all.*

T. S. Eliot once rightly asserted that the modern test for liking poetry was whether or not you liked Pope. That's still a good test—and, with just a little effort, an easy one to ace.

JEAN-JACQUES ROUSSEAU (1712–1778)
Discourses; The Social Contract; Confessions

Jean-Jacques Rousseau blew up the edifice of 2,500 years of classical and Christian thought about the nature of the soul and society. Until Rousseau, nearly everyone agreed that man was by nature sinful and vicious, and that the state, religion, and other social structures imposed a needed order on our conduct. Without higher authority to moderate passions, men and women would spend their short, nasty, and brutish lives like jungle beasts. But from religion and education we learn self-control and the ways of righteousness; from the laws and customs of society we are shaped into good and useful citizens.

Not so, said this political visionary: "Man is born free, and everywhere he is in chains." Our natural impulses are healthy and good; it is society that makes us wicked. Where once we lived in harmony with ourselves and with the world around us, now we dwell in a snakepit of appearance and inauthenticity, of competitiveness and conspicuous consumption, of inequality, prejudice, and pervasive baseness. Our institutions and governments disfigure and corrupt everything they touch. We long for happiness, without recognizing that it is the system we live under that taints our souls and leaves us alienated, despairing, and hungry for something we cannot even name.

How did we go so wrong? In the myth, or thought experiment, that Rousseau offers in his discourse *On the Origin of Inequality* (1755), he concludes that the serpent in the garden was nothing less than Reason. When people lived unmediated existences in accord with Nature and themselves, when they dwelt like animals in a perpetual present, they found life simple, fulfilling, and appropriate. On some evil day, however, one man began to compare himself with another. This led to reflection, self-awareness, and eventually competitiveness, then to specialization and a division of labor to maximize individual strengths and weaknesses, and before long the floodgates were opened to envy, accumulation, possessiveness, and excess. The clever soon exploited their fellows, stockpiled provisions, and gained superfluous wealth—and these inevitably needed to be protected. By guards, by armies, by laws and statutes. And so paradise was lost.

And lost forever. Rousseau claims there's no real going back and that recorded history is essentially the story of our degradation. But by striving to ameliorate inequities, we just might establish kindlier, small city-states (he thought of Geneva and Corsica) where governmental regulation could be minimized and civic life made human-scaled. Most of all, we can liberate ourselves.

Rousseau's contemporary, the arch-conservative Edmund Burke, labeled him "the insane Socrates of the National Assembly" (that is, of the hated French Revolution). Come the twentieth century this radical thinker had grown into the great beast of all who revere traditional institutions, worship in established churches, and either fear or exploit the common man. Yet no one, of whatever political or philosophical persuasion, would deny how deeply Rousseau's sensibility pervades the past 250 years, from the poetry of the Romantics ("one impulse from a vernal wood/ May teach you more of man . . .") to the slogans, pop songs, and lifestyles of the 1960s: Drop out, "Let it be," back to Nature, hippies, communes, self-realization. Rousseauian ideals also lie behind our unabated, unassuaged longings to live more humanely in a bureaucratic, technological, and often unjust world. Even the staunchest meritocrat or most self-satisfied scion of inherited wealth must find it hard to discount the truth of the *Discourse on Inequality*'s final ringing lines: "It is manifestly against the Law of Nature . . . that a handful of men wallow in luxury, while the famished multitudes lack the necessities of life."

Such thrillingly emotional language has always contributed to Rousseau's powerful appeal. Many philosophers have been superb prose stylists—just think of Plato, Hume, or William James—but this largely self-educated former valet may be the finest of all. Rousseau actually had to beg his readers to disregard his *"beau style"* and simply pay attention to his ideas. This is impossible. His sentences are musical and absolutely limpid, classically balanced yet often oracular and confessional. One is simply swept along, no matter what the subject.

When Rousseau decided to write about two highly moral lovers, the result was *Julie, or The New Héloïse* (1761), the most popular novel of the eighteenth century. When he published *Émile, or On Education* (1762), a Utopian pedagogical treatise, mothers turned it into a bible of child-rearing. (Largely because of Rousseau, upper-class women began to breast-feed, rather than wet-nurse, their children.) And when Rousseau finally decided to relate the story of his own checkered past, his *Confessions* (1782) established the modern autobiography and to this day remains the genre's unsurpassed and supreme achievement.

Yet self-revelation, no matter how sincere the pact to tell the whole truth and nothing but, always possesses a strategy, even an agenda. In his *Confessions,* Rousseau hopes to justify his life against detractors and critics by confessing embarrassing intimacies—such as his painful need to frequently urinate—and owning up to his most shameful memories, in particular the incrimination of an innocent servant girl for a theft he himself committed and the abandonment of his newborn children at foundling hospitals. But this public laceration serves a purpose: Before the judgment of God, can his readers maintain that their lives were any better? The *Confessions* is, at heart, an apologia.

Just a précis of Rousseau's life shows how remarkable he truly was, especially against the backdrop of *ancien régime* Europe. Born in Geneva in 1712, Rousseau was brought up by his watchmaker father, his mother having died in childbirth. At the age of twelve, he was apprenticed to an engraver; he soon ran away and eventually ended up hiking through much of Switzerland, northern Italy, and parts of France. Along the way he encountered, like any picaresque hero, beautiful ladies, con artists, kindly priests, and disdainful aristocrats. Early on he fell under the spell of a Madame de Warens, whom he called Maman, and who subsequently seduced him, rather to his dismay: He says it felt like incest. Only in his thirties did Rousseau finally settle in Paris, at first aiming for a career as a musician. Though he was largely self-taught in composition (as in everything else), his

opera *Le Devin du Village* (The Village Soothsayer, 1752) proved an
unexpected success (and is still occasionally staged today).

In Paris he met Thérèse Levasseur, a nearly illiterate young laundress, who ended up sharing the rest of his life. Choosing to earn his
way as a copyist of musical scores, he preferred the resultant poverty
to the "slavery" of patronage. But his simple life soon proved abun-
dantly rich, with time to think and time to argue with close friends
whose names are now among the most honored in French intellectual
history: Diderot, d'Alembert, Condillac. Then one day, on a walk to
Vincennes to visit a temporarily imprisoned Diderot, Rousseau happened to see an advertisement in the *Mercure de France* for an essay
contest. He entered it with his *Discourse on the Sciences and Arts*
(1750), won, and found himself famous. He was thirty-eight, and his
real career was finally beginning.

During the next dozen years Rousseau produced all his major
philosophical works, including his most famous, *The Social Contract*
(1762), which argues what most Americans believe: that the people
alone are sovereign, that they possess inalienable rights, and that
government exists to carry out the general will. Eventually, though,
this upstart thinker quarreled with the cleverest mind (and finest
writer) in Europe—Voltaire—and gradually grew apart from his old
philosophe friends. In due course the authorities decided to ban (and
even burn) *The Social Contract,* so to avoid arrest Rousseau fled into
exile, first to Switzerland (where his house was stoned), then to England (traveling there in the company of David Hume). He was
hounded, spied upon, and hunted. Yet even those with real enemies
can grow paranoid, and Rousseau became crazily suspicious of those
around him. Nonetheless, he found occasional oases of tranquillity in
his later life, and he died quietly in a house near Paris provided for
him by an aristocratic admirer. His last unfinished works, especially
the *Reveries of a Solitary Walker,* show that his prose remained unsurpassed in eloquence to the very end.

That passionate eloquence—about the human heart and the human condition—characterizes Rousseau's writing at any point in his life. As a very young man, employed as a teacher by a Lyons family, he penned a memorandum outlining his theory of pedagogy. In the middle of these proposals—which years later would find fuller exposition in *Émile*—he pauses to make an observation and ask himself a question:

> Nothing is more depressing than the general fate of men. And yet they feel in themselves a consuming desire to become happy, and it makes them feel at every moment that they were born to be happy. So why are they not?

We still argue about the answer to that question. Whether or not you agree with Rousseau's view of man's natural goodness and the evils inherent in civilization, his is a voice that simply won't go away. It echoes in the heart of nearly all men and women: Why are we not happy? Why? *Why?*

—➤◦◄—

FREDERICK DOUGLASS (1817–1895)
Narrative of the Life of Frederick Douglass, An American Slave,
Written by Himself

With the exception of Phillis Wheatley's poetry, the *Narrative of the Life of Frederick Douglass* (1845) is the first major work of African-American literature. In structure, the short book—it traces the author's life only up until his late twenties—follows that of the classic American slave narrative. That is, Douglass intends his story to rouse the reader's indignation and horror at what it truly means for one man to be the chattel of another. In this sense, the book is a polemic, an abolitionist tract, and it was so viewed and used at the time. Priced at only fifty cents, the *Narrative* sold thirty thousand copies within a few years, in large part because its author was one of the most electrifying speakers of the nineteenth century.

Douglass reveals a comparably charismatic power as a writer of plain yet beautiful English prose. His sentences are simple and direct, his tone modest and forthright, his dramatic sense masterly, and each chapter delivers a short, sharp shock. Now and again, a passage may soar into brief poetical flight, but such flowery rhetoric is rare. Instead, Douglass presents the facts of his life, states his feelings and thoughts clearly, and relies on the horror of his experiences to endow his book with a quiet, almost theological grandeur. He possesses the authority of lived experience, of witness—I was there, I suffered, I am the man.

Certainly Douglass and his book helped advance the cause of freedom for all Americans, as did his talks, newspaper writing, and friendships with the fiery abolitionist William Lloyd Garrison and, later, Abraham Lincoln. The *Narrative* even now remains a powerful—and artistic—document in an ongoing progress.

In the first chapter, Douglass tells us that he was separated from his mother when he was still an infant. The point of that separation, he suggests, was "to blunt and destroy the natural affection of the mother for the child." His mother lived twelve miles away, and could visit her little son only by walking that distance and back during the night. She managed to do this four or five times. Does love, nonetheless, conquer all? No. First, Douglass writes, with quiet pathos, "I do not recollect of ever seeing my mother by the light of day," followed by the shocking sentence, "I received the tidings of her death with much the same emotions I should have probably felt at the death of a stranger."

One of Douglass's themes is that "the peculiar institution" dehumanizes not only the slave but also the master. Through an unexpected bit of luck, the boy is sent from the Maryland countryside to help his master's relatives in Baltimore. There a Mrs. Auld, who had had little personal experience with slaves hitherto, treats him with kindness and civility, even going so far as to teach him the alphabet. Unfortunately, this was soon to change:

> But, alas! This kind heart had but a short time to remain such. The fatal poison of irresponsible power was already in her hands, and soon commenced its infernal work. That cheerful eye, under the influence of slavery, soon became red with rage, that voice, made all of sweet accord, changed to one of harsh and horrid discord; and that angelic face gave place to that of a demon.

Those sentences may be a bit declamatory, but their truth is undeniable. As Lord Acton was to observe only a few years later, "power corrupts, and absolute power corrupts absolutely." Mrs. Auld, like a good German during the Nazi Reich, or an eager student in Stanley Milgram's famous "obedience" experiments, gradually surrendered her instinctive kindness to the cruel protocols of slave ownership because she was persuaded to honor the system more than the feelings of any individual person. Indeed, the slave-holding white Marylanders nearly all possessed this corrupt double nature—neighborly and religious with each other, casually cruel and sadistic with their human "property."

Whipping is the usual punishment for the smallest infraction. The slaves could never relax their vigilance, for the master or his enforcer was always watching, waiting. Sometimes, Douglass hints at sexual sadism, as when young women are stripped before their lashings; at other times, he suggests just plain sadism. Worst of all, though, are those like the cold and inflexible overseer Mr. Gore, who possesses an almost bureaucratic inhumanity—he whips, torments, and kills without scruples or hesitation simply because it's the most efficient way of doing the job and preserving law and order.

The slave suffered from physical punishment and the psychological disorientation of never knowing when or from whom the next blow might fall, yet there was an even greater, more insistent, torture in the frequent lack of food. As Douglass says with stabbing irony: "I was seldom whipped by my old master, and suffered little from any thing else than hunger and cold." Pause and reread that sentence. Here is a condition that denies people the most basic necessities—necessities that they themselves have largely provided for their masters. The larders would be full, while the slaves barely survived on handfuls of cornmeal.

The story of how Douglass managed to teach himself to read—through chicanery, since literacy was forbidden to nearly all slaves—and how knowledge started him on the path to freedom might be likened to Benjamin Franklin's *Autobiography* or to any later American success story. It is that, certainly. Yet Douglass never lets us forget that, though he worked hard, he was basically lucky. And as he periodically reminds us, the world he describes isn't ancient history. Even while he wrote in the 1840s, the slaves he knew as friends still worked in the fields, with scarred backs and empty bellies.

Autobiography has long been a prominent genre in African-American writing, largely because its principal theme is self-transformation, the freeing of the self from social or psychological chains. It often takes the form of spiritual conversion or a newly acquired historical consciousness: "Once I was lost and now I'm found, was blind and now I see." "The fire next time." But autobiography of any kind authenticates the fundamental value of the writer as a human being, one whose life matters. What counts most in the entire *Narrative of the Life of Frederick Douglass, An American Slave* may well be the title's last proud words: "Written by himself."

=⟫·◦·⟪=

JACOB BURCKHARDT (1818–1897)
The Civilization of the Renaissance in Italy

Friedrich Nietzsche, who was briefly Jacob Burckhardt's colleague at the University of Basel, revered the older Swiss historian and called him "our great teacher" and "the profoundest student of Greek culture now living." Greek culture? Yes; for even though Burckhardt was to make his name as a historian of the Italian Renaissance, he was an equally notable authority on ancient Greece and the reign of Byzantium's Constantine the Great. In those days, many scholars refused to confine their efforts to some narrow field of specialization; in fact, they ranged across subjects with the swagger of adventurers, soldiers of fortune, condottieri.

The Civilization of the Renaissance in Italy (1860) reflects such a swashbuckling exuberance, for it is packed with anecdote, scandal, and intrigue—in short, with what most people secretly want from history: exciting stories. Discussing the murderous Borgias and their political maneuverings, Burckhardt—in S. G. C. Middlemore's standard translation—zeroes in on what we really want to hear:

> Those whom the Borgias could not assail with open violence, fell victims to their poison. For the cases in which a certain amount of discretion seemed requisite, a white powder of an agreeable taste was made use of, which did not work on the spot, but slowly and gradually, and which could be mixed without notice in any dish or goblet . . . At the end of their career father and son [Alexander and Cesare] poisoned themselves with the same powder by accidentally tasting a sweetmeat intended for a wealthy cardinal.

For Burckhardt, the Renaissance in Italy is essentially an age of energy and charisma, when a man was "forced to be either hammer or anvil." Men and women acted as true individualists, pursuing glory in the arts, business, and politics (especially in Florence, "the great market of fame"). Scholars were busy rediscovering antiquity, and the example of the Greek and Roman achievement led the contemporary Italians to emulate, even to match and sometimes exceed, ancient masterpieces. Beauty was revered—in buildings, paintings, sculpture, even handwriting. *The Courtier,* by Balthasar Castiglione, taught people how to comport themselves in polite society, to converse with ease and wit, to embody that marvelous ideal of *sprezzatura*—the performance of the most difficult tasks with nonchalance. At the same time, Machiavelli's *The Prince* taught the even more important skill of how to acquire power and then keep it.

The ideal man could handle a sword or a pen, rule a state, and cultivate the arts. Take Federigo da Montefeltro, the Duke of Urbino, who was painted by Piero della Francesca in profile (with his distinctive broken nose). The duke, Burckhardt tells us, was "an accomplished ruler, captain and gentleman" who commissioned Greek translations, mastered the science of the day, wrote poetry, studied Seneca and Aristotle, and constantly read the ancient historians. Burckhardt offers us scores of such pen portraits. The famous Cardinal Ippolito Medici "kept at his strange court a troop of barbarians who talked no less than twenty different languages, and who were all of them perfect specimens of their races. Among them were . . . North African Moors, Tartar bowmen, Negro wrestlers, Indian divers, and Turks." Sigismondo Malatesta, the tyrant of Rimini, practiced evil with a zest that Iago or Sade would envy: "It is not only the Court of Rome, but the verdict of history, which convicts him of murder, rape, adultery, incest, sacrilege, perjury and treason, committed not once but often. The most shocking crime of all—the unnatural attempt on his own son Roberto, who frustrated it with his drawn dagger—may have been the result, not merely of moral corruption, but perhaps of some magical or astrological superstition."

In *The Civilization of the Renaissance in Italy,* history itself grows operatic. Savonarola burns the luxuries of Florence on his famous Bonfire of the Vanities. A certain Buonaccorso Pitti "in the course of his incessant journeys as merchant, political agent, diplomatist, and professional gambler, won and lost sums so enormous that none but princes like the Dukes of Brabant, Bavaria and Savoy were able to compete with him." Roman prostitutes practiced witchcraft to ensnare their clients, even while philosophers in the next piazza conversed about Platonic ideals.

Burckhardt called his book an "essay," which suggests something of its tentative and personal quality. Much that he writes about has been amplified or refuted by later historians, and we no longer believe in quite so sharp a divide between the hidebound Middle Ages and the sparkling Renaissance. Burkhardt unquestionably overemphasizes the personal element, the cult of the striking individual. But his book retains its power as well as a verve equal to that of the artists and adventurers of the cinquecento itself. In these pages is the Italian Renaissance of our imaginations, a realm of overreachers and beatific courtesans, of timeless works of art and Machiavellian *Realpolitik.* Here, in short, is the bloody and exhilarating birthplace of the modern.

HENRY JAMES (1843–1916)
Collected letters; collected essays; *The American Scene;*
Italian Hours; A Small Boy and Others

Admirers of Henry James have long maintained that he is the finest of all American novelists. Yet the prospect of reading the prose of *The Golden Bowl* or *The Wings of the Dove* has been known to make even the strongest graduate student quake. All that circumlocution, those endless sentences, the accumulation of clauses circling around some fine distinction that just escapes the writer's ability to pin it down, to make it, so to speak, intensely *there*—all this has led to James's reputation as one of the best sleeping aids available without prescription.

It's true that much of the later work makes serious demands. Yet what reader would want to miss, to mention only shorter master-pieces, that most enigmatic of all psychological ghost stories, *The Turn of the Screw,* or that classic example of drily devastating irony, "The Aspern Papers," or—so lacerating to those of a certain age—the heartbreaking evocation of a missed life, "The Beast in the Jungle"? After a hundred years, Henry James remains the Master.

What is less commonly recognized is James's comparable mastery of what we now call "creative nonfiction." He was an outstanding travel writer (*The American Scene, Italian Hours*) and memoirist (*A Small Boy and Others*) and a superb all-around literary critic. More-over, throughout his life he wrote hundreds and hundreds of mag-nificent letters, which allow us to better understand why this odd, roly-poly American was so beloved by nearly everyone who met him.

Read, in particular, the letters sent during the last twenty years of his life, when the novelist was living in Lamb House, near the English seaside at Rye. Time and again, they reveal a man as sensitive and honorable as any of his characters.

When James learned that novelist Stephen Crane was dying (at only twenty-nine), he immediately sent the family fifty pounds—at a time when a novel might sell for just three hundred. In a letter to critic Edmund Gosse he praises Joseph Conrad's fiction, adding, "Un-happily, to be serious and subtle isn't one of the paths to fortune." At the same time, he can tell Owen Wister how much he liked his immensely popular western *The Virginian,* while admitting that he thirsted for more blood and less sentiment.

In a more sober vein, the aging novelist consoles Leslie Stephen— the father of Virginia Woolf, whose talent James perceived—on the death of his wife: "There is no happiness in this horrible world but the happiness we have had—the very present is in the jaws of fate." He looks on as the English poet and novelist George Meredith encounters the French novelist Alphonse Daudet at a railway station; both are old and debilitated by diseases, "each staggering and stumbling, with the same uncontrollable paralysis, into the arms of the other, so that they almost rolled together onto the line, beneath the wheels of a train." He warns his admirer Edith Wharton to concentrate on America in her novels: "Profit, be warned, by my awful example of exile and ignorance." A page later, he is reminiscing about his own New York City childhood: "I wonder if you ever kick the October leaves as you walk in Fifth Avenue, as I can to this hour feel myself, hear myself, positively smell myself doing. But perhaps there are no leaves and no trees now on Fifth Avenue."

As these letters suggest, James knew just about all the literary giants of his time, going back to the heyday of Flaubert, Turgenev, and George Eliot. When he writes an essay about their work, he usually brings a particular intimacy to his criticism as well as the insight of a fellow craftsman. He seeks, above all, to understand any writer's underlying vision. Of the author of *La Comédie humaine,* James observes, "To get on in this world, to succeed, to live greatly in all one's senses, to have plenty of things—this was Balzac's infinite; it was here that his heart expanded." Of Mérimée's ice-clear prose and dryly controlled tales of hot-blooded passion ("Carmen," "Colomba," "Mateo Falcone"), he writes that they "have gradually come to be considered perfect models of the narrative art; we confess our own admiration for them is such that we feel like declaring it a capital offense in a young storyteller to put pen to paper without having read them and digested them."

Such shrewdness and passion appear in virtually all James's reflections on writing, from his early book-length study of Hawthorne to the collected prefaces of the New York edition of his own novels. The

Hawthorne study quite openly conveys the young James's infatuation with high society and "civilization." In a famous passage, he enumerates those elements that the American scene lacks: "No sovereign, no court, no personal loyalty, no aristocracy, no church, no clergy, no army, no diplomatic service, no country gentlemen, no palaces, no castles," and so on. Without these traditional structures, the novel as James conceived it—depicting a sensitive consciousness in conflict with the strictures of society—becomes almost impossible. Decades later, however, the celebrated prefaces show how brilliantly he nonetheless managed, not only by taking as his major theme the clash between American innocence and European experience, but also by his mastery of point of view and all the other tools of the novelist's trade.

Not that any of this brought success as the world judges it—popularity and wealth. Disappointment, misunderstanding, and depression haunted him all his days. When a journalist asked James about the "port" from which he had set sail as a writer, the young reporter must have been surprised by the anguish of the response he received:

> The port from which I set out was, I think that of the essential loneliness of my life—and it seems to be the port also, in sooth, to which my course again finally directs itself! This loneliness . . . what is it still but the deepest thing about one? Deeper about me, at any rate, than anything else: deeper than my "genius," deeper than my "discipline," deeper than my pride, deeper, above all, than the deep countermining of art.

Similarly, James elsewhere observes that "existence is mainly a business in which we are constantly throwing overboard the possible to keep the actual afloat." One can hardly look upon life with fewer illusions.

At seventy, the Master found himself honored by a birthday greeting from virtually all the eminent literary figures of the day. But he still continued to work as relentlessly as ever. "I have," he characteristically wrote to his friend William Dean Howells, "at last finished my little book—that is a little book, and so have two or three mornings of breathing-time before I begin another." Which of our modern novelists is quite this tireless? The "little" book, by the way, was *The Turn of the Screw.*

Near the end of his life, the great writer found himself viciously parodied by his erstwhile friend H. G. Wells, who said that reading James's fiction was like watching a hippopotamus painfully attempting to pick up a pea. In short, the hot novelist of the younger generation dismissed James's whole approach to art—his whole life, in other words—as wrong-headed and irrelevant. Soon thereafter, the psychologist William James, his "Ideal Elder Brother," died, and then the Great War broke out, bringing the entire civilization that James so valued to a bloody end in the carnage of Passchendaele and the Somme.

By this time, James had only a short time left to live. The final sentence of what might well be his final letter reads "but the pen drops from my hand." All writers might envy such parting words, and yet even they are not quite the end. As Henry James lay unconscious on his deathbed, Mrs. William James, his brother's widow, "observed his hand moving across his bedcover as if he were writing."

W. H. AUDEN (1907–1973)
Selected Poems; The Dyer's Hand; The Enchafèd Flood; Forewords and Afterwords

W. H. Auden, who wrote much of the mid-century's most unforgettable poetry, possessed the kind of mind you'd expect to find in a mathematics teacher, a professional logician, or a follower of Thomas

Aquinas. In his many essays and lectures he liked nothing better than to create grids, diagrams, and definitions. Suggest any topic and he would instinctively break it down into its aspects and components, provide exact definitions, and suggest illustrative examples or anecdotes. Since he produced a steady stream of journalism—to pay the bills—he would turn his analytical intellect toward subjects as diverse as opera, cold weather, Mozart, ballet, Shakespeare, the moon landing, and the detective story. It seems only appropriate, then, to approach Wystan Hugh Auden in his own categorical spirit.

The Man

Joseph Brodsky: "The greatest mind of the twentieth century: Wystan Hugh Auden."

Evelyn Waugh: "A very dull and awkward writer"; "a public bore" who "writes mediocre verse."

Cyril Connolly: "A benign, austere, somewhat solitary man who is seldom contradicted, with a whimsical humour and a taste for the scatological; deeply religious, wayward, tolerant, with a fastidious aversion to passionate love, love-poetry and emotional confidences . . ."

Igor Stravinsky: "He is the dirtiest man I have ever liked."

Edmund Wilson: "He represents a reversion to the old-fashioned 'family' poet—Longfellow, Wordsworth, Browning—who can be kept around and read in bulk . . . He amuses us, converses with us, does his best to give us good advice; he sings us comic songs, supplies us with brilliant elegies on the deaths of great contemporaries; he charms us, he lulls us to sleep; he lifts us to a moment of inspiration."

W. H. Auden: "My face looks like a wedding cake left out in the rain."

The Character

In 1933 Auden published a poem titled "Meiosis"—a love lyric, of course. His classical-sounding "Ode" contains these lines: "Watching with binoculars the movement of the grass for an ambush/ The pistol cocked, the code-word committed to memory . . ." In his youth a master of slang, argot, and jazzy lingo (see the exuberant and very funny "Letter to Lord Byron"), in later years the poet casually employed words like "ubity," "oppugnant," and "osse." He was often said to have the best ear for poetry since Tennyson and wrote in virtually every verse form. In a single long work—"The Sea and the Mirror"— one finds elegiacs, terza rima, a Petrarchan sonnet, a villanelle, and a ballade. He did crosswords in ink.

Though a lifelong homosexual, Auden nonetheless proposed marriage to three, possibly four, women, including philosopher Hannah Arendt. He produced a pornographic classic, "The Platonic Blow," yet could also satirize gay stereotypes: Uncle Henry, in the poem of that name, leaves Lady Starkie to travel south to find a "fwend," "a charmin' cweature,/ like a Gweek god." A lover of nature, Auden nevertheless confessed that "tramlines and slagheaps" and "pieces of machinery" made up his "ideal scenery."

At one period Auden oversaw a group house whose tenants included, besides himself, novelists Richard Wright and Carson McCullers, composer Benjamin Britten, tenor Peter Pears, writers Paul and Jane Bowles, and, not least, ecdysiast Gypsy Rose Lee. His longtime cold-water flat in Manhattan, according to his friend Dorothy Farnam, resembled "a carpenter's shop gone awry or a public building about to be vacated."

At dinner he would often sit on a volume or two of the *Oxford English Dictionary.* Come 9:30 or 10 P.M., his regular bedtime, he would abruptly leave his own parties. He would urinate in the bathtub, liked to sleep under a heaping mound of blankets, coats, and throw rugs, and regularly wore house slippers outdoors. He sometimes dressed, and smelled, like a bum, though he was never late for an appointment and always paid his bills by return mail.

In later years, Auden deeply regretted his failure to receive the Nobel prize, not because he yearned for the honor but because he wanted the money. He asked that when he died, his body be roasted and eaten by his friends (it wasn't).

The Works

Auden edited twenty-two anthologies, translated Icelandic poetry, and wrote hundreds of book reviews and essays (many remain uncollected, including his brilliant introductions to the five-volume *Poets of the English Language*). The major essays are gathered in *The Dyer's Hand* and *Forewords and Afterwords*. Auden also composed plays (including *The Dog Beneath the Skin,* with Christopher Isherwood); opera libretti (Stravinsky's *The Rake's Progress,* in partnership with the love of his life, Chester Kallman); lyrics for Benjamin Britten songs ("Our Hunting Fathers"); voice-overs for movie documentaries (*Night Mail*); and travel books (*Letters from Iceland,* with Louis MacNeice).

The best one-volume introduction to Auden's poetry is *Selected Poems: Expanded Edition,* edited by Edward Mendelson, which reprints everything as it originally appeared and before the poet dismissed from his canon, because of alleged insincerity, such classics as "Spain" and "September 1, 1939" ("I sit in one of the dives/ On Fifty-Second Street/Uncertain and afraid"). Auden seldom revised so drastically the verse he wrote after coming to America in 1939; for this later work the hefty *Collected Poems* is the handiest source. The individual volumes from *Poems* (1930) to *The Sea and the Mirror* (1944) gather the work we most remember, such as the elegies for Yeats ("Earth, receive an honored guest") and Freud ("Every day they die/ Among us, those who were doing us some good"). Randall Jarrell once wrote, "when old men, dying in their beds, mumble something unintelligible to the nurse, it is some of those lines that they will be repeating.": "Lay your sleeping head, my love/ Human on my faith-less arm."

Some readers dismiss Auden's 1950s and '60s verse as "high-table garrulousness" (Seamus Heaney), but they forget such funny poems as "On the Circuit" or such magnificent ones as "The Cave of Making" (about his workroom). Allen Ginsberg, more appropriately, once kneeled before Auden and tried to kiss the cuff of the master's trousers.

The Teacher

During the 1940s and early '50s Auden taught at the University of Michigan, Swarthmore College, and the New School. His courses included Shakespeare, "Romantic Literature: Wordsworth to Hitler," and "The Quest in Ancient and Modern Literature." At the University of Virginia he presented three dazzling lectures on "the romantic iconography of the sea," later published as *The Enchafèd Flood* (1950). At Harvard he lectured on *Don Quixote* and admitted that he'd never been able to finish the book.

One former student remembers Auden's first assignment: "Write a story or essay in which every sentence contains a lie." For a final exam at Michigan he asked the class to learn by heart, in Italian, six cantos of Dante's *Inferno*.

Favorite Things

Literature—*The Oxford English Dictionary,* Ronald Firbank, P. G. Wodehouse, Sydney Smith, Goethe, Henry James, fairy tales, Tolkien.

Music—opera, especially Mozart, Rossini, Bellini, Donizetti, and Strauss; *Don Giovanni* and *Der Rosenkavalier* above all.

Painting—Caravaggio, Brueghel ("About suffering they were never wrong,/ The Old Masters").

Final Judgments

"Treachery, unrequited love, bereavement, toothache, bad food, poverty, etc. must count for nothing the moment one picks up one's notebook."

"In the end, art is small beer. The really serious things in life are earning one's living so as not to be a parasite, and loving one's neighbor."

"We were put on this earth to make things."

The Dark Side

Sigmund Freud spoke about the "return of the repressed." In this category we see not only its return, but its triumph. For, like icebergs, much of our real life goes on below the surface, in those submerged parts of our being that we hardly ever fully acknowledge. When Mr. Kurtz—in Joseph Conrad's *Heart of Darkness*—peered within himself, he saw only "the horror, the horror." Most of us don't even dare to look.

The writers in this category refuse to flinch. John Webster reveals the Renaissance as little more than a torture chamber and a madhouse. James Hogg takes us deep into the soul of a religious fanatic. Mary Shelley shows us the monster as scapegoat—and philosopher. In Sheridan Le Fanu's stories the sinister past reaches out to the guilty and the innocent alike. Bram Stoker's *Dracula* is immortal—and deserves to be, as our greatest tale of terror. M. R. James's deliciously atmospheric ghost stories remind us, again and again, that the devil is in the details. Certainly, those who consider murder as one of the fine arts recognize William Roughead as the master. Not least, H. P. Lovecraft strips away the stage décor of the quotidian to reveal that nothing is as it seems: We are, in fact, merely the playthings of dark gods.

JOHN WEBSTER (1580?–1625)
The White Devil; The Duchess of Malfi

Almost nothing is known about John Webster, though a contemporary poem does refer to him as "crabbèd Websterio." Over the years he seems to have co-authored plays with at least a half-dozen other dramatists, among them Thomas Heywood, John Marston, and Cyril Tourneur. Through dint of sheer thoroughness, the standard collected edition of his writing (in four thick volumes) is heavily padded with minor poetry, collaborations, and conjectural works. But in the end John Webster haunts our imaginations for only two plays, *The White Devil* and *The Duchess of Malfi*.

For many, they are the best tragedies of the period, second only to those of the genius from Stratford. But there's almost no light or humor to them, as there is in even Shakespeare's darkest plays, only a disturbing, almost Freudian, obsession with lust, madness, revenge, and murder. In Webster the grave and the charnel house are never far away from the prison, the torture chamber, and the lunatic hospital.

To some readers, these two dramas of Italian Renaissance intrigue prefigure Gothic novels or the gruesome excesses of nineteenth-century Italian opera. In *The White Devil* a brother prostitutes his married sister; in *The Duchess of Malfi* another brother, full of unacknowledged incestuous desire, orders the murder of a sister in part because her body haunts his imagination. In the first play, a cheating husband applies a deadly poison to the painted lips of his own portrait because he knows that his loving but now inconvenient wife kisses the picture each night before going to bed; in the other, a duke goes mad and believes himself transformed into a ravenous wolf. In both plays, the stage (at least in our imaginations) flickers with torch flames and shadows, where only the blade of the waiting dagger glints in the half-light, evoking an utterly immoral world of spies and traitors and whores.

The plots barely hang together and are the very stuff of Italianate mischief and feverish savagery. In *The White Devil,* the two illicit lovers—Vittoria Corombona and the Duke of Bracciano—need to get rid of their respective spouses; in *The Duchess of Malfi,* the widowed duchess secretly marries her steward and rightly fears the wrath of her two proud brothers, a brooding duke and a worldly cardinal. In the first play, Vittoria's money-hungry brother Flamineo tries to manipulate and "arrange" everything; in the second, the morose Bosola agrees to become an "intelligencer" and later an assassin. By the end of act five, all the major characters in both tragedies, and a fair number of minor ones, are dead.

So why is the morbid Webster so admired? The poet Swinburne likens him to Aeschylus, Dante, and Shakespeare. The French critic H. A. Taine maintained that "no one has equalled Webster in creating utterly desperate characters." The young poet Rupert Brooke wrote an entire book in his praise, and T. S. Eliot quotes him in *The Waste Land* ("keep the wolf far thence, that's foe to men,/ For with his nails he'll dig them up agen") and, in an important essay, points out the sheer "spiritual terror" that Webster conveys. The English scholar F. L. Lucas regards the playwright's characters as proto-existentialists, bereft of hope and drawing on nothing but "the courage of despair." This chaos, this murky theater of senseless death and blackest lust, is a bitter world we recognize as our own.

And then, in the midst of all the graveyard horror, Webster somehow flashes forth with lines of poetry as exquisite as any in the English language. Duke Ferdinand looks down at his murdered sister: "Cover her face; mine eyes dazzle; she died young." We hear of "all the weary minutes of my life" and "the friendless bodies of unburied men." We learn of "the irregular crab,/ Which though't goes backward, thinks that it goes right,/ Because it goes its own way" and shudder at the eerie vision of the conscience-stricken cardinal: "When I look into the fish-ponds, in my garden,/ Methinks I see a thing, arm'd with a rake/ That seems to strike at me." The pander Flamineo unctuously confesses, "I made a kind of path/ To her and mine own preferment" and later tells us that, "We think caged birds sing, when indeed they cry." Bracciano, fearing betrayal, agonizes, "How long have I beheld the devil in crystal?" When suffering from poison, he cries out: "On pain of death, let no man name death to me,/ It is a word infinitely terrible." At her trial Vittoria denies the charge of adultery: "Condemn you me for that the duke did love me?/ So may you blame some fair and crystal river/ For that some melancholic distracted man/ Hath drown'd himself in 't." With resignation, even the Duchess of Malfi speaks lyrically of death:

> *What would it pleasure me to have my throat cut*
> *With diamonds? Or to be smothered*
> *With cassia? Or to be shot to death with pearls?*
> *I know death hath ten thousand several doors*
> *For men to take their exits . . .*

It's hard to stop quoting.

Being a dramatist, Webster sometimes needs context or space to generate his most moving effects. In the tragedy's final scene, the remorseful assassin of *The Duchess of Malfi* is asked how Antonio came by his death. Himself dying, Bosola answers:

> *In a mist: I know not how—*
> *Such a mistake as I have often seen*
> *In a play. —O, I am gone!—*
> *We are only like dead walls, or vaulted graves,*
> *That ruin'd, yields no echo: —Fare you well—*
> *It may be pain, but no harm to me to die*

In so good a quarrel. O, this gloomy world!
In what a shadow, or deep pit of darkness,
Doth womanish and fearful mankind live!
Let worthy minds ne'er stagger in distrust
To suffer death, or shame for what is just—
Mine is another voyage.

———

MARY SHELLEY (1797–1851)
Frankenstein; or, The Modern Prometheus

Frankenstein (1818) is the greatest novel of the Romantic movement. This isn't to say that it's a masterpiece comparable to the work of Jane Austen, who was the supreme stylist of the time, or of Balzac, who depicts every aspect of society in his *Comédie humaine.* But Mary Shelley's novel explores the dark recesses of our psyches with the same intensity as so much of the poetry of that era. To read her book—which is far more complex than the movies based on it—is to realize that she offers us a philosophical fable, an archetypal journey toward death, the foundational work of modern science fiction, and a poem (in prose) nearly the equal to Coleridge's "Rime of the Ancient Mariner" and Byron's "Manfred."

Perhaps the best way to approach the book is to think back over the story and notice its themes: the persistent interconnection of sex, birth, and death; the mirroring of monster and creator; the conflict between instinctive goodness and the societal creation of the criminal; the power of nature to soften and civilize; the human yearning for spiritual sympathy and love. Think, too, of the images of the Noble Savage and the Byronic wanderer with a secret sin, the multiple allusions to Satan's fall from angel to devil and of Adam from Paradise, the sense of isolation and loneliness that results from moral transgression, and the need to confess one's crimes in the hope of being understood if not absolved. Add to these the Monte Cristo–like desire to revenge oneself for undeserved suffering, and the ever-increasing sense of doom, followed by remorse that comes too late.

The novel can be quite creepy in its implications. Victor Frankenstein immerses himself in "filth" and creates what he regards as a kind of "abortion," while his slashing destruction of the promised "female" companion prefigures the sexual brutality of Jack the Ripper. Relations always seem ambiguous: Victor marries a woman who is virtually his sister. During one daydream her image modulates into that of his mother. When the monster first observes the siblings Felix and Agathe, they behave like a young married couple. Later, the creature determines to "ravish" Victor from his happiness, saying, "I shall be with you on your wedding-night." After murdering Victor's new bride instead, he leaves her sprawled across the marriage bed as if orgasmically exhausted.

The movies have conditioned us to a lumbering half-comic lug who murmurs broken phrases like "I love . . . dead." But Shelley's original soon learns to speak with the eloquence of a European *philosophe*. He reads Plutarch, Milton, and Goethe, and repeatedly points out, like a follower of Rousseau, that society has made him a monster. At his "birth," he tells us, he instinctively turned toward the light, loved nature and the twittering of birds, found himself drawn to beauty and goodness: All to no avail. First, his creator casts him into the darkness; then, those he has admired and helped—the De Lacey family—reject him with horror; and finally he is cruelly shot and nearly killed after rescuing a peasant girl from death. Reviled and denied a happiness desperately yearned for, what soul would not gradually grow embittered at the world's injustice? The poor creature observes:

> All men hate the wretched; how then must I be hated, who am miserable beyond all living things? . . . Every where I see bliss,

from which I alone am irrevocably excluded. I was benevolent and good; misery made me a fiend. Make me happy, and I shall again be virtuous.

It is hard to miss the echoes of Adam exiled from the garden, of Satan remembering heaven, of Shelley's father, William Godwin, philosophizing.

The geography of *Frankenstein* is no less grand than its themes: Shelley takes us across Europe, from the snow-covered Swiss Alps to France, then to England and Scotland, and even to a lonely shack on one of the Orkney Islands. At one point the monster speaks of his daydream of a simple life in South America, instead of "the desert mountains and the dreary glaciers" that are his current refuge. Victor works in a truly infernal laboratory, lies feverish in a hospital, and languishes in a prison; he takes a pleasure boat down the Rhine and later finds himself adrift on an icy ocean; he visits the dreaming spires of Oxford and journeys to the desolate wastes of the north. The book embraces the known world. Best of all, the novel opens and closes on those boundless and dreary ice floes of the Arctic. There, the two implacable enemies—father and son, sexual rivals, spiritual brothers—finally realize how much they are halves of a single whole, each giving life to the other.

There are faults to Shelley's novel—the De Lacey section is overlong—but what some have dismissed as melodramatic caricatures, others may understand as archetypes: the Overreacher, the Good Old Man, the Fragile Beauty, the Shadow Self. At times the monster's speeches attain a tragic grandeur:

When I call over the frightful catalogue of my deeds, I cannot believe that I am he whose thoughts were once filled with sublime and transcendant visions of the beauty and majesty of goodness. But it is even so; the fallen angel becomes a malignant devil. Yet even that enemy of God and man had friends and associates in his desolation; I am quite alone.

At the novel's end, Frankenstein's creation foresees his death in images of light and summer warmth, in memories of the rustling of leaves and the chirping of birds. In his beginning is his end. Like many doomed romantic heroes before and since, he finally yearns only for the night. In the quiet close of the novel, this fated, ill-begotten being is "borne away by the waves, and lost in darkness and distance."

But Shelley's creation has never been forgotten. Ever since that dreary night of November, when Victor first saw the dull yellow eye of the creature open, it has been loose among us. We find his shadowy presence in works as different as Dickens's *Great Expectations,* Hugo's *Hunchback of Notre Dame,* Stevenson's *Dr. Jekyll and Mr. Hyde,* Stephen Crane's "The Monster," and Alfred Bester's science-fiction classic "Fondly Fahrenheit," among many, many others.

JAMES HOGG (1770–1835)
The Private Memoirs and Confessions of a Justified Sinner

Among connoisseurs of dark fantasy, no nineteenth-century novel is more greatly admired than James Hogg's *The Private Memoirs and Confessions of a Justified Sinner* (1824). This masterpiece is a stunning amalgam of the weird tale, the mystery story, and the madman's confession, as well as a biting satire on religious fanaticism in Scotland during the early eighteenth century (the place and time of its action). What's more, Hogg adopts a daring structural device in telling the same story twice—once, briefly, from the outside, then again, more expansively, from within. The first account, by the "editor," sets down the facts and events leading up to a young man's death; the second, called the memoir and confession, takes us inside the mind of the murderer.

Not that Robert Wringhim regards himself as a murderer; quite the contrary: He is merely an extremely devout believer in predestination, recognizing that each soul is damned or saved for all eternity and that good works avail us nothing. Only the Lord's grace matters, and those whom God has elected for heaven—the "justified"—can, in essence, do no wrong. (This is essentially the antinomian heresy, but common enough among more extreme forms of Calvinism.) For the Elect, all trespasses are venial and will be forgiven. Besides, how can any crime really matter to those who know that their names are already inscribed in the book of glory?

Wringhim grows up under the care of both his fanatically religious mother, long separated from the sinful Lord Dalcastle, and a stern fundamentalist preacher. Not so his older brother George. While Robert is pinched of mind and spirit, George is open-hearted, glad-handed, and well-loved, a youthful version of his Falstaffian father. Two brothers could hardly be less alike. But for some reason Robert, always clad in black, starts to stalk George, appearing wherever the sociable young man hopes to enjoy himself—at the tennis courts, on the playing fields, in church, even atop a lonely mountain. Gibes and mockery follow, sometimes leading to the exchange of insults or blows. George is mystified. Why is he being persecuted by this demon in human form?

In that very question lies its answer, as we gradually learn in part two of Hogg's novel. It opens with Wringhim's testimonial:

My sorrows have all been for a slighted gospel, and my vengeance has been wreaked on its adversaries. Therefore, in the might of heaven I will sit down and write: I will let the wicked of this world know what I have done in the faith of the promises, and justification by grace, that they may read and tremble, and bless their gods of silver and gold, that the minister of heaven was removed from their sphere before their blood was mingled with their sacrifices.

Clearly, young Wringhim has turned into some kind of religious nut. But how deluded is he really? A studious, lying little hypocrite as a boy, he once enjoyed pointing out and punishing the faults of others. Throughout his childhood, however, he had been deeply burdened with the fear of God's awful judgment—until the day his guardian and mother announce that they are convinced that, through their prayers, he is a member of the community of the just, his name written forever in the Lamb's book of life and "that no bypast transgression, nor any future act" can alter that decree. With this uplifting knowledge, a newly buoyant Wringhim strides out for a walk in the nearby fields.

"As I thus wended my way," he tells us, "I beheld a young man of a mysterious appearance coming towards me." With a shock, Wringhim realizes that this stranger's features are his own. How is this possible? The stranger eventually explains, "My countenance changes with my studies and sensations . . . If I contemplate a man's features seriously, mine own gradually assume the very same appearance and character." This is not all. Through this miraculous sympathy, he also gains an understanding of the other's feelings and thoughts.

Wringhim soon spends more and more time with his new acquaintance—he can't quite tear himself away and increasingly feels that they are indissolubly united. At the same time, he grows to recognize and bow to the foreigner's superior understanding, especially of every aspect of religion and the heart of man. But who can he be? His charismatic manner suggests the possibility of royal blood. Isn't Peter the Great known to be traveling incognito in Europe? The reader, of course, suspects the dark truth right away, for every line the stranger murmurs is rich with double meaning. When asked about his family, he answers, "I have no parents save one, whom I do not acknowledge." He refers to some strange kind of account book as "my Bible." He cleverly refuses to say prayers.

And, of course, he can quote Scripture to his purpose, eventually convincing the smug Wringhim that "the elect of God would be happier, and purer, were the wicked and unbelievers all cut off from troubling and misleading them." The wicked? For example, that elderly preacher who recently warned Wringhim against his illustrious friend's company, or that frivolous brother of his, or so many others. The world is full of those whose rank impiety deserves the punishment of death. If only there were someone brave enough, righteous enough, to undertake this moral cleansing, this new crusade . . .

Despite some sinful doubtings, Wringhim recognizes that he has been called upon to take up this glorious task. After all, he stands among the chosen elect, freed from all merely human strictures and laws. What a magnificent destiny will be his!

Hogg's novel offers more than a compelling plot and story. It brilliantly portrays self-delusion, revealing how people gradually come to regard even their basest desires as noble enterprises. Its claustrophobic atmosphere rivals that of Dostoevsky or Edgar Allan Poe: At his darkest moments, Wringhim grows convinced that he has become two people, and that neither is wholly himself. There are strange blanks in his life, and sometimes he seems to perceive everything in a kind of daze or fever dream. Is he in fact just a madman with an imaginary friend? Or has he truly become the Devil's plaything?

Whatever the case, *The Private Memoirs and Confessions of a Justified Sinner* is a harrowing book. For all its touches of humor, it tells as dark a story as any imaginable. Is faith an anchor or a snare? A source of comfort or the cause of torment? How can we decide? Whom can we trust? Might we be more like Robert Wringhim than we suspect? Is he, in fact, our brother, our twin?

SHERIDAN LE FANU (1814–1873)
Ghost stories; *Uncle Silas*

Sheridan Le Fanu wrote the best supernatural fiction of the nineteenth century. Only Vernon Lee (the pen name of Violet Paget) can equal him in power and artistry, and then only occasionally (in her two masterpieces, "Amour Dure" and "Oke of Okehurst"). Le Fanu's famous "Green Tea" has been called the archetypal weird tale and his even more disturbing "Carmilla" the best of all vampire stories. The finest twentieth-century practitioner of the classic ghost story—M. R. James—revered the Irish writer as his master.

Le Fanu excelled in three elements of supernatural storytelling: narrative framing, powerful descriptions (particularly of countrysides and abandoned estates), and teasing ambiguities.

His frames—in which a story is usually set in the past, then conveyed through a witness or informant, and finally written down by a narrator—encourage not so much belief as a suspension of disbelief. Le Fanu isn't asserting the truth of the fantastic, he's simply passing on what he's been told. Such layering creates a sense of documentary verisimilitude, and it reaches a mini-apotheosis in "Mr. Justice Harbottle." There we learn that two accounts of the old Harbottle case exist, and that the informant Dr. Hesselius judged the one by a Mrs. Trimmer to be the better of the pair: "It is minute and detailed, and written, it seems to me, with more caution and knowledge." But, alas, Mrs. Trimmer's memorandum of 1805 has somehow been lost. As a result our author, ostensibly Le Fanu himself, has found himself obliged to settle for a Mr. Harman's account, written thirty years later and far more polished in character. Still, we are assured by a note discovered among Dr. Hesselius's papers that this other record "exactly tallies with that furnished by Mrs. Trimmer." And so, Le Fanu neatly makes his nightmarish tale appear all the more real and convincing by avowedly printing the less-than-authoritative version of it.

Deft as this kind of trick is, Le Fanu's artistry shows up even more forcefully in his descriptions. He brings his characters and landscapes to vivid, hideous life with just a few well-chosen phrases, as when Mrs. Joliffe confronts the robot-like horror of Madam Crowl, who suddenly rises from her bed:

> And in an instant she opens her eyes, and up she sits, and spins herself round, and down wi' her, wi' a clack on her two tall heels on the floor, facin' me, ogglin' me in my face wi' her two great glass eyes, and a wicked simper wi' her old wrinkled lips, and lang fause teeth. . . . If I'd a thought an instant, I'd turned about and run. But I couldn' take my eyes off her, and I backed from her as soon as I could; and she came clatterin' after, like a thing on wires, with her fingers pointing to my throat, and she makin' all the time a sound with her tongue like zizz-zizz-zizz."

Just as brilliantly, Le Fanu can sweep clear the stage, as he does to prepare for the arrival of the midnight horseman in "The Dead Sexton":

> It was about eight o'clock, and the hostler, standing alone on the road in front of the open door of the George and Dragon, had just smoked his pipe out. A bright moon hung in the frosty sky. The fells rose from the opposite edge of the lake like phantom mountains. The air was stirless. Through the boughs and sprays of the leafless elms no sigh or motion, however hushed, was audible. Not a ripple glimmered on the lake, which at one point reflected the brilliant moon from its dark blue expanse like burnished steel. The road that runs by the inn door, along the margin of the lake, shone dazzlingly white.

While Le Fanu's frames contribute a documentary authority to his storytelling, his descriptions constantly foil this apparent scientific objectivity with their myriad touches of romance and mystery. The resulting tension imbues the narratives with much of their power. In the end, the reader is generally left in a state of some uncertainty, even allowed the hope that all was really quite natural, that a character's mysterious lingering sickness or sudden death or disappearance might have been brought about by nervous exhaustion, delusion, or despondency. Indeed, throughout his oeuvre Le Fanu shows us protagonists as skeptical as ourselves—at least up to the point when they surrender to apparent mania and mental breakdown. Yet what is the true etiology of their pathetic fates? Does seeing a demonic monkey or being constantly shadowed by a mysterious watcher drive them to madness, or does madness lead them to imagine ghosts and monsters? Escher-like, the natural and supernatural imperceptibly slide into each other before our wondering eyes.

A similar ambiguity makes itself felt in Le Fanu's unsettling "romance of terror," *Uncle Silas,* one of the dark masterpieces of Victorian fiction.

Maud Ruthvyn—seventeen at the start of the story—has been brought up in an isolated estate with little acquaintance of the outside world. Her father, Austin Ruthvyn, is an enigmatic, taciturn man, now given to pacing his study in darkness, studying the works of Swedenborg, and meeting periodically at midnight with an unsettling Dr. Bryerley. Though immensely rich, Austin feels proudest of his family name and heritage, both of which have been besmirched by his brother Silas, whom he has not seen in many years. Dissolute and profligate, elegant and hypnotically charming, Silas has squandered vast sums of money and committed unspeakable crimes, possibly even murder. Maud, naturally (or unnaturally), grows half infatuated with her Byronic uncle, over whose youthful portrait she moons.

Even in these early chapters it quickly grows clear that *Uncle Silas* is solidly built on narrative quicksand. First of all, Le Fanu leaves us unsure about the genre of novel we are reading. Is it a mystery? A ghost story? A Gothic or philosophic romance? Or is it to be a study of character, like Charlotte Brontë's *Jane Eyre* (whose plot was partly borrowed from a story by Le Fanu)? What's more, we are left unsure about who is "good" and who "wicked." Personalities initially identified as Mephistophelean may actually turn out to be angelic, or vice versa.

Against this pervasive atmosphere of disorientation and uncertainty, Le Fanu counterposes a steel trap of a plot that closes slowly but inexorably. Nothing is left to chance as our heroine—who narrates her own story—is gradually steered by unknown forces toward several close misses with a fate worse than death, and then, it would seem, toward death itself. We fear for Maud constantly, as when she awakens one morning not at a London hotel but in what is clearly a brothel.

However, Maud is to suffer a far more dreadful destiny than to find herself shanghaied for an "establishment" on the continent. After the young woman travels to meet her white-haired uncle in the flesh—in the corpselike and bloodless flesh—*Uncle Silas* adds mounting paranoia to its exploration of moral ambiguity and sexual innuendo. The aged man tells Maud that in his household everyone loves each other very "cordially," and he beckons to his slatternly daughter:

> He extended his thin, white hand with a chilly smile toward Milly, who bounced up, and took it with a frightened look; and he repeated, holding her hand rather slightly I thought, "Yes, I hope, very cordially," and then turning again to me, he put it over the arm of his chair, and let it go, as a man might drop something he did not want from a carriage window.

No wonder that *Uncle Silas* ranks with Wilkie Collins's *The Woman in White* and John Meade Falkner's *The Nebuly Coat* in suspensefulness, or that Le Fanu's other great thriller, *The House by the Churchyard,* elicited the admiration of James Joyce, who drew on aspects of it in *Finnegans Wake.* Sheridan Le Fanu is a writer who can keep you on tenterhooks—either with or without ghosts.

<hr>

BRAM STOKER (1847–1912)
Dracula

The one important fact about Bram Stoker's *Dracula* (1897) is that the novel remains, despite countless films, sequels, copies, and parodies, among the scariest books ever written. Popular culture may have assimilated the vampire and turned him into a slightly kitsch figure—"I vant to drink your blood"—but Stoker's original is straight out of nightmare.

The first third of the book could hardly be bettered in its carefully designed journey into fear, one that starts quietly and gradually ratchets up the tension. Consider its elements: Jonathan Harker's gradual penetration into ominous Transylvania, the folkloric warnings and fear-struck Carpathian peasants, the hellish coach ride to Dracula's castle, the destruction of the young lawyer's mirror, the sight of Dracula descending the castle wall face downward like a giant bat, Harker's languorous surrender to the ministrations of the voluptuous "sisters"—"there are kisses for us all"—and the count's interruption of their anticipated banquet with the hideous and triumphant cry, "This man belongs to me!"

Leaving us uncertain about Harker's fate, Stoker then shifts the action to sunny England, where the two friends Lucy Westenra and

Mina Murray discuss with girlish innocence the men in their lives. One of Lucy's suitors, Dr. Seward, manages an insane asylum where a certain inmate has begun to act very strangely, ravenously devouring flies and even small birds, growing oddly agitated at various times of the day. What ails Renfield? And why does he murmur, on the night when he temporarily escapes his cell and flees to nearby Carfax Abbey: "I am here to do Your bidding, Master. I am Your slave, and You will reward me, for I shall be faithful. I have worshipped You long and afar-off. Now that You are near, I await Your commands, and You will not pass me by, will You, dear Master, in your distribution of good things?"

Stoker modeled his novel after Wilkie Collins's *The Woman in White,* unfolding its tense narrative through letters and journals. This allows him to build suspense to a breaking point, then suddenly change key, forcing the reader to squirm with apprehension. Once in England, Dracula moves in, slowly, methodically, relentlessly, on Lucy Westenra. Only the Dutch doctor Van Helsing finally understands the wasting sickness that leaves the young woman increasingly pale and listless. Can he save her in time?

Today more than ever, *Dracula* seems a text built, if only half consciously, on sexual anxieties. The conventionalized heroes all fear awakened female sexuality. The count himself, like many nineteenth-century vampires, is tacitly modeled after the darkly charismatic Lord Byron—a romantic outcast, bisexual, incestuous, electrifyingly attractive, "mad, bad, and dangerous to know." What woman would deny, could deny, such a lover anything? In the novel, the appalled heroes burst into a locked bedroom to discover one of their nice girls sucking from the monster's breast, in an act of what is clearly symbolic fellatio. "Unclean, unclean!" Another of the women progresses from a sweet and blushing maiden to a fearful yet excited bride surrendering to hitherto unsuspected ecstasies, before ending up a provocative and brazen voluptuary.

Ghosts, werewolves, or Frankenstein's monster may be frightening or life-threatening, but our fear of the vampire lies in his seductiveness. He threatens our values, our public socialized selves; he tempts us from the path of salvation. Once our suppressed desires, our innermost demons, are released, how can we ever contain them again? Dracula is as much Dionysus as the Devil, and it's no surprise that he appeared at the end of the Victorian era, when readers were drawn to the Great God Pan, Dr. Jekyll and Mr. Hyde, and handsome Dorian Gray with his wicked portrait. In the vampire's smothering embrace, we discard our most publicly cherished values and, fearfully but almost gratefully, open our arms to all that is inexpressible and shudderingly intense. Little wonder that the lord of the night has been adopted as the icon of transgressive sexuality, from the 1920s vamp to Anne Rice's Lestat. For don't we secretly envy Dracula? What's truly disturbing about the Undead, after all, is not that virtuous and likable people become blood-sucking fiends but that they take so completely to the lifestyle.

Bram Stoker never again wrote anything half as good as *Dracula*. He didn't need to, having somehow produced the greatest of all novels of terror. At times he can be long-winded or sentimental, and Van Helsing's accent can be wearisome, but how few are such cavils. The repulsive Renfield is alternately frightening and pitiable: "The blood is the life." There is no better, fiercer storm in all of Western literature than the one that brings the *Demeter,* Dracula's ghost-ship, to Whitby. Scenes of mist and snow, of wolves and rats, of a figure—or something—with red eyes barely glimpsed in the shadows, are wonderfully presented. At times one can hardly force oneself to read for sheer anxiety, and then one can hardly stop for the same reason. But, then, such speed should only be expected in a novel like this, for as Bram Stoker tells us, "The dead travel fast."

—>•◦•<—

M. R. JAMES (1862–1936)
Collected Ghost Stories

What Sherlock Holmes's adventures are to the mystery, M. R. James's thirty or so "ghost stories of an antiquary" are to horror and the supernatural. In his lifetime James was the greatest English authority on the New Testament apocrypha, a bibliographer of medieval manuscripts, an amateur expert on early church architecture and decoration, a Cambridge don, and eventually the provost of Eton. All these contribute their part to what are widely regarded as the finest ghostly tales in English.

Originally, James's stories of revenants, demons, and black magic were intended to be enjoyed as shivery Christmas treats. After the seasonal feast and good cheer, "Monty" would read one or two aloud to his friends at Cambridge or his students at Eton. By a single candle, after all other lights had been extinguished, the bespectacled scholar would gradually create a sense of unease, of growing eeriness and expectation.

Many of the stories begin quite casually, often when a middle-aged bachelor, typically a don, visits an old church or country house, or takes a holiday in Denmark or France, and there stumbles across something from the past—an old diary, an enigmatic inscription on a tomb, puzzling symbols in stained glass, or even an eighteenth-century maze in which one never feels quite alone. In "Canon Alberic's Scrap-book," Mr. Dennistoun spends an afternoon of his holiday abroad sketching the interior of a decaying French cathedral. Toward evening, he notices that "the church began to fill with shadows, while the curious noises—the muffled footfalls and distant talking voices that had been perceptible all day—seemed, no doubt because of the fading light and the consequently quickened sense of hearing, to become more frequent and insistent."

Invariably, James's heroes shrug off what at first seems only "curious." Who wouldn't? Those muffled sounds must be some odd echo or sympathetic vibration from the thick stone walls, that shadow a trick of the light, and the unexpected nervousness of the locals a normal response to a stranger in their midst. Could it, though, just possibly be something else? There is that old legend . . .

No matter what the exact circumstance, the past eventually reaches out into the present, and the most seemingly ordinary object or discovery may serve to summon up the horror. In "The Mezzotint," Mr. Williams orders a print of an English manor-house, one that seems disappointingly unexceptional—aside from the hideous skeletal figure crawling on all fours across the front lawn. Taking a vacation at Barnstow, Professor Parkins strolls along the beach and almost literally stumbles upon the ruins of a Templar preceptory. There among its crumbling tombstones he unfortunately makes a small discovery:

> It was of bronze, he now saw, and was shaped very much after the manner of the modern dog-whistle; in fact it was—yes, certainly it was—actually no more nor less than a whistle. He put it to his lips. . . . He blew tentatively and stopped suddenly, startled and yet pleased at the note he had elicited. It had a quality of infinite distance in it, and, soft as it was, he somehow felt it must be audible for miles round.

Quite a nice little archeological find, but Parkins can make out only part of the Latin inscription, something about somebody coming. Back in his hotel quarters he decides to blow the whistle again: "Goodness! What force the wind can get up in a few minutes! . . . It's enough to tear the room to pieces." The story—one of James's supreme achievements—takes its deliciously ominous title from a slightly modified line of Robert Burns: "Oh, Whistle, and I'll Come to You, My Lad."

James's scholars and antiquaries generally bring their fates upon themselves, sometimes inadvertently or through simple bad luck, but often because they give in to a form of passion. Not sexual, of course—heaven, forfend—but rather the passions typical of the academic life: the allure of an arcane discovery, perhaps a spiteful desire for revenge on a colleague, sometimes just the thrill of figuring out a riddle or solving a historical mystery. Anyone, of course, might wish to go after "The Treasure of Abbot Thomas," some "ten thousand pieces of gold laid up in the well in the court of the Abbot's house of Steinfeld." Clever Mr. Somerton learns of their location by deciphering an elaborate cryptogram; mistakenly, however, he fails to pay sufficient attention to the full coded text, which ends with an enigmatic phrase: The abbot, a dabbler in the dark arts, warns that he has "set a guardian" over his wealth.

Atmosphere—James himself called it mood—is all-important to the cozy style of the English ghost story. Indeed, that nostalgia-laden period flavor is what we now value most in fiction from the late Victorian and Edwardian era.

So it may sound less than heretical to say that James's supernatural tales aren't really all that frightening to a modern reader. To begin with, they are elaborately framed, often set in the past, and laced with a dry humor. Moreover, the main characters are lightly sketched, and James never makes us care greatly about their fates. (In this regard, he's rather like Agatha Christie.) In truth, what we most deeply enjoy is the storytelling itself, starting with the titles—"Casting the Runes," "A Warning to the Curious," "Count Magnus." Reading along, we do more than suspend our incredulity, we surrender to the spirit of the game. As James deftly creates an atmosphere of suggestion and anticipation, we wonder just how and when his various hobgoblins will appear. He is, in fact, a great master of reticence, a quality he much admired in life as in narrative art. Nothing gross or gruesome is described; it is only hinted at. Instead, James will usually deliver a single memorable shock. Let me quote an example, without giving away the story's title:

> Then he dozed, and then he woke, and bethought himself that his brown spaniel, which ordinarily slept in his room, had not come upstairs with him. Then he thought he was mistaken: for happening to move his hand, which hung down over the arm of the chair within a few inches of the floor, he felt on the back of it just the slightest touch of a surface of hair, and stretching it out in that direction he stroked and patted a rounded some-thing. But the feel of it, and still more the fact that instead of a responsive movement, absolute stillness greeted his touch, made him look over his arm. What he had been touching rose to meet him.

James's other gift is a flair for pastiche. In life he was noted as a mimic, adept at replicating the mannerisms and idiosyncrasies of his colleagues. His stories abound with fabricated antiquarian docu-ments. In "Mr. Humphreys and His Inheritance," James recreates a seventeenth-century religious tract, one that tells of a man who ven-tured into a certain maze in search of a great treasure:

> He went merrily on, and without any Difficulty reached the Heart of the *Labyrinth* and got the Jewel, and so set out on his way back rejoycing: but as the Night fell, *wherein all the Beasts of the Forest do move,* he begun to be sensible of some Creature keeping Pace with him and, as he thought, *peering and looking upon him* from the next Alley to that he was in; and that when he should stop, this Companion should stop also, which put him in some Disorder of his Spirits. And, indeed, as the Dark-ness increas'd, it seemed to him that there was more than one . . .

In all his stories M. R. James aimed to create what he called "a pleasing terror," and this oxymoron hints at his artistry. More precisely, he remains unrivaled in evoking ominous foreboding—and of how easy it is to awaken the unwanted attention of things that should sleep quietly in their tombs or hiding places.

⸻⸻⸻

WILLIAM ROUGHEAD (1870–1952)
Tales of the Criminous (1906–1946)

To aficionados of "true crime," the Shakespeare—or, better yet, the John Webster—of the genre is the Scotsman William Roughead. Having inherited enough money so that he didn't need to pursue an active career as a lawyer, Roughead nonetheless attended every notable murder trial in his hometown of Edinburgh for more than fifty years. He also collected books, letters and newspaper clippings on the great cases from earlier periods of British criminality, and read widely in the literature of blood and intrigue, especially Elizabethan revenge tragedy, Victorian sensation fiction, and the novels of Charles Dickens and Joseph Conrad. In due course, Roughead turned to writing and publishing accounts of favorite murder cases, paying close attention to atmosphere, dramatic pacing, and irony in the telling, but also adopting a comfortable, conversational tone, albeit one marked by a slightly formal and sometimes *recherché* diction. Trying to sum up his artistry, mystery novelist Dorothy L. Sayers concluded that "William Roughead is far and away the best showman that ever stood before the door of a Chamber of Horrors."

What kind of horrors? In his 113 "tales of the criminous"—a phrase used as the title for a retrospective collection edited by his son—Roughead covers every sort of homicide, every sort of criminal, and every sort of trial, including several that resulted in quite obvious miscarriages of justice. His dramatis personae include the notorious body-snatchers Burke and Hare; the hypocritical and unctuous Dr. Pritchard, who slowly poisoned both his wife and mother-in-law; and, of course, that sweetheart of all true-crime writers, the almost legendary Miss Madeleine Smith, who cheated the gallows by beguiling the judge and jury into the notorious Scots verdict of "Not Proven." These are famous cases, but Roughead may be at his personal best describing the rather less well known, such as the poisoning of Charles Bravo, possibly by his beautiful young wife (who had been the mistress of a quite elderly doctor), possibly by her horrid companion, Mrs. Cox. Periodically, too, Roughead makes us aware of egregious favoritism and class prejudice in the justice system—the guilty rich get off, the innocent poor are frequently set up (Oscar Slater, a victim of judicial prejudice, was released—after twenty years' imprisonment—largely through the efforts of Sir Arthur Conan Doyle, among others).

In 1827, Thomas De Quincey brought out what remains the ground-breaking theoretical essay for any effective "study in scarlet": "On Murder Considered as One of the Fine Arts." There he notes that "something more goes into the composition of a fine murder than two blockheads to kill and be killed, a knife, a purse, and a dark lane. Design, gentlemen, grouping, light and shade, poetry, sentiment, are now deemed indispensable to attempts of this nature." De Quincey notes that one can experience moral revulsion to killing, and yet—after the fact, when the deed cannot be undone—still appreciate the esthetics of a work well executed by a "bold artist." (Oscar Wilde was to develop this notion of art's amorality in "Pen, Pencil and Poison," an essay built about the career of Wainewright the Poisoner.) For all his own appreciation of such "artistry," Roughead's own pieces do portray genuine evil and often convey moral outrage, either at the crime itself or the inadequacies of the courtroom judgment. It is no

accident that Roughead determines that the one common element to
nearly all his "bold artists" is self-conceit, the satanic sin of pride.

In his prose, Roughead can be coolly factual but also slightly arch
or humorous:

> Pondering upon this problem the partners [Burke and Hare]
> had a brain-wave. Why await the tardy operations of Provi-
> dence? Surely, there were to be found in the purlieus of the city
> many homeless wanderers whom it were mere charity to relieve
> of the weary burden of existence, so as it could be done wisely
> and with safety. . . . I have long had an uneasy feeling that I did
> not do justice to Dr. Pritchard, either as a man or as a mur-
> derer. . . . In the spring of 1856 the flirtation developed into an
> intrigue, the changed relations of the lovers being reflected in
> the tropical and abandoned tone of the fair correspondent [note
> the genius of that adjective "tropical"] . . . Lord Advocate Mon-
> creiff's masterly address, strong, restrained, convincing, was
> then, as now, unduly eclipsed by the brilliant, emotional speech
> of John Inglis for the defence, held to be the finest ever delivered
> in a Scots court.

For those who might worry about the detrimental moral effect on
Roughead of so much knavery and malice, he reassures us that "the
study of criminology has by no means made me a cynic; it has en-
couraged my admiration for the ingenuity of the race."

Readers who succumb to William Roughead's "witchery" (to use
the word of his admirer Henry James) should look for the work of
the compeers he himself recommended: F. Tennyson Jesse (*Murder
and Its Motives,* 1924); William Bolitho (*Murder for Profit,* 1926); and
the various collections by Roughead's friend, correspondent, and disciple Edmund Pearson, starting with *Studies in Murder* (1924), which

includes the classic account of Lizzie Borden. The Scots master's own works are collected in many volumes, as well as several "best of" compilations such as *The Evil That Men Do* (1929) and *Classic Crimes* (1951).

In these days of rampant urban violence, serial killers, and global conflict, we have grown sadly inured to violent death, provided it doesn't touch us in some direct fashion. But once upon a time—and indeed, not so long ago—murder was still rare enough to be shocking, and some homicides bizarre or mysterious enough to pass into the popular imagination. Now and again, we still thrill to a well-told murder, as in the masterly accounts of Truman Capote's *In Cold Blood* and John Berendt's *Midnight in the Garden of Good and Evil*. But the gold standard of the genre remains the work of William Roughead, the writer whom Victorian scholar Richard Altick neatly describes as "the great Edinburgh connoisseur of human error."

⸺⟫•⟪⸺

H. P. LOVECRAFT (1890–1937)
Selected short stories; *The Case of Charles Dexter Ward;* *At the Mountains of Madness*

Howard Phillips Lovecraft is undoubtedly the most important and influential American writer of weird fiction since Poe. Yet to subsequent practitioners in the three overlapping genres of horror, fantasy, and science fiction, his legacy is so fraught and problematic it generates an anxiety similar to that which the English Romantics felt about the influence of John Milton. In such cases, young writers might start out by copying the earlier master's style, while more mature writers work hard to escape from it as soon as possible, if only to develop identities of their own.

Such contradictory reactions merely testify to the ongoing power of a Milton—or a Lovecraft. Like them or not, both have created distinctive cosmic visions of great and overwhelming authority. You may find their language portentous, overblown, or rebarbative, but that's your problem, not theirs. In Lovecraft's case, if people know anything at all about this self-educated semi-recluse, they probably know that he favored fancy words like "eldritch," "Cyclopean," and "eidolon"; referred frequently to Miskatonic University's rare copy—one of six extant—of the accursed *Necronomicon* of the mad Arab Abdul Alhazred; and created a pantheon of evil gods (who are actually extraterrestrials) with nearly unpronounceable names such as Nyarlothotep, Yog-Sothoth, and Shub-Niggurath (a.k.a. "The Black Goat of the Woods with a Thousand Young").

All the common and implicitly dismissive impressions of Lovecraft's art are perfectly true—up to a point. Yet what makes this daring writer so addictive isn't his pervasive philosophy of "cosmicism"— which reduces mankind's role in the universe to a bit part, hardly even a walk-on—or his sometimes overheated prose, or even the Grand Guignol character of his plots (revival of the dead, the exchange of minds, aliens among us). What matters is that Lovecraft possesses the storyteller's greatest gift, the one that Nabokov called *shamanstvo,* the "enchanter quality." Before his visions we shudder and believe. This narrative sorcery derives, to a great extent, from Lovecraft's mastery of atmosphere. Read almost any story's opening sentence—most are quietly suggestive of a world grown suddenly uncanny—and the spell is cast:

> When a traveler in north central Massachusetts takes the wrong fork at the junction of Aylesbury pike just beyond Dean's Corners he comes upon a lonely and curious country. ("The Dunwich Horror")

After twenty-two years of nightmare and terror, saved only by a
desperate conviction of the mythical source of certain
impressions, I am unwilling to vouch for the truth of that which
I think I found in Western Australia on the night of July 17–18,
1935. ("The Shadow Out of Time")

West of Arkham the hills rise wild, and there are valleys with
deep woods that no axe has ever cut. ("The Colour Out of
Space")

Note that the voice of these narrators—often academics—is
calm, logical, nearly reportorial; here are no fanciful speculations but
hard facts and clear-eyed, if somewhat unsettling, observations. Lovecraft firmly believed that the successful weird tale should be utterly
realistic except for the one shattering incursion from the Outside.
Nonetheless, from the very first words his stories constantly hint that
something is awry, off-kilter, not quite right. To convey a growing and
pervasive uneasiness, his most powerful word is often nothing more
fancy than "too":

The trees grew too quickly, and their trunks were too big for any
healthy New England wood. There was too much silence in the
dim alleys between them, and the floor was too soft with the
dank moss and mattings of infinite years of decay.

As the various stories progress, the prose usually starts to grow
more luxuriant and extravagant, and that initial Apollonian tone
gradually modulates into the ecstatic language of Dionysus as the narrator attempts, in vain, to describe violations of nature and visitations
by the absolutely Other. Moreover, Lovecraft can be genuinely shocking, whether in the licentious and incestuous implications of "The
Thing on the Doorstep" or the echos of the Crucifixion in the clos-

ing pages of "The Dunwich Horror." Sometimes he doesn't quite say anything at all, yet causes the reader to suspect very disturbing things indeed:

> She was one of the Innsmouth Waites, and dark legends have clustered for generations about crumbling, half-deserted Innsmouth and its people. There are tales of horrible bargains about the year 1850, and of a strange element 'not quite human' in the ancient families.

In his earliest tales—those written before the late 1920s—Lovecraft tends to focus on human-scaled horrors: he wants, in the words of Dickens's Fat Boy, "to make your flesh creep." His later work, however, often turns to the grander dimensions and concomitant sense of wonder of science fiction. He seeks, as he says in his masterly essay "Supernatural Horror in Literature," to excite "in the reader a profound sense of dread, and of contact with unknown spheres and powers, a subtle attitude of awed listening, as if for the beating of black wings or the scratching of outside shapes and entities on the known universe's utmost rim." The notion of "awed listening" is particularly potent, for many of his ill-starred characters seem, just before their doom, to be listening for something—the scurrying of rats or a strange whistling, perhaps a peculiar buzzing sound or even "a rhythmical surging or lapping, as of the waves at some level beach."

"The most merciful thing in the world," claims the narrator of Lovecraft's key work, "The Call of Cthulhu," is "the inability of the human mind to correlate all its contents. We live on a placid island of ignorance." In story after story, some character gradually detects an unexpected pattern behind various oddities, folkloristic rituals, or ancient legends—and this dossier of anomalies brings him to the abyss as surely as it brought Conrad's Mr. Kurtz. After horrible imaginings these scholar-scientists finally arrive at even more horrible certainties, and are then crushed or driven mad by the ghastly import of their knowledge.

At its most "cosmic," Lovecraft's supernatural horror aims to create in the reader a psychological vertigo akin to that experienced by his racked protagonists. Could all history, in fact, be a sham, and the earth's true masters be hidden from us? Are we the playthings of a great race from beyond the solar system? Is our very identity uncertain and friable? Lovecraft answers yes to all these questions—even if poor forked humanity cannot bear the burden of quite this much reality. After all, who really knows? Old Ones and crablike fungi from Yuggoth may lurk in backwoods New England. Somewhere under the waves Great Cthulhu could lie dreaming in his nightmare corpse-city of R'lyeh, patiently waiting for the stars to come right again. There are doubtless things at the South Pole that don't belong there. And some lost souls have unfortunately peered into, and can never forget, the pit of the Shoggoths.

Traveler's Tales

The poet Charles Baudelaire once observed that the only true travelers are those who travel simply to travel, finding constant renewal in distant places, unusual experiences, and encounters with strange and interesting people. In life the journey, not the arrival, matters.

In a category embracing all kinds of armchair adventure we join expeditions to an ideal society, down to the center of the earth, and around an ordinary apartment. We visit, to adopt another phrase from Baudelaire, "torrid Africa and languorous Asia." A patriotic Englishman shows off his country's bounty, and a decadent Frenchman creates a world of his own. All these places are, as guidebooks say, "worth the trip."

If half the titles in *Classics for Pleasure* might be fitted under the category "Love's Mysteries," the other half might be slipped into this one. Is there, after all, any kind of story more fundamental to narrative than that of the marvelous journey? Here, then, are a few accounts of travels over the hills and far away, beyond the fields we know, there and back again.

———>•◦•<———

THOMAS MORE (1478–1535)
Utopia

Early on in *Utopia* (1516)—described on its title page, in Latin, as a "golden handbook" to the "best state of a commonwealth"—Thomas More tells us about the Achorians. Their Greek-derived name suggests "people from nowhere," just as Utopia itself means "no place." The story More tells, in Robert M. Adams's translation, sounds eerily all too familiar:

> Long ago, these people went to war to gain another realm for their king . . . When they had conquered it, they saw that keeping it was going to be as hard as getting it had been. Their new subjects were continually rebelling or being attacked by foreign invaders. The Achorians had to be constantly at war for them or against them, and they saw no hope of ever being able to disband their army. In the meantime, they were being heavily taxed, money flowed out of their kingdom, their blood was being shed for the advantage of others, and peace was no closer than it ever was. The war corrupted their own citizens by encouraging lust for robbery and murder, and the laws fell into contempt because their king, distracted with the cares of two kingdoms, could give neither one his proper attention.

A twenty-first-century reader cannot help but sigh and murmur: *Plus ça change, plus c'est la même chose.*

Lawgivers, philosophers, and revolutionaries at least since the time of Plato have periodically imagined ideal communities, but Thomas More was clever enough to choose a name for his that stuck. We all know that a utopia is the civic equivalent of the biblical Garden of Paradise or of antiquity's Golden Age. In our own time it

might take the daydream form of a worker's republic or a Fabian socialist city-state or an Ayn Randian enclave of genius-libertarians. In
general, though, modern literature tends to picture utopias as secretly
rotten. In Ursula Le Guin's short story "The Ones Who Walk Away
from Omelas," the city of Omelas is essentially heaven on earth, but
its perfection can be maintained only through the constant and pro-
longed torture of a small child. Isn't the happiness of many worth the
torment of one?

In *Utopia* itself, More describes a highly disciplined, egalitarian
community, part communistic, part monastic. Everyone works,
mainly at some agricultural activity or simple trade. Personal wealth
isn't allowed, and gold is used principally for chamber pots and the
heavy chains that weigh down criminals. Learning remains highly valued, but the Utopians chiefly believe that one should seek moderate
pleasures in life. Their customs are at once sensible and revolutionary:
Any two people contemplating marriage must first view each other
naked; a crime attempted is as bad as one committed; and lawyers are
unneeded, since the laws are few, simple, and clear. In wartime the
Utopians hire mercenaries, and they always refuse to persecute anyone for religious reasons "because they are persuaded that no man can
choose to believe by a mere act of the will." In Utopia no man owns
anything, yet everyone is wealthy in what counts: "For what can be
greater riches than for a man to live joyfully and peacefully, free from
all anxieties, and without worries about making a living? . . . Each
man can feel secure of his own livelihood and happiness and of his
whole family's as well."

Ever since Thomas More published *Utopia,* readers and scholars
have argued over its meaning. Some view it as an extended *jeu d'esprit,*
almost a kind of learned joke; others believe it a serious political blue-
print; still others consider it a critique of sixteenth-century society.
Whatever the case, the book is, in the apt words of Robert M. Adams,
"one of those mercurial, jocoserious writings that turn a new profile

to every advancing generation, and respond in a different way to every set of questions addressed to them."

<hr>

DANIEL DEFOE (1660–1731)
A Tour Through the Whole Island of Great Britain

What is the most famous scene in English literature? Dozens of possibilities come to mind, but certainly near the top of the list is the spine-tingling moment when Robinson Crusoe discovers a footprint in the sand and realizes with a shock that he is no longer alone on his desert island. Even people who've never cracked a book know about Crusoe; he has passed into myth, like Sherlock Holmes and Tarzan.

Many readers will also know one or two of Daniel Defoe's other books: most likely that seamless mix of fact and fiction, *A Journal of the Plague Year,* or the picaresque adventures of *Moll Flanders.* Aficionados of the supernatural duly honor Defoe for the most famous ghost story of the early eighteenth century, "A True Relation of the Apparition of one Mrs. Veal." In fact, this prolific writer's complete works, most of them anonymous political or satirical pamphlets, are thought to number about five hundred, though there may be many more.

There is, however, one superb and exceptionally entertaining book by Defoe that should be more widely read: *A Tour Through the Whole Island of Great Britain,* an epic guidebook that originally appeared in three volumes (1724–26). Modern editions tend to be abridged, but most partly make up for this by including an abundance of contemporary illustrations.

For almost four centuries *A Tour* has been mined by historians for information about early eighteenth-century Britain, but what makes the book so much fun for the ordinary reader are its anecdotes, its odd bits of social history, its glimpses of Defoe's personality, and its sturdy plain prose. The bedrock of all these characteristics is the author's confident authority. Defoe—businessman, soldier, journalist, spy, ex-con—always knows what he's talking about. When he arrives in a new town, he looks it over as a real-estate speculator would, judging its merits, tallying social debits and credits, surveying the buildings, and debriefing major citizens.

Stopping in the damp coastal village of Wyvenhoo, Defoe learns—from what he calls with striking modernity "oral tradition"— that its men are said to go through as many as fourteen or fifteen wives, chosen from women who live in the nearby hills. The husbands "took the young lasses out of . . . their native air into the marshes among the fogs and damps" and "there they presently chang'd their complexion, got an ague or two, and seldom held it above a year at most. . . . Then," blithely concludes Defoe's informant, "we go to the uplands again, and fetch another." At Newmarket, our author visits a famous race-horse trainer who—by chicanery—always manages to secure good betting odds for his favorites. If a horse "was so light as the wind, and could fly like a meteor, he was sure to look as clumsie, and as dirty, and as much like a cart-horse as all the cunning of his master and the grooms could make him."

Though Defoe displays a personal interest in merchants and entrepreneurs, he also mingles with the upper crust. At Tunbridge Wells, famous for its healthful waters, "company and diversion . . . is the main business of the place; and those people who have nothing to do any where else, seem to be the only people who have any thing to do at Tunbridge." After describing the pleasures of this town of flirtation and self-indulgence, he adds:

> Tunbridge wants nothing that can add to the felicities of life, or that can make a man or woman completely happy, always provided they have money; for without money a man is no-body at

Tunbridge, any more than at any other place, and when any man finds his pockets low, he has nothing left to think of, but to be gone, for he will have no diversion in staying there any longer.

Here, clearly, one detects the voice of a man who once went bankrupt to the lively tune of 17,000 pounds.

Naturally, Defoe visits Windsor Castle, and he relates a charming anecdote:

On the outside [of the castle] was added, the Terrace Walk, built by Queen Elizabeth, and where she usually walked for an hour every day before her dinner, if not hindered by windy weather, which she had a peculiar aversion to; for as to rainy weather, it would not always hinder her; but she rather loved to walk in a mild, calm rain, with an umbrella over her head.

Such unexpected bits of trivia add an airiness, even a sweetness, to this sprawling love letter to Great Britain.

For Defoe loves his country immensely. One village grows the most delicious cherries anywhere; the town of "Chedder" makes "the best cheese that England affords, if not, that the whole world affords"; the Royal Exchange is "the greatest and finest of its kind in the world." Every page carries its superlative. Some of them may sound jingoistic, but what shines through is a deep patriotic pride. *A Tour* focuses not on vanished glories but on present achievements, especially those dealing with trade and business. Defoe writes enthusiastically about the wool industry, mining, spinning, agriculture, fishing, and building. He describes herds of up to a thousand turkeys and geese being driven to London.

Like some modern travel guides, *A Tour Through the Whole Island of Great Britain* is logically organized into seventeen circuits, taking in all the counties of England, Wales, and Scotland. At the very center of the book lies the description of London, which for Defoe is England's hub, the boisterous, rudely healthy capital that devours the produce, livestock, and goods of the rest of the country. You can tell that it's also his home and that he wouldn't live anywhere else.

⎯⎯►●◄⎯⎯

XAVIER DE MAISTRE (1763–1852)
A Journey Around My Room; A Nocturnal Expedition Around My Room

Confined to his quarters for forty-two days as punishment for dueling, the French soldier Xavier de Maistre decided to undertake a journey around his room. By treating his bed, his armchair, the artworks on the wall, and his small library as major tourist sites, he planned to reflect upon their history, their importance to him, and the philosophical questions that they brought to mind. Just as some Shelleyan romantic might stand in awe before the grandeur of Mont Blanc or weep amid the ruins of the Parthenon, so de Maistre would confront the ordinary objects around him—and really see them for the first time. As he proved to himself (in Andrew Brown's translation), "The perceptions of the mind, the sensations of the heart, the very memories of the senses, are inexhaustible sources of pleasure and happiness for man."

William Blake claimed that one could "see a world in a grain of sand/ and a heaven in a wild flower/ Hold infinity in the palm of your hand/ And eternity in an hour." De Maistre's *A Journey Around My Room* (1795) and its sequel, *A Nocturnal Expedition Around My Room* (1825), might be test cases for that proposition. Life, after all, gains value from the intensity of one's engagement with it. By acts of concerted attention, we can invest even the most ordinary activities or objects with meaning, purpose, and satisfaction. "A bed," writes de

Maistre, "witnesses our birth and death; it is the unvarying theatre in which the human race acts out, successively, its captivating dramas, laughable farces, and dreadful tragedies. It is a cradle bedecked with flowers; —it is the throne of love; —it is a sepulchre."

As de Maistre embarks on "the long journey we still have to make if we are ever to reach my desk," he reflects on the bliss of lying warm under the duvet or seated before an evening fire. Before long, he picks up letters that call to mind friends who died young, finds a faded rose, which summons up a memory of the beloved who proved untrue, notes the lessons in fidelity and kindness he has learned from his dog Rosine and his servant Joannetti. Sometimes he even considers the poor living on the street outside in Turin, or recalls the terrors of the French Revolution.

Anything is grist for this restless and digressive *Tristram Shandy*–like imagination because "there's no more attractive pleasure, in my view, than following one's ideas wherever they lead." At one point de Maistre takes up and considers various prints and paintings, including one of his current mistress, over which he sighs—until his servant complains that the portrait's eyes seem to follow him around the room, that the painted beauty seems to smile at every visitor. Ah, reflects de Maistre, the fickleness of women! While studying himself in a mirror, he charmingly observes that it alone frames "a perfect picture, one with which it is impossible to find fault." In judging the arts, he decides that painting should be viewed as superior to music because it is less prey to fashion: "The paintings of Raphael will delight posterity just as they delighted our ancestors."

De Maistre has sometimes been likened to Descartes, who hunched over a stove in an inn and built an entire philosophy from scratch (*cogito ergo sum*—I think, therefore I am). The introspective soldier maintains that he is himself a dual being—a soul and an Other, which he sometimes calls the Beast. The two do not always work together, for there are times when we surrender to the body and other times when the soul wings its way into spiritual realms or "the enchanting land of imagination." In particular, though, de Maistre repeatedly finds himself obsessing about the passage of time, as in this paragraph that presages Lamartine's famous poem "Le Lac" (The Lake):

"O Time! Dread deity! It is not your cruel scythe that fills me with terror; I fear only your hideous children, Indifference and Forgetfulness, who turn three quarters of our lifespan into a long death." In the darkest nights of the soul, he cries out, "all that remains in the depths of my heart are regrets and empty memories; a melancholy brew, on which my life continues to swim, just as a vessel smashed by the tempest continues to float for a while on the stormy sea!" Time, he concludes, "is nothing more than a punishment of the mind."

Soon, however, de Maistre is explaining how he'd like to make love to all the women in the world, indeed to all the women who ever lived; he's imagining conversations among the illustrious dead, or inviting the Dear Reader to sit down to breakfast with him; and finally, upbeat again, he's reminding us that "we should allow ourselves to laugh, or at least to smile, each time an innocent opportunity to do so presents itself."

A Journey Around My Room and *A Nocturnal Expedition Around My Room* may seem mere sports, literary *jeux d'esprit,* but their ancestors and progeny are many. Hamlet maintains that were it not for his bad dreams, he could be "bounded in a nutshell and count myself the king of infinite space." Milton's Satan boldly announces that "the mind is its own place, and in itself/ Can make a heav'n of hell, a hell of heav'n." Novellas such as Diderot's *Rameau's Nephew* and Dostoevsky's *Notes From Underground* examine, in microscopic detail, the rapid fluctuations of consciousness. Modern literary solipsists—from Proust and Beckett to Nicholson Baker—have dissected themselves and the quotidian world with delicate intensity and seriocomic exhaustiveness. Perhaps the most direct homage to *A Journey Around My*

Room, though, is Daniel Spoerri's captivating *An Anecdoted Topography of Chance,* in which the author relates the histories—with footnotes—of the various objects on his worktable. Clearly, Xavier de Maistre belongs to a long literary tradition of *multum in parvo*—much in little.

———⋙•◦•⋘———

JULES VERNE (1828–1905)
A Journey to the Center of the Earth;
Twenty Thousand Leagues Under the Sea;
Around the World in Eighty Days; The Mysterious Island; other works

To begin to understand Jules Verne's genius, simply call to mind any of his best-known titles out of the sixty or so *"Voyages Extraordinaires": A Journey to the Center of the Earth* (1864), *Twenty Thousand Leagues Under the Sea* (1869–70), *Around the World in Eighty Days* (1873), or *The Mysterious Island* (1874–75). These are all largely accounts of marvels and monsters, or eyewitness reports about realms from which no traveler has ever returned—until now. But Verne imaginatively enhances the traditional "marvelous journey" by grounding it in the new wonders of the foundry and the laboratory or by drawing on the latest geographical explorations and discoveries.

As a writer, Verne's goal was never simply to dazzle; he aimed to instruct as well as entertain. His brisk, clear prose deftly mixes the real and the almost real in a fact-filled style that employs, according to the poet Apollinaire, "nothing but nouns." His books are sometimes journalistic, at other times scientific, but they are always replete with news items, historical events, and leisurely descriptions of how things work. In the preface to *The Adventures of Captain Hatteras* (1866) Verne writes that he aims to "sum up the geographical, geological, astromagnetic, and physical knowledge accumulated by modern science and to refashion, in an appropriately attractive form, the history of the universe."

For all its ambition, Verne's work has suffered three grievous literary misfortunes. First, it was badly translated into English, occasionally bowdlerized, and sometimes actually rewritten. Second, it was largely relegated to the children's bookshelf, even though Verne aimed for an audience of all ages. And third, much of the late and posthumously published fiction was written either entirely or in large part by Verne's son Michel, who blithely signed his father's lucrative name to the title page. Such cavalier publishing practices soon created the common image of Verne as a sloppy, tin-eared author for the semiliterate.

It probably didn't help that he was also dubbed the father of science fiction (Mary Shelley being the mother). In fact, Verne's books are more accurately what he himself called "novels of science," and many are essentially realistic travelogues to distant lands, or even ludic, experimental texts, such as *The Will of an Eccentric* (1899), in which the human characters are all players in a kind of Monopoly game using the United States itself as the board. (Not surprisingly, some of the most innovative twentieth-century writers, such as Raymond Roussel and Georges Perec, look to Verne as an inspiration.) Several of this visionary writer's most interesting books even despair that science might harm the world instead of improve it.

For example, the early thriller *The Begum's Millions* (1879) is best read as a cautionary political fable, part dystopian satire, part Dickensian social tract. In it a deranged German industrialist aims to destroy whole cities with a weapon of mass destruction: a super-cannon whose gigantic shells deliberately break apart to rain down fire over vast areas. But he has, in reserve, something even more insidious, an early version of the neutron bomb: a special projectile filled with compressed liquid carbon dioxide that, when released, instantly lowers the surrounding temperature to 100 degrees below zero centigrade, quick-freezing every living thing in the vicinity. As the madman proudly explains, "thus, with my system, there are no wounded, just the dead."

Throughout his work, Verne insists that scientific and technological developments need to be viewed in a social context. In the light-hearted *Dr. Ox's Experiment* (1874), a callous researcher transforms a placid village into a raging cauldron of emotion by piping pure oxygen into homes and public buildings. Every feeling is intensified, metabolisms are sped up, and an opera that normally takes six hours to perform is zipped through in eighteen minutes. In *Master of the World* (1904), the once relatively thoughtful hero of *Robur the Conqueror* (1886) returns as a megalomaniac who spreads shock and awe with his powerful battle station, a combination tank-plane-ship-submarine called, simply, The Terror. Finally, in *The Barsac Mission* (1919)— posthumously published as the last *"Voyage Extraordinaire"*—we are taken to a fortress city in Africa, from which a criminal mastermind uses the inventions of a brilliant if blithely unaware scientist to wreak global havoc and mayhem.

The Barsac Mission was completed by son Michel Verne, though it reflects the elderly Jules's increasingly pessimistic outlook. That despair reaches its acme in the famous short story, also by both Vernes, "The Eternal Adam" (1910): A scientist of the far future named Zartog Sofr-Ai-Sr is chastened to discover that archeological evidence reveals that the men and women of the inconceivably distant past— that is, of our era—were intelligent and civilized, and were almost completely wiped out when the oceans suddenly rose, engulfing the continents. There is, concludes Zartog, no progress to history, only unending, senseless repetition.

These bleaker aspects of Verne's work shouldn't overshadow the pure pleasure of his more famous novels. Surely the various eccentricities of Phileas Fogg, nothing if not an orderly English gentleman, make for much of the charm of *Around the World in Eighty Days*. Moreover, Verne always makes sure that his "marvelous journeys" are always, no matter how technical, didactic, or humorous, tales of wonder and adventure. *Mathias Sandorf*—appropriately dedicated to the memory of Alexandre Dumas—offers a Vernean take on the immortal revenge saga *The Count of Monte Cristo*. In *A Journey to the Center of the Earth*, three men climb down through the chimney of a volcano to discover another world underground. Like such swashbuckling authors as C. S. Forester, Rafael Sabatini, and George MacDonald Fraser, Verne seldom lets up on the excitement.

This is certainly true of his two most ambitious novels, *Twenty Thousand Leagues Under the Sea* and its semisequel *The Mysterious Island*. The first is dominated by the figure of the romantic antihero Captain Nemo, and by the wondrous submarine he has constructed to revenge himself on a world that—we eventually learn—destroyed his family. In *The Mysterious Island*, we discover among other things the ultimate fate of Nemo and the *Nautilus*, even as Verne offers us a nineteenth-century version of *Robinson Crusoe*. (I might add that as a boy of thirteen or so, I checked out *The Mysterious Island* from my local library and turned the pages of its thick illustrated edition steadily, unstoppably, for three glorious never-forgotten days.)

To read Jules Verne when young is one of the great treats of childhood. To read Jules Verne later in life is to discover a writer just as satisfying but even richer, one who is not only a natural storyteller but also a mythmaker, a social critic, and an innovative artist. In France, Verne is now studied seriously as an innovative literary figure, and thanks to fresh, accurate English translations, more and more of his work is available to American readers in reliable texts.

J. K. HUYSMANS (1848–1907)
A Rebours (Against Nature); *Là-Bas* (Down There)

In Oscar Wilde's *The Picture of Dorian Gray,* the ever-youthful hero picks up a certain "yellow book" and idly begins to turn its pages. Before long he cannot tear himself away from the "poisonous" volume: "One hardly knew at times whether one was reading the spiritual ecstasies of some medieval saint or the morbid confessions of a modern sinner." Wilde never gives the book's title, but his description—"a novel without a plot, with only one character"—leaves no doubt that Dorian has discovered J. K. Huysmans's *A Rebours* (Against Nature, or Against the Grain, 1884), the acknowledged bible of decadence.

Huysmans's epicene hero, Des Esseintes, has wearied of the vulgar, bourgeois world and come to feel, in Robert Baldick's translation, "sapped by disillusionment, depressed by hypochondria and weighed down by spleen." So he retreats to a specially designed refuge in the country, where he plans to spend the rest of his life alone with his memories and his books. It is, in effect, a temple devoted to the most rarefied pleasures and reveries, an artifical world where Des Esseintes can daydream his life away. Surely, he insists, "the imagination could provide a more-than-adequate substitute for the vulgar reality of actual experience."

Des Esseintes orchestrates every element of his various rooms, from the furniture to the lighting (ecclesiastical candles). After carefully choosing the dominant colors of his study—mainly orange, with some blue trim—he decides that the décor needs more vibrancy. So he acquires a tortoise, then encrusts its carapace with gilt and jewels so that the animal will pass slowly along the floor like a moving bouquet or floor-level chandelier. When bored, he sometimes plays his "mouth" organ, in which various stops on the instrument release different liqueurs, allowing one to taste as well as hear the music. At one point, in a fever of heightened perversity, Des Esseintes fills his house not, as one might expect, with artificial flowers, but with real flowers that only look as if they were fake.

A decadent's taste in art naturally—unnaturally?—merges the perverse and the sadistic. On the walls of the library are Gustave Moreau paintings of Salome, "the symbolic incarnation of undying Lust," whose voluptuousness can rouse the sleeping senses with "the charms of a great venereal flower, grown in a bed of sacrilege, reared in a hot-house of impiety." Other rooms display grotesque scenes of torture or nightmarish visions of horror. Everything aims either to soothe or provoke the senses.

A bedroom, Des Esseintes tells us, should be either devoted to sensual pleasure and nocturnal delectation or fitted out like a monastic cell for meditation and solitude. In his younger days, he had organized his Paris apartment for depravity—a great white lacquered bed providing extra titillation through its being "apparently designed for innocent children and young virgins"—but here in the country he prefers the austere simplicity of the Trappist. Nonetheless, Des Esseintes often calls to mind his past amours, most notably with a female ventriloquist who, to rouse and stimulate his already doubtful energies, would cast her voice and pretend to be a drunken lover or angry landlord, yelling outside the bedroom door, "Open up, damn you . . . you slut, you'll get what's coming to you."

Des Esseintes's library is considerably more refined and exquisite. He was "really interested only in sickly books, undermined and inflamed by fever." The select volumes on his shelves are specially printed on exotic papers, then bound in rare leathers, sometimes like missals with metal clasps. What he likes best is a particular "gamey" quality to an author's prose, certain "Byzantine flowers of thought and deliquescent complexities of style." Thus he favors writers like Petronius and Apuleius, minor ecclesiastics, the more charnel works of Edgar Allan Poe and Barbey d'Aurevilley, and such then-modern poets as Baudelaire, Verlaine, and Mallarmé. Alas, "how few books there are worth reading again." His mind, he tells us, no longer has room "for anything but superfine sensations, religious doubts and sensual anxieties."

His favorite literary genre is the prose poem, "an intellectual communion between a hieratic writer and an ideal reader . . . an aesthetic treat available to none but the most discerning." In this sense, *A Rebours* itself may be regarded as a kind of extended prose poem. Flaubert used to hope that he might one day construct a novel about "nothing," and Huysmans's novel comes close to that austere ideal. It is a marvelous sickly-sweet orchid of a book, at once bizarre, campy, luxurious, and unforgettable.

Readers taken with Huysmans should also look for his other famous novel, the notorious and "satanic" *Là-Bas* (Down There), which weaves together the monstrous Gilles de Rais, a war between two nineteenth-century necromancers, and a detailed re-creation of a black mass. Little wonder that shortly after these two decadent masterworks were published, Huysmans took instruction at a monastery and converted to Catholicism. As Barbey d'Aurevilley said when he read *A Rebours:* "After such a book, the only choice left open to the author is between the muzzle of a pistol and the foot of the cross."

———————

ISAK DINESEN (1885–1962)
Out of Africa; Seven Gothic Tales; other stories

Isak Dinesen thought of herself as a storyteller and often identified with Scheherezade of *The Arabian Nights*. While a novel usually loads on backstory, complex psychological analysis, and other sorts of furniture, the tale strips away all this gaudy excess for a piercing brevity and directness, avoiding needless circumlocution. A tale's characters, like the Italians in "The Roads Round Pisa," always speak "fluently under the wildest passions, as if life were, in any of her whims, a comedy which they had already rehearsed."

The storyteller's art lies in balance—in establishing just the right tone, in juggling many smaller stories into the pattern of a larger one, in surprising or even shocking us as some dark truth is eventually revealed. In all these narrative skills, Dinesen commands comparison with the greatest, with Prosper Mérimée, E. T. A. Hoffmann, and Heinrich von Kleist. Like most of their work, her "Gothic" or "Winter's" tales are generally set in the late eighteenth or early nineteenth century, but Dinesen's are deliberately suffused with a courtly and refined decadence. Cross-dressing, incest, rape, and murder are just what you'd expect from her dissolute cardinals and demon-haunted prioresses, foppish counts, impotent princes, and diabolical actors. No matter how black their deeds, all of them display the most complete self-possession and suavity, an almost glacial correctness even in the face of death.

Dinesen's heroes and heroines may be damned, but they approach life as esthetes, as epicures of experience. Her great theme is the working out of fate or nemesis, and her tales can veer from the supernatural ("The Monkey") to the touching ("Babette's Feast"). Such as it is, her moral might be that it's better to welcome a tragic fate with polite hauteur than to settle for an insipid and quotidian obscurity. True to this principle, Dinesen once said that she had sold her soul to the Devil in return for the power to tell stories.

The old-world formality of Dinesen's syntax and diction seems common to writers who learn English as a second language—Joseph Conrad and Vladimir Nabokov are other examples. In the case of Dinesen, born in Denmark as Karen Blixen, the resulting coolness and patrician elegance add just the right patina to her chronicles of romantic intrigue:

During the first quarter of the last century, seaside resorts became the fashion . . . The romantic spirit of the age, which delighted in ruins, ghosts, and lunatics, and counted a stormy
night on the heath and a deep conflict of the passions a finer
treat for the connoisseur than the ease of the salons and the harmony of a philosophic system, reconciled even the most refined
individuals to the eternal wildness of the coast scenery and of
the open seas . . . ("The Deluge at Norderney")

During her lifetime Isak Dinesen's admirers ranged from Eudora
Welty, Carson McCullers, Marianne Moore, and Lawrence Durrell to
John Gielgud, Cecil Beaton, and Edmée de la Rochefoucauld. Upon
receiving the Nobel prize for literature in 1954, Hemingway said it
should have gone to Dinesen. Certainly her stories invite such enthu-
siastic as well as refined appreciation, but the memoir *Out of Africa*
elicits something more, a kind of holy rapture. The critic Rebecca
West once wrote about this account of a decade on an African farm:
"It gives me that strange sense of peace I always feel in the presence
of my superior." Holden Caulfield, the hero of J. D. Salinger's *Catcher
in the Rye,* grants its author his very highest encomium: "I wouldn't
mind calling this Isak Dinesen up."

The memoir opens simply: "I had a farm in Africa, at the foot of
the Ngong Hills." In her subsequent pages, Dinesen memorializes a
world she has lost: the idyllic landscape and wildlife of Kenya from
1913 to 1929, the native people who cared for her and tended the cof-
fee plants she grew, the dashing English hunter and guide she came
to love. *Out of Africa* is one of the great prose elegies of our time:

A Masai warrior is a fine sight. Those young men have, to the
utmost extent, that particular form of intelligence which we call
chic—daring, and wildly fantastical as they seem, they are still
unswervingly true to their own nature, and to an immanent

ideal. Their style is not an assumed manner, nor an imitation of a foreign perfection; it has grown from the inside, and is an expression of the race and its history, and their weapons and finery are as much part of their being as are a stag's antlers.

To an even greater degree, the Masai possess the serene and noble integrity—minus the perversity—that Dinesen admires in the self-assured European aristocrats of her stories.

Anecdotes and vignettes abound in *Out of Africa.* When the Masai want Dinesen to recite some poetry, they ask her to "speak like rain." After she explains the plot of *The Merchant of Venice,* they are shocked that Shylock gave up his rightful pound of flesh. " 'But what else could he do,' I said," 'when he must not take one drop of blood?' " A Somali tells her: "Memsahib, he could have used a red-hot knife. That brings out no blood."

All around Dinesen's farm live British expatriates and old colonial hands, most of them eccentrics or dandies. One Englishman drinks a bottle of Champagne out in the forest every morning at eleven, and is shocked when Dinesen provides him with coarse and ordinary wineglasses instead of the finest crystal. Another elderly gentleman reveals that he was once the lover of La Belle Otero. When the famous courtesan's memoirs appear, Dinesen asks if he's in the book. Yes: "She writes that I was a young man who went through a hundred thousand for her sake within six months, but that I had full value for my money." To which Dinesen laughingly says, "And do you consider that you did have full value?" "He thought my question over for a very short moment. 'Yes,' he said. 'Yes, I had.' "

For all the bucolic happiness that Dinesen evokes in *Out of Africa,* there's also plenty of death—a servant is accidentally killed, the African campaigns of World War I start up, a close friend perishes in an airplane crash. Soon thereafter Dinesen breaks down and sells the farm, which had already been heading toward bankruptcy.

The dying fall in the last chapters of *Out of Africa* reminds us, once again, that all the real paradises are lost. Yet this one is at least preserved on the page, down to the most mundane farmyard chores, which are suddenly touched with magic:

> Charcoal-burning is a pleasant job. There is undoubtedly something intoxicating about it, and it is known that charcoal-burners see things in a different light from other people; they are given to poetry and taradiddle, and wood-demons come and keep them company.

ROBERT BYRON (1905–1941)
The Road to Oxiana

Robert Byron was, for a long time, merely a name that would crop up occasionally in the letters of Evelyn Waugh or Nancy Mitford, yet another one of those esthetes who blossomed at Oxford during the bright golden springtime of the early 1920s. This changed when the admired literary scholar Paul Fussell published *Abroad: British Literary Traveling Between the Wars* and in it devoted an entire chapter to Byron. "What *Ulysses* is to the novel between the wars and what *The Waste Land* is to poetry," he stated, "*The Road to Oxiana* is to the travel book." Readers everywhere rushed to acquire this masterpiece, only to discover that it had never been published in America. Since then, the book has appeared in multiple editions.

The Road to Oxiana (1937) appears to be a haphazard journal of Byron's travels in Persia and Afghanistan during the early 1930s. In fact, the text is carefully composed, though deliberately fragmented, and in this resembles the works of Joyce and Eliot. Byron's ostensible aim in crossing Central Asia to the Oxus River was to visit certain famous monuments, chiefly the Gumbadi-Kabus, a tower built as a mausoleum for an ancient king. As a result, his book proffers detailed descriptions of the excavations at Persepolis, of the interior of the Friday Mosque at Isfahan, and of various other tomb-temples. These sections constitute perhaps a quarter of the text and, though valuable, will hardly lure the ordinary reader to the book. What will are Byron's ear for the absurdities of colonial conversation and his flair for evocative description.

The book opens with the kind of brittle observation made famous by the Bright Young Novelists of the 1920s: "Lifar came to dinner. Bertie mentioned that all whales have syphilis." These soon stretch into little dialogues of noncommunication, their tone that of proto-Beckett or slapstick Kafka: "Mr. Trump-of-Raphael gave a tea party . . . I sat between the English bishop and a Kajar prince. 'Why are you out here?' asked the bishop angrily. 'Travelling.' 'What in?'"

Byron is equally adept with the epigrammatic jab: "But Persians, broad as their views on religion are, drink mainly for the sin of it and care little for the taste." "Water is the main difficulty of such a journey, as sufferers from syphilis of the throat, who are numerous, are apt to choose the wells to spit in." "When evening came we put out the beds beside the lorry. Mosquitos the size of eagles collected as though to a dinnerbell."

Of Byron's more lyrical moments, perhaps none better suggests his richness than this catalog aria on the color green:

> We came out onto the steppe: a dazzling open sea of green. I never saw that colour before. In other greens, of emerald, jade, or malachite, the harsh deep green of the Bengal jungle, the sad cool green of Ireland, the salad green of Mediterranean vineyards, the heavy full-blown green of English summer beaches,

some element of blue or yellow predominates over the others. This was the pure essence of green, indissoluble, the colour of life itself.

With lingering memories of this brilliant verdancy, Byron a few pages later depicts a more somber scene: "After Akcha, the colour of the landscape changed from lead to aluminum, pallid and deathly, as if the sun had been sucking away its gaiety for thousands and thousands of years; for this was now the plain of Balkh, and Balkh they say is the oldest city in the world."

Byron wrote other fine books—in particular *The Station,* which is an account of Mount Athos, and *The Byzantine Achievement*—but he died young, killed during World War II at the age of thirty-six. Something of his wry spirit, however, can be found in the work of other sandy-haired young Brits traveling for adventure, such as A. W. Kinglake's classic *Eothen* (adventures in the Levant during the 1830s) or W. H. Auden and Louis MacNeice's captivating *Letters from Iceland,* Wilfred Thesiger's celebrated *Arabia Deserta,* Freya Stark's *The Valleys of the Assassins,* and Eric Newby's almost whimsical *A Short Walk in the Hindu Kush.* Even the most admired travel writer of the 1980s, Bruce Chatwin, confessed that he closely studied *The Road to Oxiana* before composing his own masterpiece, the lapidary and scintillant *In Patagonia.*

The Way We Live Now

A novel, observes Stendhal, can be likened to a mirror traveling down a roadway. Christopher Isherwood begins one of his novels with the words "I am a camera." Critics speak of "photographic realism" and authors title their books *Scenes of Clerical Life* or *Pictures from an Institution*. Such phrases remind us that "mimesis," the representation of reality, is central to Western literature, and especially to fiction since Cervantes.

The various authors of "The Way We Live Now" show us recognizable people making their way through "the real world." Here are the genteel and the down-and-out, spinsters and philanderers, con men and clergymen, the lazy, the industrious, the corrupt, the angry, and the good-for-nothing. Each writer, from Petronius to Welty, is offering up snapshots—unretouched, warts and all—from the real life of a person who just happens to be imaginary.

This intense focus on psychological portraiture lies at the heart of the traditional novel. (By contrast, in fantasy, science fiction, the adventure story, and much experimental writing we may be more interested in the book's ideas, plot, distinctive language, or the protagonist's existential dilemma.) In "realistic" books, what interests the reader is a character's traumatic or dramatic life and the eventual revelation of his or her destiny. We learn to care about these people and gradually come to see ourselves in them, not as in a glass darkly but face-to-face. Much of the time we never quite know whether to laugh or cry.

———≫•◦•≪———

PETRONIUS (first century)
Satyricon

The *Satyricon*, observed the English critic Cyril Connolly, is a magical book and Petronius a "Roman Proust":

> How little known to generations of boring novelists is the secret
> of his rapidity of style, of his visual clarity, biting dialogue, in-
> tellectual fastidiousness, or of the haunting fugacity of the pica-
> resque—that art which keeps characters on the move from
> waterfront to waterfront, brothel to palace, adventure to adven-
> ture. . . . The analysis of such a book could help many young
> writers to give movement and montage to their characters, the
> lilt of transience which is the breath of readability.

The *Satyricon* has come down to us only in fragments; what we
possess seems to be sections of Books 14 through 16, suggesting that
the full text might have been as long as *War and Peace*. Insofar as we
can reconstruct the plot, it appears—like Lucian's *True History*—to
be a kind of parody of the *Odyssey*. The hero Encolpius travels from
Marseille to Italy to Egypt, observing the world, engaging in various
con games and scams, and carrying on love affairs with both men and
women. However, at some point he offends Priapus, the somewhat
comical Roman god of sex, who renders him impotent. Part of the
bawdy humor of the book involves several attempts to remove this
curse.

We know nothing for sure about the novel's author, but it has
been conjectured that he must be the same Petronius described by the
historian Tacitus as Nero's "arbiter of taste," a man who turned hedonism and luxury into a fine art. This Petronius was eventually forced
to commit suicide, which he did by opening his veins, then spending

his remaining hours by dining with friends and making jokes. It's ru-
mored that as a final flourish he sent Nero a scandalously frank glos-
sary of all of the emperor's favorite sexual practices, along with a list
of his various partners.

The title *Satyricon* is itself uncertain of meaning, as it may refer
to satire, satyrs, or simply the mix of prose and verse then commonly
dubbed Menippean satire. (Menippean satire was to have a long history, from Boethius's vastly influential *Consolation of Philosophy* to
Dante's *Vita Nuova* to Jean Toomer's *Cane*.) By hearsay alone, and in
this case not without reason, Petronius's book stands for sexual titillation and moral degeneracy. Our surviving fragments focus on
Encolpius's passion for the boy Giton, though we are told of earlier
entanglements with a noted courtesan and, just as the book closes,
about our antihero's seduction by a beautiful lady in a garden. Its
most famous chapter, virtually complete, describes a feast at the house
of the millionaire freedman Trimalchio.

At first Trimalchio appears as a shallow buffoon, but he gradually
deepens (or thickens) into a vivid first-century Falstaff. The gossipy
conversation during the dinner party itself is wonderfully funny, vulgar, and colorful, as seen in William Arrowsmith's translation:

> That boy would have grubbed in the gutter for a coin and
> picked it out with his teeth too . . . I knew him for ages, and he
> was horny, right to the end. By god, I'll bet he even pestered the
> dog. Boys were what he really liked, but he wasn't choosy: he'd
> jump anything with legs. . . . Why, darling, it's been just ages
> since I've seen you.

One drunken guest hilariously skews the story of the Trojan War;
another tells a spooky tale about a werewolf. Eventually, the guests
start cavorting by the pool and singing the current pop songs. By then
completely drunk, Trimalchio insists on reading aloud from his will

and later stretches out and pretends to be dead: "I want each of you to say something nice about me." The saturnalia comes to an end only when someone blows a horn, which summons the fire brigade. Men with axes and buckets break down the doors and Keystone Kop–like confusion reigns, allowing our hero and his latest "friend" to steal away into the night.

The *Satyricon* is throughout just this kind of bouillabaisse of sophisticated and low humor, full of sex, picaresque adventure, poetic doggerel, magic and fantasy, contemporary satire, and much else, all of it conveyed with tireless gusto. In fact, the novel was probably meant to be recited aloud, for it is highly dramatic and conversational, a sea of many voices. Some modern critics view the book as profoundly amoral, if not immoral; others judge it a critique of moral corruption. There doesn't seem to be a single truly admirable character in the whole novel. The women, in particular, hunger after only one thing: sex.

Whatever the activities of his lowlife characters—voyeurism, bedroom kinkiness, excretory misfortunes—Petronius blithely describes them in a style that is generally quite refined and even literary. An aged homosexual works away on Encolpius, who is bound hand and foot, until "a river of sweat and perfume was streaming down his face, leaving his wrinkled cheeks so creviced with powder that he looked like some cracked wall standing desolate under a pelting rain." The poet Eumolpus pronounces a genuinely moving speech over the body of the drowned Lichas: "Shipwreck is everywhere," and yet "we scheme and hope, stuffing our foolish hearts with dreams, scrimping and saving, hoarding the wealth we win by wrong, planning our lives as though we had a thousand years to live! . . . The great house you built falls in, crumbles, buries you in the rubble of your dreams."

Aside from the "Dinner at Trimalchio's," the most celebrated section of the *Satyricon* is that famously cynical short story about the fickleness of women, "The Widow of Ephesus," in which a young widow dishonors her late husband's corpse to save the life of her new lover. Much admired, too, are the closing fragments, in which Encolpius and his friends agree to pretend that Eumolpus is immensely rich so that the legacy hunters of Croton will entertain them royally in the hope of inheriting his supposed fortune. Many of these late pages possess a Middle Eastern allure—scented gardens, bewitching women, secret rites.

There is at least one passage from the *Satyricon* known to readers of modern literature. T. S. Eliot chose a few of its lines as the Latin epigraph for *The Waste Land,* his own medley of reflections on the fallen contemporary world. Translated, they tell us that the Sibyl of Cumae had once been captured and locked in a cage. Boys mock her by asking, "Sibyl, what do you want?" and she answers: "I want to die."

As the critics and scholars repeatedly say, there's nothing in all of ancient literature quite like Petronius's *Satyricon.*

ELIZABETH GASKELL (1810–1865)
Cranford; other works

My copy of *Cranford*—published in New York at some unknown date, but probably around the turn of the last century—identifies its author only as Mrs. Gaskell. No first name is indicated anywhere. Nowadays, Elizabeth Gaskell is much studied and admired as the first biographer of Charlotte Brontë as well as the author of *North and South, Mary Barton,* and other novels about social problems and working-class life in Victorian Britain.

Yet the name Mrs. Gaskell seems appropriate for this series of sketches, loosely organized into a novel: *Cranford* (1853) is the portrait of a small town, in the 1840s and '50s, and it mainly depicts life among a group of middle-class spinsters and widows. Much admired by Dickens, who originally published the chapters in his magazine *Household Words,* the book was long revered for its low-keyed humor, beautifully rendered accounts of card parties, female rivalries, and social distinctions, and its tender evocations of love and affection between "elderly" people in their, ahem, fifties. Gaskell's prose is clear, graceful, and often neatly comic. The conclusion of her book may skirt close to sentimentality, but in general *Cranford* more than lives up to its reputation as "a prose idyll."

That said, the novel is far from smarmy. Several major characters die; one ends up ruined because of a bank failure; lovers fail to marry when they should and then spend their entire lives alone, content enough but fundamentally incomplete. Miss Matty, the principal "heroine," is almost too unassuming and kind, but her friends can be deliciously vain, snooty, and set in their ways. Throughout, Gaskell shows us a society in the midst of change—the old rural habits of eighteenth-century England, of good sturdy yeomanry gradually being supplanted by the industrial age, represented by the railroad and the bank.

These darker elements raise the characters above mere "humors," and the book can be surprisingly touching. Yet Gaskell's wit remains appealingly restful, a mixture of Trollope, the Lucia novels of E. F. Benson, and the pastoral comedies of Angela Thirkell. A young woman of Cranford is sternly informed that when making a social visit, she is never to stay longer than a quarter of an hour.

> "But am I to look at my watch? How am I to find out when a quarter of an hour has passed?"
>
> "You must keep thinking about the time, my dear, and not allow yourself to forget it in conversation."

In such a circumscribed world, an earth-shaking event may be the purchase of a carpet for a drawing room. To protect their new rug from fading, Miss Matty and her older sister Miss Jenkyns spread newspaper over the areas exposed to the sun. They keep shifting the paper all afternoon. When they plan a party, they spend hours "in cutting out and stitching together pieces of newspaper so as to form little paths to every chair set for the expected visitors, lest their shoes might dirty or defile the purity of the carpet."

In such a world, an elderly bachelor farmer owns exactly "six and twenty cows, named after the different letters of the alphabet." One old reprobate confesses to a credulous widow that while out in India he accidentally "shot a cherubim." Still another ancient gentleman frets so about wasting paper that when envelopes come into general use, "the only way in which he could reconcile himself to such waste of his cherished article was by patiently turning inside out all that were sent to him, and so making them serve again." Even the book's narrator, a younger woman named Mary Smith, confesses that she can't bring herself to use rubber bands: "To me an india-rubber ring is a precious treasure. I have one which is not new—one that I picked up off the floor nearly six years ago. I have really tried to use it, but my heart failed me, and I could not commit the extravagance."

Apart from its pervasive melancholy over the lost chances of life, *Cranford* pulses with amusing incidents. Widespread panic rips through town as its ladies grow hysterical over imagined robbers prowling the night. When the conjuror Signor Brunini announces his forthcoming magic act, all Cranford is convinced that "such a piece of gayety was going to happen as had not been seen or known of since Wombwell's lions came, when one of them ate a little child's arm." (That could be a sentence in Saki.) And then, of course, what can one say of the rumor—it's absolutely shocking, not to be believed—that the widowed Lady Glenmire has agreed to wed a Mr. Hoggins, the local surgeon? As if that weren't enough, it's bruited that she will actually take the name Mrs. Hoggins! Some of the book's humor even seems to approach camp: "The next morning I met Lady Glenmire and Miss Pole setting out on a long walk to find some old woman who was famous in the neighborhood for her skill in knitting woolen stockings."

Still, there is that melancholy. At one point, Mary Smith helps burn some old correspondence, chiefly love letters between the long-dead parents of the two spinsters Miss Matty and Miss Jenkyns:

> I never knew what sad work the reading of old letters was before that evening, though I could hardly tell why. The letters were as happy as letters could be—at least those early letters were. There was in them a vivid and intense sense of the present time, which seemed so strong and full, as if it could never pass away, and as if the warm living hearts that so expressed themselves could never die, and be as nothing to the sunny earth. I should have felt less melancholy, I believe, if the letters had been more so.

Eventually, Mary reads one announcing the birth of a child, who is described as "the prettiest little baby that ever was seen" and who, it is predicted, will grow up to be a regular beauty. "I thought," writes Mary, as the sad truth emerges, "of Miss Jenkyns, gray, withered, and wrinkled."

I suspect that anyone who enjoys the works of Jane Austen (or any of the authors mentioned above) will find *Cranford* particularly engaging. Little wonder that in just one decade—1899 to 1910—Elizabeth Gaskell's book reportedly went through seventy-five editions in Britain and the United States and that it is still in print, and still much and deservedly loved.

————

IVAN GONCHAROV (1812–1891)
Oblomov

Nineteenth-century Russian fiction is one of the undisputed glories of world literature. *Crime and Punishment, War and Peace, Fathers and Sons*—who does not know, if only by name, these masterpieces of Dostoevsky, Tolstoy, and Turgenev? Perhaps one might add Gogol's *Dead Souls* to this list, or even Lermontov's *A Hero of Our Time.* Yet suppose one were to mention *The Tales of Belkin, A Lady Macbeth of Mstsensk Dictrict,* or *The Golovlyov Family.* How many people would recognize these similarly wonderful books by Pushkin, Leskov, and Saltykov-Schedrin?

In this same elite category of the too-little-known belongs *Oblomov* (1858), one of the most popular novels ever published in Russia, and certainly the most winsome and delightful of all the works just mentioned. Its pages relate the story of a man who fundamentally never wants to get out of bed, and who remains throughout his life as guileless, simple, and kindly as a Slavic version of Forrest Gump. In a preface to the best translation of the book, that by Stephen Pearl, the novelist Tatyana Tolstoya suggests that simply on the basis of this single novel its author, Ivan Goncharov, might be Russia's "true national writer." That may be exaggerated, but even Chekhov—who really is Russian's national writer (to my mind, anyway)—did claim that Goncharov stood "10 heads above me in talent."

Tolstoya argues that "there is something deeply Russian in the character of Oblomov, something that strikes a chord in every Russian heart. This something lies in the seductive appeal of laziness and of good-natured idleness, the golden conservation of a serene, untroubled childhood when everyone loves one another and when life with its anxieties and demands is still over the horizon. It is to be found in the tact and delicacy of 'live and let live,' in taking the path of least resistance, in unassertiveness, and an aversion to fuss and bother of any kind. It manifests itself in insouciance about money matters and . . . in trustfulness."

Ilya Ilyich Oblomov prefers daydreaming to actually doing . . . anything. Such charming indolence is distinctly un-American, in sharp contrast to the get-up-and-go of Oblomov's close friend Andrei Stolz. But then Stolz is half-German, which explains his practicality, efficiency, and no-nonsense approach to everything, from business to romance. If Theodore Dreiser had been writing this book, Stolz would have been the hero.

The novel opens with Oblomov—about thirty, somewhat plump, and definitely out of shape—lying on his divan wrapped in an old dressing gown. For the next hundred pages he pretty much remains just where he is, as a series of friends drop by to say hello, invite him out, or try to cadge some money. Money is, in fact, a bit of a problem just now since our rentier-hero relies on his estate to pay his expenses in St. Petersburg, and the bailiff has written with lots of unpleasant news: Drought has ruined the harvest; peasants have started to run off; the old homestead is falling down. This clearly makes for a crisis, and Oblomov finds himself "faced with the grim prospect of having to think of some way of doing something about it." Despite the sound advice of Stolz, that something doesn't include actually going home to check up on matters himself. Far easier just to forget about the letter for a while, and maybe everything will somehow turn out okay.

Besides, there's far worse on the immediate horizon. Oblomov's landlord plans to renovate the apartment building and wants his slothful tenant to move out right away. Move! Who can face such an overwhelming prospect? At least not just now, when it's time for a little nap.

"Oblomov's Dream," which makes up the whole of chapter nine, was published by itself in a magazine long before the novel came out.

On its own, this reminiscence of things past offers thirty-seven of the most wonderful pages you will ever read. Oblomov's memories of the sleepy summer days and cozy winter nights of his childhood waft us into an Edenic paradise of "placid and unruffled calm," a world where nobody does much of anything at all. After a heavy lunch, nearly every living being falls into an afternoon slumber until teatime, as if a fairy had passed a wand over the estate. People doze away the decades. When feeling unusually energetic, Oblomov's mother might spend a busy three hours with a tailor discussing how to make her husband's quilted jacket into a coat for her little boy.

At Oblomovka, even a letter from an old friend, who wants the recipe for the family's homemade beer, demands far too much effort to actually answer. During long winter evenings, though, people will laugh and laugh as they recall how Luka Savich's sled fell to pieces as he was sliding down the hill. And what about the day the cows and goats broke through the old garden fence and ate all the currant bushes? Oh, that was a time! By contrast with Oblomov's childhood home, the sleepy, sun-dappled Blandings Castle of P. G. Wodehouse is a veritable hive of industry:

> The people of Oblomovka found it difficult to believe in painful emotions; to them the constant drive for movement and activity could not be described as life and overpowering emotion was something they avoided like the plague.

Not surprisingly, the grown Oblomov has inherited this disposition to take it easy and go with the flow—he calls it *oblomovschina*—when suddenly his entire manner of half-life is overturned: Stolz forces him out into the world and there, one evening, he meets Olga. Or rather, Olga! Olga! Love encourages our hero to buy some new clothes, read the newspapers, attend the theater, and actually write that letter to his bailiff. Goncharov's (somewhat long) account of how love sneaks into the hearts of two innocents re-creates the almost embarrassingly true-to-memory course of youthful infatuation. There are the long strolls in the garden, the little spats, the make-up kiss. Ah, first love! Yet can any grand amour, no matter how grand, actually overwhelm the power of *oblomovschina*?

There are many surprises yet to come in Goncharov's quietly humorous, touching, and thought-provoking book. How, for instance, should we finally judge Oblomov? Is he an aristocratic parasite, a holy fool, or a kind of Buddhist saint? Academical readers will note the expert control of time in the way the novel slows down and speeds up. But anyone will admire how Goncharov brings the subsidiary characters to vivid life, especially Oblomov's sullen but fanatically loyal servant, Zakhar; his bovine landlady, Agafy Marveyevna (whose elbows fascinate her tenant); and his supposed friend, the shameless scoundrel Tarantyev. Little wonder that Tolstoy declared himself "in rapture over *Oblomov*" and kept going back to it again and again.

⎯⎯⎯⎯➤◦◄⎯⎯⎯⎯

JOSÉ MARIA EÇA DE QUEIROS (1845–1900)
The Crime of Father Amaro; Cousin Bazilio; The Maias

Eça de Queiros is generally regarded as Portugal's greatest novelist, author of some half-dozen masterpieces that bear comparison with the work of Flaubert and Zola. *The Crime of Father Amaro* (1876, revised 1880), his mesmerizing first novel, is by turns comic, sexy, and harrowing.

Eça's plot is as sensational now as then: A priest, prey to erotic reverie and without a true clerical vocation, half seduces, half falls in love with the daughter of his landlady. The first two-thirds of *The Crime of Father Amaro* depicts the burgeoning desire between these two young people; the last third charts the consequences of their illicit passion. Aside from a bitterly clear-eyed doctor and a saintly old priest, all the people in the book would benefit from quite a bit of time in the confessional.

The love story—as classic as Abelard and Héloïse—provides the motor for the novel, but its chief pleasure lies in its cynical humor, crisp narration, and slightly exaggerated characters, all of them observed by the author with a disdainful acceptance of human frailty and divine indifference.

Consider Amaro at the seminary, to which he had been consigned as an orphan. "Before he had even made his vows," writes Eça in Margaret Jull Costa's translation, "he was already longing to break them." Praying at night before a lithograph of the Virgin Mary, he sees merely "a pretty blonde girl." He would actually "cast lubricious glances at her as he undressed; in his curiosity he would even imagine himself lifting the chaste folds of the image's blue tunic to reveal shapely forms, white flesh. . . ." In fact, Amaro is infected with a sentimental *Bovarysme,* a longing for the heightened existence of the dashing aristocratic protagonists of romantic fiction. He notes that one young woman's glittering eyes are "like black satin covered with water" and practically swoons when she plays a "plangent" passage from *Rigoletto.*

Gradually, Eça builds up the character of his priest-hero— resentful of his tonsure, susceptible to the decadent mores of those around him, weak-willed and timorous, self-deluding and increasingly callous. Amaro periodically daydreams that the Inquisition has returned and that he can torture his enemies and terrorize proud, beautiful women. By contrast to her conflicted lover, Amelia is all youthful vitality—eager, sensual, malleable—and yet touchingly devout and trusting. Early in her infatuation she admits that she "had only one idea now: to throw her arms around his neck and kiss him, oh, yes, kiss him! And then, if necessary, die." Later, however, she is taught to enjoy "humiliating herself before him, offering herself up, feeling that she was all his, his slave . . . She lived with her eyes fixed on him, in a state of animal obedience; she only looked away and down when he spoke or when the moment came to unbutton her dress." Later still, she settles into "a confused feeling in which hatred glimmered beneath her continuing desire." This is an author who understands sex.

All the clergy in the book, with one exception, are corrupt—gluttonous, vengeful, scheming, believers in expedience, hypocrisy, and self-indulgence:

> Father Brito was the strongest and most stupid priest in the diocese; he had the appearance, manners and rude health of a sturdy peasant from the Beira who handles a crook well, drinks a skin of wine, happily ploughs his fields or plies the trowel when there's any building to be done and, during hot June siestas, has his brutal way with the girls on the maize ricks.

Father Natario lives with his two nieces, who are very, very attached to him, and has made himself the willing tool of the government: "He had come to an arrangement with a missionary, and on the eve of the election, people in the parish had received letters from Heaven, all signed by the Virgin Mary, in which they were asked, with promises of salvation and threats of eternal damnation, to vote for the government candidate."

The most influential man in town is the supercilious Dr. Godinho, "whose virtues paraded slowly by, solemn and sublime, leaving in their train a host of noble adjectives." Another worthy administrator spends "his office hours gazing from his balcony through a pair of binoculars at the wife of Teles the tailor." The dried-up Doña Josefa, under attack by Satan, glimpses "St. Francis Xavier in the nude," followed by a vision of the "whole of Heaven's court . . . throwing off their tunics and their habits and dancing imaginary sarabands stark naked."

Eça employs all sorts of comedy—lighthearted satire in the inane conversations among the guests of Doña Joannierra, broad humor in his depiction of a drunken printer turned revolutionary, and even a kind of loathsome kitsch in his description of a vicious old maid who torments Amelia but goes into nightly ecstasies when kissing her relic of a piece of the baby Jesus's diaper. Every page here is amusing or savage: Good wine "'contributes to the dignity of the holy sacrifice,'" says Amaro gravely, "meanwhile stroking Amelia's knee."

Cousin Bazilio, translated by the poet Roy Campbell, is another tale of seduction, in which a young married woman succumbs to the blandishments of her sophisticated and grossly predatory cousin. At first the story recalls *Madame Bovary*—Luiza daydreams over too many French novels—but Eça soon adds echoes of Balzac's *Cousine Bette.* A cruel and jealous servant turns to blackmail after she discovers Luiza's transgression. First she appropriates her mistress's clothes, then demands money, and finally takes to lounging in bed while the errant, regretful wife laboriously irons the clothes and cleans the house. Yet even at that low point, Luiza has only begun her degradation. This is a devastating, razor-edged novel, even if the great Brazilian novelist Machado de Assis thought it salacious.

If you are taken with these two books, you should go on to *The Maias,* a masterwork partly about a love affair between a brother and sister, or *The Relic,* a comic tale about a young scapegrace who tries to appear holy in order to inherit his aunt's fortune. Then there's *The Illustrious House of Ramires* and the stories collected in *The Yellow Sofa.* Eça de Queiros is a major writer and a delicious one, too.

—————»-o-«—————

ANTON CHEKHOV (1860–1904)
Short stories; letters; plays

Anton Chekhov claimed that after he was dead people would say he was "a good writer but not as good as Turgenev." For once, he couldn't have been more wrong: There is no short-story writer (or modern dramatist) so admired as Chekhov. More surprisingly, there are few human beings who seem quite so admirable.

A true artist, according to George Bernard Shaw, will let his wife starve, his children go barefoot, and his mother drudge for his living at seventy sooner than work at anything but his art. It's a good thing nobody told this to Chekhov. The grandson of a serf, he started writing humorous sketches in his teens to bring in cash to support his indigent parents and spendthrift siblings. He wrote fast—"I don't remember a single story over which I have spent more than 24 hours"— because he needed time for his medical studies. As he said (in one of his inspiring letters), "What aristocratic writers take from nature gratis, the less privileged must pay for with their youth."

Once he became a doctor, Chekhov treated cholera victims, started a sanitorium for tuberculosis patients, and journeyed across Russia—before the Trans-Siberian railway—to the penal colony of Sakhalin, where he cared for prisoners, conducted a census, and worked for prison reform. Later, after he had made some money, his villa was open to all, and he lived surrounded by peasants needing medical care, actresses wanting parts, brothers looking for drinks, editors calling for stories, and fans requesting autographs. For most of his short life (he died at just forty-four from tuberculosis), Chekhov kept juggling the demands of family, friendship, medicine, and writing. In no aspect of life did he swerve from his ideals of tolerance and forgiveness: "I hate lying and violence whatever form they may take . . . My holy of holies is the human body, health, intelligence, talent, inspiration, love and absolute freedom—freedom from force and falsehood." As Ivan Ivanovitch, in "Gooseberries" (translated by Constance Garnett), adds: "There is no happiness, and there ought not to be; but if there is a meaning and an object in life, that meaning and object is not our happiness, but something greater and more rational. Do good!"

Chekhov's fiction deals, unblinkingly, with every aspect of what it is to be human. In the harrowing "A Dreary Story," an aging professor peers at his wife:

> I gaze at my wife and wonder like a child. I ask myself in perplexity, is it possible that this old, very stout, ungainly woman, with her dull expression of petty anxiety and alarm about daily bread, with eyes dimmed by continual brooding over debts and money difficulties, who can talk of nothing but expenses and who smiles at nothing but things getting cheaper—is it possible that this woman is no other than the slender Varya whom I fell in love with so passionately?

Not only do his readers regard Chekhov with admiration; other writers look to him with awe and humility. Here are a few typical comments:

Robert Stone: "Chekhov brought the priceless gift of clarity. He is one of those writers who seem to work without artifice; we experience above all his humane intelligence and his perception. He is an athlete, a hero of perception."

William Maxwell: "Though no Church has seen fit to canonise him, he was nevertheless a saint. The greatest of his stories are, no matter how many times reread, always an experience that strikes deep into the soul and produces alteration there. The reader who has lived through 'Ward No. 6' knows forever after that his own sanity is only provisional. As for those masterpieces, 'The Lady with the Dog,' 'The

Horse-Stealers,' 'Sleepy,' 'Gooseberries,' 'About Love,' 'In the Ravine'—where else do you see so clearly the difference between light and dark, or how dark darkness can be?"

Vladimir Nabokov: "Chekhov managed to convey an impression of artistic beauty far surpassing that of many writers who thought they knew what rich beautiful prose was. He did it by keeping all his words in the same dim light and of the same exact tint of gray, a tint between the color of an old fence and that of a low cloud. The variety of his moods, the flicker of his charming wit, the deeply artistic economy of characterization, the vivid detail, and the fade-out of human life—all the peculiar Chekhovian features—are enhanced by being suffused and surrounded by a faintly iridescent verbal haziness." He adds, "Those bleak landscapes, the withered sallows along dismally muddy roads, the gray crows flapping across gray skies, the sudden whiff of some amazing recollection at a most ordinary corner—all this pathetic dimness, all this lovely weakness, all this Chekhovian dove-gray world . . ."

William Trevor: "Chekhov . . . fashioned the art of the glimpse. . . . In story after story, explosions of truth make his point for him. Escapism has no place; all human sentiment, however humble its manifestation, is worthy of investigation."

Cynthia Ozick: "Each story, however allusive or broken-off, is nevertheless exhaustive—like the curve of a shard that implies not simply the form of the pitcher entire, but also the thirsts of its shattered civilization."

Harold Brodkey: "Consider his powers of description: night, day, horses, men, buildings, smiling women all are more brilliantly present in him than in Tolstoy . . . He has conferred more meaning on us than any other artist of the century."

V. S. Pritchett: "What Chekhov brings out, as he makes his people tell their own story without listening to one another, is their absurd pride in their own history and their indifference to everyone else's." The comedy, tragedy, and pathos of his tales lie in "the collision of these solitudes."

Autumn is the traditional time to pick up a volume of Chekhov: One imagines a gray and threatening afternoon, the slightly feverish reader reclined on a sofa, the chipped teapot near at hand. Yet this cozy picture is partial, limited. The great Russian is deeper and more various than this, capable of the lighthearted satire of "The Darling" as well as the harrowing journeys of "A Dreary Story," "Gusev," and "Ward No. 6." His epiphanies suddenly arise to surprise his characters as much as his readers: the moment in "The Lady with the Dog" when Grusow realizes that he has truly fallen in love with the married woman he so casually seduced; the climax of "The Bishop," when the consumptive prelate's old mother—who has stood in awe of her glorious son—kneels at his deathbed to caress him and call him her little Pavel.

For storytelling genius, creation of character, and sheer human sympathy, it seems to me that Chekhov stands with Chaucer, Balzac, and Dickens. As for his rightly celebrated plays—*The Sea Gull, The Three Sisters, Uncle Vanya*—all that needs be said is this: Go see them.

⊸•⊷

JEAN TOOMER (1894–1967)
Cane

*C*ane (1923) is arguably the first great classic of African-American fiction. Before Jean Toomer, one could read moving poems (by Phillis Wheatley, among others), stirring memoirs (*Narrative of the Life of Frederick Douglass*), and influential works of cultural thought (W. E. B. Du Bois's *The Souls of Black Folk*), but in the realm of fiction, perhaps only the powerful stories in Charles W. Chesnutt's *The Conjure-Woman* might be put forth as a rival claimant for priority. *Cane* appeared just as the Harlem Renaissance was taking off, and it stood then and stands now as the most distinguished fictional work of the movement.

Or does it? Jean Toomer himself never liked any racial labels applied to his book or its author. He regarded himself as simply an artist, a modernist writer who—like Hemingway and Faulkner—learned from Sherwood Anderson, often published in avant-garde journals such as *Broom, The Double Dealer,* and *The Little Review,* and preferred to hang out with Hart Crane more often than with Langston Hughes. Eventually, Toomer was to disclaim his "Negro" heritage entirely and devote his later life to philosophical and occult thought, largely as a disciple of the Russian mystic G. I. Gurdjieff. He never published a work of fiction again.

Unsurprisingly, then, the vexed issues of race and identity inform the jazzy medley of sketches, poems, and stories that make up *Cane.* In part one, Toomer presents glimpses of southern black life when it is still in touch with its passional, archetypal roots. But this is an era fast disappearing, and in the stories (as well as the short poems interspersed between them) Toomer laments the loss of a fundamental naturalness. Sex haunts these threnodies in prose:

> Men had always wanted her, this Karintha, even as a child, Karintha carrying beauty, perfect as dusk when the sun goes down. Old men rode her hobby-horse upon their knees. Young men danced with her at frolics when they should have been dancing with their grown-up girls. God grant us youth, secretly prayed the old men. The young fellows counted the time to pass before she would be old enough to mate with them. . . . Karintha, at twelve, was a wild flash that told the other folks just what it was to live. . . . Karintha's running was a whir.

Alas, as it turns out, "the soul of her was a growing thing ripened too soon."

In the middle section of *Cane,* the scene shifts to Washington and Chicago. Here we observe black souls yearning for love and understanding yet constrained by decorum, hemmed in by modern urban civilization or by the mere thought of crossing not only the color line but any line at all. In the third and last section of his book, Toomer presents a long story about a light-skinned black intellectual who returns to the South of his roots. There he encounters a representative cross-section of his race—the elegant pseudo-white school principal; a wandering preacher; the accommodating wagonsmith who espouses a Booker T. Washington cult of manual work; an ancient ex-slave who lives, unmoving and almost mute, in a dark cellar; a girl who seems to represent a hope for the future, and several others. The book ends on a despairing note.

Throughout this mix of fiction and poetry we are shown the diversity of African-American life, and the presentation ranges from the naturalistic to the dreamlike to the positively surreal. (In "Rhobert," a man wears a house on his head.) There are scenes of grotesquerie— such as a staged fight between dwarfs—and of psychological extremis, as when a shy young woman, racked by sexual fantasies about a powerful preacher, hypnotically goes to a sporting house and offers herself to him. In these pages people are shunned, knifed, and burned alive. The characters display every skin color from jet black to pale white, yet all of them are "Negro."

In form Jean Toomer's book is probably most like Sherwood Anderson's *Winesburg, Ohio* or Ernest Hemingway's *In Our Time.* It is certainly as fine as either of these near contemporaries. Among works by later African-American writers, its only peers are Zora Neale Hurston's *Their Eyes Were Watching God,* Richard Wright's *Native Son,* Ralph Ellison's *Invisible Man,* and Toni Morrison's *Beloved.* In the intensity and beauty of its ecstatic prose, *Cane* has no rivals.

——>·•·<——

WILLA CATHER (1873–1947)
Death Comes for the Archbishop; A Lost Lady; other books

Willa Cather hated to see her fiction anthologized or used as a school text. She feared that instead of discovering her stories and novels on their own, children would grow up with unpleasant memories of being forced to read her work. Unfortunately, this has happened. *My Antonia* is a staple of high-school English classes, but seldom a favorite with students, especially teenage boys.

In some ways, Cather is the perennial "lost lady" of twentieth-century American fiction, and like England's Ford Madox Ford is constantly being rediscovered. We tend to forget that three of her finest books—*A Lost Lady* (1923), *The Professor's House* (1925), and *Death Comes for the Archbishop* (1927)—are contemporary with the best work of F. Scott Fitzgerald and Ernest Hemingway. (Indeed, Fitzgerald once wrote Cather to apologize for a chapter of *The Great Gatsby* that closely echoes one in *A Lost Lady.*) In recent years, Cather has been claimed by feminists as a lesbian writer, just as she was once regarded as the laureate of Nebraska or the celebrant of the Southwest.

Such categorization is anathema to a true artist, and Cather was as devoted to her art as anyone since Flaubert. Without being precisely a recluse, she avoided publicity and self-advertising, content to be left alone to get on with her work. She took to heart the advice given to her by Sarah Orne Jewett (author of *The Country of the Pointed Firs*): "You must find a quiet place. You must find your own quiet center of life and write from that . . . To write and work on this level we must live on it—we must at least recognize it and defer to it at every step."

In college, Cather majored in classics, and many readers have remarked the Virgilian clarity, lyricism, and elegance of her prose. One sees this throughout her work, from *The Song of the Lark* to *My Mor-*

tal Enemy, but particularly in *Death Comes for the Archbishop.* The most serenely beautiful of her books, it seems scarcely a novel at all, more a kind of New World pastoral, evoking the beauty of the desert Southwest, lamenting the passing of traditional Native culture, and glorifying the lives of two saintly Catholic missionaries as they spread their faith in a harsh land. Its pages are full of stories, including several about wicked priests who are sensualists, misers, or hedonists, but everything unfolds without the roil of present passion. *Sunt lacrimae rerum*—there are tears in things. *Death Comes for the Archbishop* is as much reverie as historical novel.

On the surface, such a work might well seem tedious, even hokey and pious. That it is none of these is partly because of Cather's low-keyed wit and lyricism. Is there a better Christmas dinner in American fiction than the one cooked by Father Vaillant and shared with his friend Bishop Latour? Is there a more moving scene than the one in which, on a cold winter's night, the bishop discovers an old Mexican woman praying and weeping before the altar? Sada, a slave owned by an irreligious family, has been forbidden to attend mass, but on this night she has stolen away to spend a few minutes in the house of God. She tells the bishop it has been nineteen years since she was allowed to partake of the sacraments. At the chapter's climax, the two pray together and the bishop humbly tells himself that truly "this church was Sada's house, and he was a servant in it."

Cather lovingly depicts the Southwestern landscape—the tamarisk trees and steep-faced mesas and ancient caves, the occasional gardens of fruit and vegetables, the Indian hogans and adobe huts, the sand and the willows and the sky. When the aging bishop returns briefly to France, to his birthplace, he soon finds himself growing restless:

> In New Mexico he always awoke a young man; not until he rose
> and began to shave did he realize that he was growing older. His
> first consciousness was a sense of light dry wind blowing in

through the windows, with the fragrance of hot sun and sage-brush and sweet clover; a wind that made one's body feel light and one's heart cry, "To-day, today," like a child's.

Cather espoused the virtues of a clean, stripped-down art—*démeublé* (unfurnished) was the French word she used for her ideal. Rather than stuff her books with descriptions of interiors and the plethora of detail we associate with Balzac or Dickens, she preferred to suggest rather than blatantly spell out:

> Whatever is felt upon the page without being specifically named there—that, one might say, is created. It is the inexplicable presence of the thing not named, of the overtone divined by the ear but not heard by it, the verbal mood, the emotional aura of the fact or thing or the deed, that gives high quality to the novel or the drama as well as to poetry itself.

As she wrote further, in an essay on Jewett, every great story "must leave in the mind of the sensitive reader an intangible residuum of pleasure, a cadence, a quality of voice that is exclusively the writer's own, individual, unique. A quality that one can remember without the volume at hand, can experience over and over again in the mind but can never absolutely define . . ." Certainly that serene beauty, beyond time, characterizes Cather's own best work.

And what of *A Lost Lady*? Might one just say that it is among the most perfect short novels in our language, and that its tale of the courtly and beautiful overwhelmed by venality and corruption breaks our heart? One of the most horrifying scenes in modern fiction, and a highly symbolic one, occurs in chapter two when the evil Ivy Peters takes a little blade and slits the eyes of a frightened woodpecker and then, gloating, releases the poor bird:

The woodpecker rose in the air with a whirling, corkscrew motion, darted to the right, struck a tree-trunk,—to the left, and struck another. Up and down, backward and forward among the tangle of branches it flew, raking its feathers, falling and recovering itself. . . . There was something wild and desperate about the way the darkened creature beats its wings in the branches, whirling in the sunlight and never seeing it, always thrusting its head up and shaking it, as a bird does when it is drinking.

A Lost Lady, like nearly all of Cather's work, is set largely in the past, most of it "thirty or forty years ago" when the narrator was a boy or young man. This imbues the portrait of Marian Forrester with a hazy *sfumato* that softens some of its painful revelations. Once there was something lovely and kind and pure—but no longer. All that remains of that vanished Midwest, the time of civility before the Ivy Peterses took over the world, is the memory of—to use good Captain Forrester's favorite toast—"Happy days!" Alas, one by one those days slipped away unseen, and were soon gone forever.

⟶➤◆◄⟵

LOUIS-FERDINAND CÉLINE (1894–1961)
Death on the Installment Plan; Journey to the End of the Night

Louis-Ferdinand Céline refused to write fiction that sounded as if it had been composed in a library with a quill pen. Instead he celebrated the living language of the people, full of argot, profanity, and savage street rhetoric. To this he added a taste for gallows humor and a view of life as something far more nasty and brutish than anything ever imagined by Hobbes. Céline's American descendants range from

Henry Miller and Kurt Vonnegut to William Burroughs and William T. Vollmann.

Journey to the End of the Night (1932) opens with its semi-autobiographical hero's grim experiences during World War I, in the African jungle, and in America (where he works on the Ford assembly line in Detroit), and ends with Bardamu as a down-and-out doctor in Paris. The sentences of this brutal, despairing book might have been ripped from his guts, leaving only breathless fragments:

> Here's how it started. I'd never said a word. Not one word. It was Arthur Ganate that made me speak up. Arthur was a friend from med school. So we meet on the Place Clichy. It was after breakfast. He wants to talk to me. I listen . . .

Still, this prose is relatively controlled, aside from its magnificent rants, at least by comparison to the sordid, horrific, and very funny *Death on the Installment Plan* (1936). Here we learn about the childhood, family life, and early adventures of Céline's hero (now called Ferdinand), in sentences that spool out as nonstop memories, shrieks and monologues about the horrors of poverty and the wretchedness of life. As Céline says of one of his characters, "She didn't believe in sentiments. She took the lowest view and she was right."

In its quiet opening, the novel at first suggests the weariness and despondency usually associated with Samuel Beckett: "Here we are, alone again. It's all so slow, so heavy, so sad . . . I'll be old soon. Then at last it will be over." (This could be a passage from *Malone Dies.*) At first Ferdinand talks about the gruesomeness of his life as a doctor, treating the poor and syphilitic, but then he describes his ongoing literary project, a kind of Arthurian romance about King Krogold. But "you get sick of everything," he tells us, "except sleeping and daydreaming." Even daydreams, though, can hardly ward off grim reality. Soon Ferdinand takes us back to his childhood.

He grew up surrounded by filth. As a boy he stank from the dried feces on his bottom; one of his aunts became a whore, an uncle went crazy and disappeared with a circus. When the little boy tried to help his mother sell lace and trinkets to a rich old lady, the gross biddy pulled up her dress and asked for kisses on her pudendum. In hopes of collecting some small rent on a hovel, his grandmother first had to clear a blocked-up toilet with a pole. ("The pole alone wouldn't do it. She plunged in with both arms.") This is a book that doesn't shy away from mentioning snot, vomit, menstrual blood, and urine.

Meanwhile, little Ferdinand loses one job after another, victimized by his bosses and abused by his coworkers. In a last attempt to give him a chance to make something of himself, his parents scrimp to send the boy to a run-down boarding school in England. There Ferdinand watches over an idiot child while fantasizing about sex with the wife of the headmaster. Meanwhile, that distinguished educationalist sits around naked playing with children's toys, as Madame herself starts to drift into a kind of Ophelia-like dream world.

Upon his return to Paris, having learned absolutely nothing, not even a little English, Ferdinand quarrels with his father and nearly strangles the old man. The boy manages to find temporary asylum with his Uncle Edouard, who then sets him up as an unpaid assistant to the immortal Roger-Martin Courtial des Pereires.

Des Pereires runs a "scientific" journal called *Genitron* and publishes pamphlets on just about everything: *Poultry Raising at Home, Hindustani Revelation, Be Your Own Doctor, The True Language of Herbs, Electricity Without a Bulb, The Complete Works of Auguste Comte Reduced to the Dimensions of a Positivist Prayer in Twenty-Two Acrostic Verses.* He is, in fact, one of the most shameless scam artists of modern letters, a rival in flim-flammery to W. C. Fields, Groucho Marx, and Professor Marvel himself (i.e., Oz, the Great and Powerful), with whom he shares a passion for ballooning. When des Pereires begins to orate, all the reader wants to do is listen:

Ladies and gentlemen, if I'm still flying a balloon at my age, it's not out of vain bravado . . . you can take my word for that . . . not out of any desire to impress the crowd . . . Take a look at my chest! You see before you all the best known, most highly prized, most envied medals for merit and courage! If I take to the air, ladies and gentlemen, it is for purposes of popular education . . . that is my life-long aim! Everything in my power to enlighten the masses! We are not appealing to any morbid passion, to sadistic instincts, to emotional perversity! . . . I appeal to your intelligence! Your intelligence alone!

(Ralph Manheim's translation)

Note, by the way, those ellipses, which are Céline's hallmark. To give his book the stream-of-consciousness rush of nonstop memories or the staccato rhythm of actual speech, his prose relies on regular use of those three dots. As a result, the sentences never quite end. The ellipses work like a man catching his breath, or perhaps gagging, even as he simultaneously breaks out in a *cri du coeur,* a hallucinatory rage, or a carnival spiel.

Eventually, Pereires and Ferdinand find themselves conducting a contest for a workable system of perpetual motion, then in a hunt for sunken treasure. After those projects run into certain difficulties, Pereires convinces himself that his system of Radiotellurism will promote the growth of gigantic vegetables. While waiting for his crop of super-potatoes to come in, he founds a school, appealing to the "Anguished Fathers of France" to send their dear children out to the country, where they will grow vigorous and healthy in the fresh air as members of the "Renovated Familistery for the Creation of a New Race."

And so it goes in a book that lurches from gallows humor to the realities of starvation and death. It ends with the young Ferdinand about to join the army, where he will soon set out on the ghastly, heartbreaking maturity already chronicled in the earlier *Journey to the End of the Night.*

Céline brings an astonishing vitality to the page—but he's hardly an admirable man, whether viewed through these semi-autobiographical confessions or as an actual human being. Note, for instance, that ominous phrase "the creation of a New Race": During the Second World War Céline collaborated with the Germans and some of his later books add virulent anti-Semitism to his general revulsion for mankind's all-around "crumminess." As a result, some people may not be able to stomach any of his work, early or late. Yet Céline's Swiftian disgust and despair, in both *Journey to the End of Night* and *Death on the Installment Plan,* are oddly tonic, leaving us not only shocked but also strangely exhilarated by so much misanthropic gusto.

———⟶•⟵———

ZORA NEALE HURSTON (1891–1960)
Their Eyes Were Watching God

Published in 1937, Zora Neale Hurston's *Their Eyes Were Watching God* was well received by critics, but gradually sank into the limbo of the little read and then into that of the half forgotten. To later literary historians, it was merely a minor work of the Harlem Renaissance, from an author best known for her anthropological studies of black folk culture (*Mules and Men,* 1935). Worse still, toward the end of her life, Hurston actually condemned the Supreme Court's decision to outlaw segregation. Who would bother with such a book, by such an author? Besides, its title made it sound vaguely "religious."

Yet since Hurston's death, *Their Eyes Were Watching God* has come to be regarded as one of the classics of American fiction. The novel's rediscovery was originally spearheaded by women writers and scholars like Alice Walker, Sherley Anne Williams, and Mary Helen Washington, who found in the protagonist Janie an emblem of their own experience. Here was a black woman who was neither mammy nor mulatto, who sought to find real love and fulfillment. Through the poetic beauty of its language and its attention to the details of ordinary people's lives, *Their Eyes Were Watching God* now seems a novel of self-discovery as potent as James Joyce's *Portrait of the Artist as a Young Man.*

Janie is reared by her grandmother, a former slave, who wants above all to protect the child from the harsh world. So Nanny arranges a marriage with the successful farmer Logan Killicks, who's "got a house bought and paid for and sixty acres uh land right on de big road." But the vibrant sixteen-year-old finds the older man as dull and plodding as his mules. She wants to feel love, passion, and excitement. "Lawd have mussy!" says her grandmother. "Dat's de very prong all us black women gits hung on. Dis love! Dat's just whut's got us uh pullin' and uh haulin' and sweatin' and doin' from can't see in de morning till can't see at night."

After her grandmother's death, Janie runs off with a passing go-getter named Jody Stark, who soon takes over the all-black town of Eatonville, Florida (where Hurston actually grew up). Jody dotes on Janie as essentially arm candy, and wants her to stay aloof from the common folk around them. (As one local says to another, "You can't git her wid no fish sandwich.") But Janie, stuck at the cash register of the Stark general store, longs to join in the porch life around her, to swap tales and flirt and laugh over uppity mules. (Mules and blossoming are two of the key symbols in the novel.) Instead she is imprisoned in a kind of bell jar by her increasingly distant and ambitious husband: "She was a rut in the road. Plenty of life beneath the surface but it was kept beaten down by the wheels."

Only on her husband's deathbed does Janie reveal her truest feelings:

You done lived wid me for twenty years and you don't half know me atall. And you could have but you was so busy worshippin' de works of yo' own hands, and cuffin' folks around in their minds till you didn't see uh whole heap uh things you could have . . . Ah run off tuh keep house wid you in uh wonderful way. But you wasn't satisfied wid me de way Ah was. Naw! Mah own mind had tuh be squeezed and crowded out tuh make room for yours in me.

There, in a couple of sentences, Janie expresses the condition of many American women—white as well as black—before the feminist revolution.

For a while Janie fends off various offers of marriage. Then she meets Tea Cake, a seemingly no-account gambler and roustabout, a man a dozen years her junior, no less. Against all odds, he turns out to be as much in love with her as she with him. She gives up her finery and high life in Eatonville to stand by her man and even follow him into the hard labor of the bean fields. But in return he gives her springtime and laughter and happiness. And then . . .

Their Eyes Were Watching God shows us many aspects of African-American culture—from Nanny's brutal memories of slavery to the idyllic vision of daily life with Tea Cake, a time when, as Janie says, "we aint got nothin' tuh do but do our work and come home and love." But there's much more than a woman's life in this superb novel, as Hurston lingers over tall tales, Saturday-night dances, gambling with dice and cards, jealousy, racial self-hatred, folk customs, and even a hurricane and a murder trial. The novel grows a bit melodramatic toward the end and its language is at times a little too histrionic, but the main characters are as striking as any in our literature. Who can forget old Nanny's weariness when she says, "Put me down easy, Janie. Ah'm a cracked plate."? And what woman has not yearned for a Tea Cake sometime in her life?

—>-o-<<—

EUDORA WELTY (1909–2001)
Collected stories

A young writer might learn as much from Eudora Welty's character as from her art. For most of her life, "Miss Welty" simply stayed put in her hometown of Jackson, Mississippi, residing in a modest house, working steadily at the short stories that are her chief glory. With steely determination, she never wavered in her resolve to follow her imagination wherever it led.

As a result, shortly before her death, Welty found herself enshrined as the first living author to be included in the prestigious Library of America. Her work had already been compared to that of James Joyce (by the learned critic Guy Davenport), and for many scholars her place in modern Southern fiction was second only to William Faulkner's. The great Canadian writer Alice Munro once said, straight out, that "A Worn Path" was the best story in the world.

And yet, consider this: "Why I Live at the P.O."—one of Welty's masterpieces—was rejected by the *New Yorker, Collier's, Harper's Bazaar, Good Housekeeping, Mademoiselle,* and *Harper's Magazine.* At the famous Bread Loaf Writer's Workshop, "the unanimous opinion was that nobody would ever buy" her equally famous story "Powerhouse." Amazingly, she was unable to live on the earnings from her books until the success of two late novels, *Losing Battles* (1970) and *The Optimist's Daughter* (1972). By then she was in her sixties.

Welty's first collection, *A Curtain of Green* (1941), gathers many of her best-known stories, including the three just mentioned. In another, "Petrified Man," she captures perfectly the voice of a gossipy small-town beautician named Leota. One could happily listen for hours to Leota babble on to Mrs. Fletcher about husbands, pregnancy, the glamorous Mrs. Pike, a traveling carnival, the little boy Billy she minds at her shop, and any number of people in town:

"Well, ugly? Honey, I mean to tell you—their parents was first cousins and all like that. Billy Boy, git me a fresh towel from off Teeny's stack—this 'n's wringin' wet—and quit ticklin' my ankles with that curler. I declare! He don't miss nothin'.'"

While *A Curtain of Green* and then *A Wide Net* (1943) often display a certain easy folksiness and humor, Welty's last collection, *The Bride of the Innisfallen* (1955), is considerably more demanding. The stories sometimes resemble visions or fantasies, paying less and less attention to mere plot and sometimes taking place very far from Mississippi. In "Circe" the sorceress relates her encounter with Odysseus. ("Welcome," we learn, is "the most dangerous word in the world.") In the haunting and sexually charged "No Place for You, My Love," two Northern strangers meet by accident at Galatoire's restaurant in New Orleans and embark on a day's car ride into the delta. There, land and water and air all seem to blend together into a phantasmagoric world where anything is possible. Still, nothing overt happens between the couple, only a momentary bestowal of grace when they suddenly dance together:

> Surely even those immune from the world, for the time being, need the touch of one another, or all is lost. Their arms encircling each other, their bodies circling the odorous, just-nailed-down floor, they were, at last, imperviousness in motion. They had found it, and had almost missed it: they had had to dance. They were what their separate hearts desired that day, for themselves and each other.

Welty's *The Golden Apples* (1949) is her only other collection, and her own favorite. Reminiscent of Sherwood Anderson's *Winesburg, Ohio*, it offers a series of seven interrelated but independent stories about the main citizens of Morgana, Mississippi. In "Shower of Gold" we hear about King MacLain, who marries the albino Snowdie

Hudson and then disappears to wander in and out of her life and that of the town, gradually turning into a semi-mythic ladies' man and adventurer. He reappears in "Sir Rabbit," a kind of country-and-western version of Yeats's poem "Leda and the Swan." "June Recital" portrays the music teacher, Miss Eckart, and her effect on the town's children, especially Virgie Rainey, the daughter of the narrator of "Shower of Gold." "Moon Lake" takes place at a girl's summer camp, and its hero is the viewpoint figure of "June Recital." In "Music in Spain" and "The Whole World Knows" we glimpse the later lives of King and Snowdie's twin sons, Ran and Eugene. Finally, "The Wanderers" brings the book to a close with the funeral of Mrs. Rainey and Virgie's escape from Morgana.

But to describe these stories in this crayon-like way is like calling a Brahms symphony a series of rousing tunes. *The Golden Apples* is thickly structured, rich with allusions to classical myths and Yeats poetry, marked by intricate time shifts and internal monologues, startling in its symbolic details and revelations about small-town life and almost cruelly matter-of-factual about the sense of failure and compromise we all live with.

The Golden Apples is one of the most pitiless and loving and deeply literary books of twentieth-century American fiction. In her sentences Welty can be concise and epigrammatic: "The prospective audience turned out in full oppression"; "the night descended like a bucket let down a well." She can also be true to the unconscious heartlessness of the young. When an orphan appears to have drowned, another says, "If Easter's dead, I get her coat for winter, all right." Children ardently wish for a train wreck "so they could get the bananas." Miss Eckart's life is as sad as you expect it will be. While the wild and free-spirited Virgie Rainey is "always wishing for a little more of what had just been," she also asks herself "Could she ever be, would she be, where she was going?" At the end of "The Wanderers," the now forty-year-old Virgie finally comes to understand herself and to act on her dreams.

Eudora Welty once wrote, "Every good story has a mystery—not the puzzle kind, but the mystery of allurement. As we understand the story better, it's likely that the mystery does not necessarily decrease; rather it simply grows more beautiful." Certainly her own stories are as mysterious, alluring, and beautiful as any in our literature.

Realms of Adventure

R isk and danger are fundamental to the adventure story. For the experience of a lifetime one must start by giving up all that ordinary life most values, starting with safety, comfort, and family. Little wonder, then, that the great age of the adventurer is also the heyday of the aesthete. Both are in quest of intensity. As Walter Pater writes in his famous conclusion to *The Renaissance*:

> Not the fruit of experience, but experience itself, is the end. A counted number of pulses only is given to us of a variegated, dramatic life. How may we see in them all that is to be seen in them by the finest senses? How shall we pass most swiftly from point to point, and be present always at the focus where the greatest number of vital forces unite in their purest energy? To burn always with this hard, gemlike flame, to maintain this ecstasy, is success in life.

Such a paragraph might describe the life of T. E. Lawrence ("of Arabia") or mountaineer George Mallory as much as any fin-de-siècle poet. After all, Going Too Far—the journey into the unknown or the forbidden territory—alone generates that quality of danger needed for the highest excitement, the greatest thrill. As that aesthete-adventurer Peter Pan appropriately concluded, even "to die will be a very great adventure."

As one might expect, this category includes some of the most memorable works in all of world literature. Just murmur a phrase or two from any of the books: "Here begins the Great Game . . . They were the footprints of a gigantic hound . . . She-Who-Must-Be-Obeyed . . . Eloi and Morlocks . . . The Man Who Was Thursday. . . . the little gray cells . . . The black bird." I envy anyone who has yet to discover *She, The Adventures of Sherlock Holmes, Kim, The Murder of Roger Ackroyd, The Time Machine,* and *The Maltese Falcon,* among many others. So prepare for excitement—"The game is afoot!"

H. RIDER HAGGARD (1856–1925)
She; King Solomon's Mines

H. Rider Haggard's *She* (1887) has never been out of print. For good reason: Its heroine haunts our imaginations as much as Helen of Troy, Faust, Frankenstein's monster, or Dracula—all of whom She occasionally resembles. From Wilkie Collins and J. M. Barrie to C. S. Lewis and Henry Miller, *She* has never lacked ardent admirers. Freud himself recommends Haggard's masterpiece in *The Interpretation of Dreams,* calling it "a strange book, and full of hidden meaning." Jung frequently refers to *She* as one of the most vivid literary representations of the anima, the eternal feminine within us. Other critics have spoken of the book's "bewildering power," named it "the greatest effort of pure imagination in the English language," and included it among "the great patterning works in fantastic literature." The whole story, Haggard confessed, was set down, "at white heat, almost without rest," in a little over six weeks. As Rudyard Kipling told the author, "You didn't write *She,* you know; something wrote it through you."

Within *She's* pages, moreover, one may find the germs of half our more spectacular movies and bestsellers. An astonishingly handsome young man named Leo Vincey has been brought up and educated by the learned, ugly, and even baboon-like Horace Holly. Just before committing suicide, Leo's father had insisted that his then five-year-old boy be made to study ancient Greek and Arabic, and that on his twenty-fifth birthday he should open a small box that Holly must guard with his life. When the time is right, Leo and his guardian lift the box's cover and discover a broken potsherd covered with writing in various languages; it traces the Vincey family back into ancient times.

The earliest fragment, by "Amenartas, of the Royal House of Hakor, a Pharaoh of Egypt," speaks of "a magician having a knowledge of all things, and life and loveliness that does not die." This sorceress murdered the writer's beloved husband, Kallikrates, but Amenartas herself escaped and bore a son whom, in this testament, she implores to "seek out the woman, and learn the secret of life, and if thou mayest find a way to slay her." Generation after generation passes, but no one comes close to fulfilling the quest until Leo's father. He doesn't succeed, but does enclose an account of his attempt. At the age of 19, he made his way south:

> On the coast of Africa, in a hitherto unexplored region, some distance to the north of where the Zambesi falls into the sea, there is a headland, at the extremity of which a peak towers up, shaped like the head of a negro, similar to that of which the writing speaks. I landed there, and learnt from a wandering native who had been cast out by his people because of some crime which he had committed, that far inland are great mountains, shaped like cups, and caves surrounded by measureless swamps. I learnt also that the people there speak a dialect of Arabic, and are ruled over by a beautiful white woman who is seldom seen by them, but who is reported to have power over all things living and dead.

As C. S. Lewis once said, "What story in the world opens better than *She?*"

Soon Leo, Holly, and their cockney servant, Job, have set sail for Africa. Of their initial adventures there is no need to speak: Every reader should enjoy these afresh. In due course, however, the small expedition is carried to mysterious Kôr, ruled by a veiled sovereign known only as She-Who-Must-Be-Obeyed.

Because Leo is suffering from fever, Holly alone is brought before the queen, who first appears to him swathed in a "soft white gauzy material" from head to foot so that he likens her to "a corpse in its grave clothes." Holly naturally wishes to view her face, and is duly warned: "Never may the man to whom my beauty has been unveiled put it from his mind." But the Englishman's curiosity is too strong, and his ugliness has hardened his heart against all women. What he discovers, however, is not mere radiant loveliness but "beauty made sublime," even though the "sublimity was a dark one—the glory was not all of heaven . . . Though the face before me was that of a young woman in perfect health, and the first flush of ripened beauty, yet it had stamped upon it a look of unutterable experience, and of deep acquaintance with grief and passion." When Holly sees Ayesha—to give her real name—a second time, he falls at her feet and confesses that he would trade his immortal soul to marry her. To which She answers: "Oh, so soon, oh Holly! . . . I wondered how many minutes it would take to bring thee to thy knees."

She is the story of an immortal love, of a passion stronger than time itself. Having bathed naked in the fires of life, Ayesha has gained near-immortality, but over the years has mutated into a force to rival Providence itself, a power beyond good and evil—"Canst thou not understand, oh Holly, that I am above the law?" Haggard's story is pervaded by the imagery of death and reincarnation, of religious mystery and sacrilege. Is She a revived corpse, a Lilith ("her beauty was greater than the loveliness of the daughters of men"), a "beatified spirit," or even a supra-human being, whose brightness is too much for mortal men to bear and who speaks with the authority of Christ: "Let thyself go, and trust to me"?

In numerous ways, *She* is far more than its subtitle: "a history of adventure." Leo and Holly are transformed by their experience. Even today the novel feels dangerous, constantly touching on issues that haunt our culture: the theory of evolution (both physical and spiritual), the "woman question," reincarnation, racial theories, eugenics (at some point, "She-who-must-be-obeyed" breeds giants and, later, deaf-mute servants), colonialism, the relationship of Africa and Egypt, Jungian psychology, religion and morality, the corruptions of absolute power. When Ayesha tells an incredulous Holly that a native woman, who may be the reincarnation of Amenartas, will simply be destroyed, she explains: "Where is her sin? Her sin is that she stands between me and my desire."

Haggard's romance is, in truth, a great mystical poem of love and death, of love beyond death. The nineteenth-century work it most resembles is Wagner's opera *Tristan und Isolde*.

Before he wrote the immortal *She,* Haggard produced one of the best of all Victorian adventure stories—*King Solomon's Mines* (1886). He had reportedly boasted that he could write a better novel than Robert Louis Stevenson's *Treasure Island.* His brother challenged him to prove it, and *King Solomon's Mines* was the result. It opens as all good thrillers should—with a dying man and a crumbling map pointing the way to hidden treasure. Before long, Sir Henry Curtis and Captain John Good, joined by the grizzled hunter Allan Quatermain, have set out with the Zulu Umbopa to cross unexplored Africa in search of Solomon's fabled wealth. On their trek the band encounters rogue elephants, blistering deserts, and traitorous guides; they discover a lost kingdom, fight pitched battles, suffer torture and imprisonment, and foolishly defy the curses of the witch-woman Gagool. By the story's end, though, a chief will be restored to his throne, evil defeated through great sacrifice, and fabulous gems unearthed. Is it better than *Treasure Island*? As a boy I thought so, but happily there's no need to choose between them.

⟫•⟨

ARTHUR CONAN DOYLE (1859–1930)
The Adventures of Sherlock Holmes; The Lost World;
The Captain of the 'Polestar' and Other Stories

Most writers do their best to make their fictional characters lifelike, but Arthur Conan Doyle managed far more than that: His consulting detective Sherlock Holmes has walked right off the page and into the world, becoming more real than even his creator. The hawklike profile, the deerstalker cap, the Inverness cape, and the calabash pipe—all these are recognizable the world over. To this day, people address letters to 221B Baker Street, and even now rumors abound that Holmes still lives in retirement, somewhere on the Sussex Downs, keeping bees and finishing his masterwork on the whole art of detection.

For well over a century readers have tried to understand what makes the Sherlock Holmes stories so magical. As children, we probably thrill most to the mysteries and their solution. Why would a red-haired man be needed to copy page after page of an encyclopedia? What could the strange marks called the Dancing Men actually mean? Is it really a hound from the bowels of Hell that haunts the moors at night to visit violent death upon Baskerville Hall? As we grow into showoffy adolescence, we begin to savor more fully those moments when Holmes casually displays his deductive skills, perhaps most notably in his analysis of an unknown visitor's hat in that ingenious Christmas story "The Adventure of the Blue Carbuncle":

"It is perhaps less suggestive than it might have been," he remarked, "and yet there are a few inferences which are very distinct, and a few others which represent at least a strong balance of probability. That the man was highly intellectual is of course obvious upon the face of it, and also that he was fairly well-to-do within the last three years, although he has now fallen upon evil days. He had foresight, but has less now than formerly, pointing to a moral retrogression, which, when taken with the decline of his fortunes, seems to indicate some evil influence, probably drink, at work upon him. This may account also for the obvious fact that his wife has ceased to love him."

To those who come to love what Holmesians call the Canon or the Sacred Writings—fifty-six stories and four novels—a mere name, title, or quotation can set off little explosions of wistfulness and affection: Irene Adler "of dubious and questionable memory"; Professor Moriarty, mathematician turned criminal mastermind; the slothful Mycroft Holmes, who at times *is* the British government; Colonel Sebastian Moran, "the second-most dangerous man in London"; "The Giant Rat of Sumatra," just one of those tales "for which the world is not yet prepared," and on and on. It has even been said that the most famous line in twentieth-century literature is "Mr. Holmes, they were the footprints of a gigantic hound!" Dr. Mortimer's exclamation in *The Hound of the Baskervilles* is rivaled only by the celebrated exchange between the great detective and Inspector Gregory in "Silver Blaze":

"Is there any other point to which you would wish to draw my attention?"
"To the curious incident of the dog in the night-time."
"The dog did nothing in the night-time."
"That was the curious incident," remarked Sherlock Holmes.

To those of middle age, however, the Holmes stories are no longer merely dazzling mysteries or virtuosic displays of logic. We know who done it and why. Instead we return to our worn volumes of the collected adventures just to hear Watson's comforting voice: "It was in the spring of 1894 . . ." or "I had called upon my friend, Mr. Sherlock Holmes, one day in the autumn of last year . . ." or "On glancing over my notes of the seventy odd cases. . . ." In those opening pages we discover a quiet refuge from our crowded lives as we glance again around the familiar flat with its chemical retorts, blazing fire, the bullet holes in the wall forming the initials V. R. Outside the fog rolls in or the rain beats down, but Mrs. Hudson is even now bringing up a cheering supper. Soon, there will be a knock on the door and a distressed gentlewoman will enter, or a puzzled policeman or a disguised nobleman, and the next grand adventure will begin. As Vincent Starrett observed: "they still live for all that love them well: in a romantic chamber of the heart, in a nostalgic country of the mind, where it is always 1895."

For such wistful readers, the Holmes canon might well be subsumed under a title like "The Lost World," except that Conan Doyle already adopted that phrase for his great South American tale of derring-do. In *The Lost World,* Professor George Edward Challenger leads a small expedition up the Amazon to a mysterious plateau, deep in the jungle. There, the intrepid band discovers that frightening stories of monstrous behemoths are more than legends: Dinosaurs from the Jurassic era have survived into our own time. It is a classic adventure story, worthy of its epigraph: "I have wrought my simple plan/ If I give one hour of joy/ To the boy who's half a man,/ Or the man who's half a boy."

No matter what the genre, Doyle could hardly write a bad story. Think of the Napoleonic adventures of Brigadier Gerard; the piratical exploits of Captain Sharkey; the grim or touching supernatural tales such as "Lot No. 249," "The Horror of the Heights," and "The

Captain of the Pole-Star." These should be at least as well known as
the Sherlock Holmes mysteries. There have been great ages of literature throughout history, yet the great age of story, at least in English,
remains the seventy years between roughly 1865 and 1935. Sir Arthur
Conan Doyle (1859-1930) was clearly the right man in the right time.

RUDYARD KIPLING (1865–1936)
Kim; short stories

Many years ago, a colleague at the *Washington Post Book World* used
to say to me, "Dirda, you've got to read *Kim.* It's soooo good." But I
resisted. As a boy, I had discovered "Rikki-Tikki-Tavi" and a few of
the short stories about Mowgli (from *The Jungle Book*), and I still
have a vague recollection of an elementary school teacher discussing
"How the Camel Got His Hump" (one of the *Just-So Stories*). At
some slightly later point I'd also run across "If," that barracks-room
ballad of advice to the young: "If you can force your head and nerve
and sinew/ To serve your will long after they are gone,/ And so hold
on when there is nothing in you/ Except the will which says to them
'Hold on . . .'" Not only did I like the poem, I memorized it.

When I grew up, however, I was politely informed that Kipling
was old-fashioned and second-rate, as well as imperialist, sexist, and
racist. I tried to forget "If."

Only gradually did I come around again to Kipling. If he was
such a second-rater, as I was told, how was it that the consummately
refined Henry James served as the best man at his wedding? Why did
T. S. Eliot edit an anthology of Kipling's verse? Would Somerset
Maugham—hardly given to gratuitous compliments—lie when he
insisted that Kipling was "our greatest story writer. I can't believe he
will ever be equaled. I am sure he can never be excelled"?

Certainly, George Orwell seemed right in saying that Rudyard Kipling, even if one disagreed with his politics, had generated more memorable lines than any other twentieth-century author: "East is East and West is West, and never the twain shall meet . . . The Female of the species is deadlier than the Male . . . The White Man's Burden . . . The Captains and the Kings Depart . . . Lest we forget, lest we forget." And so gradually I started to read Kipling again.

The short fiction proved a revelation. "Without Benefit of Clergy"—about the love between an Englishman and a native Muslim—must rank as one of the most tender and heartbreaking stories ever written. "The Phantom Rickshaw," in which a man is haunted by the woman he cruelly spurned, manages to be a chilling ghost story, a psychological study of guilt, and a moral tale about the wages of sin. The beautiful fable "The Miracle of Purun Bhagat," in which a prominent Indian government official abandons his westernized past to become a wandering holy man, could easily appear in a volume of saints' lives. In fact, Kipling seemed able to turn his hand to any kind of narrative. "The Man Who Would be King," like so much of his writing, mixes humor, pathos, and the macabre in a tale of two layabout Englishmen who seize power in a remote section of Afghanistan. Late works like "Mary Postgate" and "Dayspring Mishandled" could be enigmatic or even cruel, while some of his more famous stories almost resemble jokes ("The Village That Voted the Earth Was Flat") or *jeux d'esprit*. In "Wireless" the spirit of Keats inspires a feverish young lover, while in "The Finest Story in the World" another young man recalls— or imagines?—his previous incarnations.

Still, none of these fully prepared me for *Kim* (1901). Yes, the novel celebrates the British in India, but it also offers a magnificent panorama of subcontinental life in all its variety and splendor. Nirad C. Chaudhuri once said that, whatever its faults, it was still the best novel written about his country. It is also an adventure story as good as any—and one of the foundation works of the modern espionage thriller. For Kim is groomed, like a young horse, to compete in "the Great Game," the clandestine war for the control of central Asia. As one unlikely secret agent says, "We of the Game are beyond protection. If we die, we die. Our names are blotted from the book. That is all."

The novel's plot traces the exotic upbringing of young Kimball O'Hara, an Irish orphan reared by native people, who makes himself the disciple of a holy man from the Himalayas. The lama is searching for a river that will bring him deliverance from the Great Wheel of Life. Kim, at first, is mainly on the lookout for fun, but he remains devoted to his Holy One, even when forced to part from him for long periods. During their travels together on the Grand Trunk Road and elsewhere, they encounter Pathan horse dealers like the mysterious Mahub Ali; a gossipy maharanee; numerous priests, beggars, and whores; and the shrewd English spymaster Colonel Creighton. No reader ever forgets the charismatic antiques dealer Lurgan Sahib, who possesses the power to cloud men's minds, or the wonderfully adaptable, almost Pickwickian Hurree Babu (who is one of the most surprisingly adept agents of the Game), or the lonely woman from Kulu who offers herself to Kim. There are dozens of other characters, including a pair of much put-upon Russian spies. In its portraits of the men and women traveling along, or living near, the Grand Trunk Road, *Kim* rivals the humanity of the *Canterbury Tales*:

> She liked men and women, and she spoke of them—of kinglets she had known in the past, of her own youth and beauty, of the depredations of leopards, and the eccentricities of Asiatic love . . .

Though Kim soon comes to accept his alien heritage, and agrees to serve the English government, this "little friend to all the world" nonetheless feels fully alive only when he loses himself in the bustling throng that is India. The book moves from the museum of Lahore—known as The Wonder House—to St. Xavier's Academy in Lucknow to the high mountains and valleys of the Himalayas. Throughout, Kim's devotion to his Holy One is unswerving, as is the lama's for his *chela,* his disciple. In the end, this great adventure story is really about love, a love for life in all its wondrous and infinite variety, and the love between an old man and a young boy. By the time I finished the novel, I could well understand why *Kim* is for many readers their favorite "comfort book," reread every year or turned to in times of trouble. For as the Holy One so rightly says, "*Chela,* this is a great and a terrible world."

⇒•✦•⇐

H. G. WELLS (1866–1946)
The Time Machine; other works

H. G. Wells always claimed that he was born with a very ordinary mind. But, in compensation, he was blessed with extraordinary drive and self-discipline. The son of a dressmaker and a gardener, he rapidly transformed himself into a novelist, journalist, historian, and social philosopher. Yet at his death, or soon thereafter, much of his work was read only by specialists in Edwardian fiction or the few people who appreciated the wit and insight of *The History of Mr. Polly, Kipps,* and *Tono-Bungay.*

Wells would be largely forgotten today were it not for a single decade in which he produced absolutely marvelous and marvel-filled novels, starting with *The Time Machine* in 1895 and followed by *The Island of Dr. Moreau, The War of the Worlds, The Invisible Man,* and *The First Men in the Moon.* There are at least a dozen comparably fine short stories, including "The Crystal Egg," "The Truth About Pycraft," "Pollock and the Porroh Man," "The Sea Raiders," "The

Plattner Story," and "The Country of the Blind." All this intensely imaginative work established H. G. Wells as the single most pivotal figure in the history of what we now call science fiction. Mary Shelley may have invented the genre in *Frankenstein,* and Jules Verne probably possessed an even more fertile imagination and pen, but Wells remains the author who first explored science fiction's central tropes and obsessions.

The Time Machine may be Wells's most hauntingly poetic work. The novel begins in a comfortable English drawing room, where representative men of business are relaxing after a good dinner and listening to their host discuss the seemingly absurd possibility of travel through time, "the Fourth Dimension." The novel ends roughly a week later, in the same room, when the host—in torn clothes, looking wild-eyed—suddenly emerges from his laboratory with a fantastic, scarcely credible story. He has, we soon learn, just returned from a journey into the future.

The Time Traveller, as Wells calls the otherwise unnamed host, offers his audience a harrowing vision of what awaits mankind. After stopping his machine—made up of a saddle, a metallic framework, quartz handlebars, a pair of levers, and bits of nickel, ivory, and rock crystal—some 800,000 years from now, he discovers that human beings have evolved into the pretty, doll-like Eloi, who eat nothing but fruit and live laughingly in an Edenic germ-free garden. But where do their clothes come from and why do they fear the night, clustering together like sheep or cattle? What is the meaning of the mysterious wells that dot the landscape? Gradually, the Time Traveller unearths the horrific truth.

Then, under dramatic circumstances, he zooms forward 30 million years, to a time when a steady twilight broods over the earth and a huge red sun lies low in the sky. He brings his machine to a halt on a forlorn shoreline and surveys the bare sand and boundless sea. The air is thin, the dark is rising. "I cannot," he tells us, "convey the sense of abominable desolation that hung over the world." In this emptiness he nonetheless catches a glimpse of what may be the final destiny of man: "It was a round thing, the size of a football perhaps, or, it may be, bigger, and tentacles trailed down from it; it seemed black against the weltering blood-red water, and it was hopping fitfully along."

If mankind can evolve, may it not also devolve? Perhaps the gung-ho industrialism and Darwinism of the nineteenth century might not after all lead to people growing better and better every day, in every way. While among the Eloi, The Time Traveller discovers the remains of a library, where now-blank pages—"brown and charred rags"—are all that remain of the world's knowledge and literature. Is this the way civilization will end, not with a bang but a whimper? Wells, being a political reformer as well as an artist, suggests that at least some of this dismal future might be avoided by fostering social and economic justice now. He also touchingly shows, through the Eloi woman Weena, that "even when mind and strength had gone, gratitude and a mutual tenderness still lived on in the heart of man."

In his later work (such as his screenplay for "Things to Come"), Wells began to foretell a shining, chrome-bright future, built on the model of Fabian socialism, but it is his more fearful early visions that most haunt us. In *The Island of Dr. Moreau,* which forms a dyptich with *The Time Machine,* evolution again goes awry as a renegade scientist meddles with genetic design. In *The First Men in the Moon,* one of the explorers meets the Grand Lunar—nothing but a huge brain atop a small, withered body. (Note the similarity to the football-shaped being on the terminal beach.) When the Martians invade earth in *The War of the Worlds,* they prove immeasurably our superiors and mankind survives through the sheerest luck.

Like so many of the writers who shape our imaginations, H. G. Wells may at first appear to be just another rattling good storyteller. But his beautifully crafted visions don't merely entertain; they provoke, trouble, and warn. As works of art they possess something of the compact power of parables. Wells extrapolates the future from the present, asking again and again the essential question, "If this goes on, what will happen?" Science fiction, after all, is a literature that presses hard against all the boundaries, not only those of time and space.

———————➤•◦•◄———————

G. K. CHESTERTON (1874–1936)
Essays, journalism, and short stories; the Father Brown mysteries;
The Man Who Was Thursday

Gilbert Keith Chesterton spent his life as a professional Fleet Street journalist, which means that he wrote a lot, far more than seems possible for one man, even a jolly fat one. GKC, as he was widely known, could no more resist forming an opinion than he could resist making that opinion the subject of an essay or newspaper column. Were he alive today, Chesterton would be featured on the Op-Ed pages of newspapers or writing a regular feature for a magazine—probably several magazines. His genuine feeling for ordinary people, his light touch with serious issues, his ability to turn sentences into aphorisms, his flair for paradox as a way of making us see the world afresh, his valuing of tradition and religious belief, the passion that he brought to whatever he wrote about—all these make for the kind of exciting, contrarian journalism that gives life to the whole profession.

Journalism is only the bedrock, however, of Chesterton's astonishing oeuvre. While filling up practically all of *G. K.'s Weekly* and contributing to the *Illustrated London News,* he was also producing mystery stories, philosophical novels, comic verse, serious poems, and biographies of saints (including Francis of Assisi), painters (G. F. Watts), poets (Robert Browning, William Blake), and philosophers (Thomas Aquinas). He turned out cultural and political tracts (*Orthodoxy*); travel books; Catholic apologia; some of the best studies ever written of the Victorian age, Dickens, Chaucer, and George Bernard Shaw; pictures for books by his friend Hilaire Belloc; a number of plays; dozens of lectures, and much else.

What makes nearly all this writing lastingly rereadable is Chesterton's style, both as a thinker and as a master of pungent English prose. Consider the paradoxes—"Anything worth doing is worth doing badly"; the concise criticisms—"Dickens was designless without knowing or caring; Sterne was designless by design"; "Emily Brontë was as unsociable as as storm at midnight, Charlotte Brontë was at best like that warmer and more domestic thing, a house on fire." Recall the striking phrases—" 'My country right or wrong' is a thing like saying, 'My mother drunk or sober' "; the aphorisms—"Men are men; but Man is a Woman"; the rhetorical flights—"Behind all these ordinary merits lie the mean compromises, the craven silences, the sullen vanities, the secret brutalities, the unmanly visions of revenge." Then there is his genial self-mockery: "I need not say that, having entirely failed to learn how to draw or paint, I tossed off easily enough some criticisms of the weaker points of Rubens or the misdirected talents of Tintoretto."

Most of Chesterton's talents come together at their finest in his 1907 novel *The Man Who Was Thursday.* Subtitled "A Nightmare," it is both Dickensian and Kafkaesque, as witty as it is exciting. The religious thinker Ronald Knox likened this philosophical mystery to *The Pilgrim's Progress* retold in the style of the *Pickwick Papers,* but the novelist Kingsley Amis bluffly sums it up even better: "It remains the most thrilling book I have ever read."

The Man Who Was Thursday opens with the description of an outdoor dinner party in London's Saffron Park: "This particular evening, if it is remembered for nothing else, will be remembered in that place for its strange sunset. It looked like the end of the world." What follows is the story of how the poet (and secret agent) Gabriel Syme tricks his way onto the elite General Council of the Anarchists of Europe, a group that plans nothing less than the destruction of civiliza-tion. Each of its seven members bears the name of a day of the week, and their leader is the all-powerful Sunday. Soon Syme finds himself the new Thursday, and is duly entangled in a series of bizarre, even grotesque, adventures, wherein nothing is ever quite what it seems. As always, Chesterton's capacious genius mingles wit, paradox, Gothic effects, and blatant melodrama.

Consider, for example, how the young poet first meets the head of the super-secret agency that has sent him to infiltrate Sunday's or-ganization. He is led into a pitch-black room. "Are you the new re-cruit?" says a heavy voice. "And in some strange way, though there was not the shadow of a shape in the gloom, Syme knew two things: first, that it came from a man of massive stature; and second, that the man had his back to him." Syme protests that he is unfit for this new assignment:

> "You are willing, that is enough," said the unknown.
> "Well, really," said Syme, "I don't know any profession of which mere willingness is the final test."
> "I do," said the other—"martyrs. I am condemning you to death. Good day."

That taste for the dramatic flourish characterizes almost all of Chesterton's fiction. In the opening to "The Tremendous Adventures of Major Brown," an old soldier wanders, entirely by chance, down an aimless-looking lane and there meets a burly fellow pushing a bar-row full of pansies, the major's favorite flower. After chatting a bit, the man casually mentions that there's a really magnificent display of pan-sies on the other side of a nearby wall. After some persuasion, the major pulls himself up the wall to see these splendid flowers. "But for once it was not their horticultural aspects that Major Brown beheld, for the pansies were arranged in gigantic capital letters so as to form the sentence: DEATH TO MAJOR BROWN. A kindly looking old man with white whiskers was watering them."

And so we are off on a whole series of fantastic adventures, as the major, naturally enough, descends into the garden. There he meets a beautiful woman, who informs him that she must keep her face averted from the street until the stroke of six. As she tells him this, a voice rings out from nowhere: "Major Brown, Major Brown, where does the jackal dwell?" Only a reader with a soul dead to all romance could put down the book at this point.

This story comes from the collection *The Club of Queer Trades,* but the fifty Father Brown stories are replete with such teasers and puzzles. Among them are "The Blue Cross," "The Hammer of God," "The Oracle of the Dog," "The Sins of Prince Saradine," and, not least, the celebrated "The Invisible Man," which explains how a murderer can remove the body of his victim from an apartment in broad daylight without being seen.

Nearly all aficionados of the mystery agree that Father Brown is second only to Sherlock Holmes as a detective. Little wonder, then, that when Agatha Christie, Dorothy L. Sayers, and Anthony Berkeley formed the Detection Club, its first president, unanimously elected, was Chesterton. At roughly the same time, the distinguished medievalist Etienne Gilson happened to comment on an oddly titled little book called *Thomas Aquinas: The Dumb Ox:* "Chesterton makes one despair. I have been studying St. Thomas all my life and I could never have written such a book. . . . I consider it as being without possible comparison the best book ever written on St. Thomas. Nothing short of genius can account for such an achievement."

It is even more astonishing to realize that, according to his old secretary, Chesterton dictated the first half of that book straight off the top of his head, and merely skimmed a stack of scholarly authors before dictating the rest. How could he do it? Genius, indeed.

AGATHA CHRISTIE (1890–1976)
The Hercule Poirot mysteries; the Jane Marple mysteries

Hercule Poirot was as much a dandy as a detective. A mere five feet four inches tall, with an egg-shaped head, brilliantined hair, and curling moustaches, the dapper Belgian investigator favored elegant formal clothes and patent leather shoes. Courtly in manner and kind-hearted toward the young (lovers especially), he was nonetheless fussy, vain, and proud as any bantam cock.

His constant preening and fractured English notwithstanding, Hercule Poirot ranks among the greatest detectives of all time. Sherlock Holmes possessed an unapproachable glamour and Father Brown an even more subtle mind, but Poirot took on problems of greater variety and ingenuity. He solved locked-room mysteries, thwarted international terrorists, dealt with serial murderers, reopened cases nearly twenty years old, and revealed, again and again, that absolutely everyone must be suspected. In his most dazzling exploits—*The Murder of Roger Ackroyd, Murder on the Orient Express, The ABC Murders*—he startled the world by figuring out crimes that have never been equaled for sheer audacious cleverness.

As a detective Poirot constantly asserted the importance of imagination, precise intelligence, and psychology. He observed, listened, and remembered. Where Holmes would pounce on a burnt match or frayed bit of rope, Poirot disdained such scrounging and preferred to use his "little gray cells." His general practice was simply to encourage people to talk about themselves, their activities at the time of the murder, and the victim. Some personality trait, a casual discrepancy in alibi, the smallest, least likely detail might be enough to set his orderly mind on the right track. He would then meditate on his "little ideas" until he discovered the one pattern that would explain every anomaly. "The power of the human brain," he once told his Watson,

Captain Hastings, "is almost unlimited." While Father Brown liked to think himself into the murderer's state of mind or soul, Poirot usually preferred to focus on the deceased: "Until you know exactly what sort of a person the victim was, you cannot see the circumstances of a crime clearly."

Most writers would be content with the creation of one great detective. Not Christie. A good many readers prefer her novels about Jane Marple, an elderly spinster living in a quiet English village, whose penetrating blue eyes miss absolutely nothing. Not surprisingly, the Miss Marple novels often examine domestic or familial tragedies. *What Mrs. Magillicuddy Saw* (a.k.a. *The 4:10 from Paddington*) suggests that a father might do away with his own sons; *The Mirror Crack'd* explores a family darkened by a child's unfortunate birth, then riven by sexual blackmail and destroyed by murder and mercy killing; and *The Moving Finger* traces the repercussions when a series of poison pen letters lays bare the secrets of a small village. Miss Marple reveals yet again that, as Sherlock Holmes once observed, the countryside is just as teeming with crime as the big city.

Agatha Christie is the most popular novelist of the twentieth century, her books having been translated into all the world's major languages. Sales figures don't indicate merit, of course, and among serious readers Dorothy L. Sayers is generally regarded as the better and wittier English mystery novelist; I myself bow to no one in my admiration for *Gaudy Night*. But Christie offers something unusual. If we look to her for the more obvious literary qualities—distinctive prose style, rich characterization, a picture of society and contemporary life—she's not even in the same library as a Sayers or a Michael Innes. Her sentences are simple, straightforward, and transparent, and she uses the same agreeable stock company in book after book— the retired colonel, the village gossip, the local doctor, the independent young woman, the shrewd governess. They, and the victim, are no more real to us than the characters in a game of Clue.

Where Christie excels is in her plotting, that most essential of the elements of fiction. (As E. M. Forster emphatically insisted, "Oh yes, the novel tells a story.") Like a poet who writes only sonnets or a composer working out a set of variations, Christie accepts the conventions of the mystery and then seeks to surprise us with her originality. A creative-writing student could usefully study her novels just to learn the art of narrative construction. Take apart *And Then There Were None*—which features neither Poirot nor Marple—and you will see how she deftly controls the reader's understanding throughout, tantalizing and diverting and manipulating his attention at every turn.

To this profound mastery of the rhetoric of plot Christie adds the pleasures of the familiar, the cozy, the traditional. Her world is the now-vanished one of country-house England, of travels on the *Orient Express,* of cruise ships and luxury hotels, of shooting in Scotland and holidays in the Levant. When the time arrives for the final deductions, all the suspects dutifully reassemble at the scene of the crime, and they include both the upstairs aristocrats and the downstairs staff. Here is a lost realm of comfort, order, and duty, so unlike our own world, our own lives. To read an Agatha Christie is as soothing as a steaming demitasse of Hercule Poirot's favorite hot chocolate or a cup of tea with Jane Marple in her cottage sitting room.

In a famous essay, "The Guilty Vicarage," W. H. Auden insists that the most satisfying detective stories require a "closed society"—a village, a university, a snowbound resort—so that the murderer isn't any random psycho merely passing by. What's more, that society must at first be perceived as good, upright, in a state of grace. The murder discloses that someone in that Eden has fallen out of grace, so that his identification by the detective is necessary to allow the restoration of innocence to the Great Good Place.

This pattern certainly contributes to the satisfaction of a Christie novel, but one mustn't overlook the more purely ludic elements— the appeal of a puzzle and the gratification of watching a complex, seemingly random or even apparently supernatural tangle of events (see John Dickson Carr's "how-dun-its") gradually given order and purpose. In our own lives we often feel ourselves the playthings of fate or the gods, but in the mystery we are comforted by entering a universe where everything, no matter how bizarre and improbable, can be shown to make sense.

——➤•◀——

DASHIELL HAMMETT (1894–1961)
The Maltese Falcon; other works

> "It's a black figure, as you know, smooth and shiny, of a bird, a hawk or falcon, about that high." She held her hands a foot apart.
> "What makes it important?"

To answer Sam Spade's question to Brigid O'Shaughnessy: What makes it important is that it's the McGuffin, as Alfred Hitchcock would say, for the most famous American detective novel ever written, *The Maltese Falcon* (1930).

Everyone wants to get his or her hands on the black bird, which is no mere statuette. As the fat man, Casper Gutman, tells Spade, it started off as a tribute to the medieval Emperor Charles V from the immensely wealthy Knights of Rhodes, "a glorious golden falcon encrusted from head to foot with the finest jewels in their coffers. And—remember, sir—they had fine ones, the finest out of Asia." But since then it has become—as Spade says, though only in the classic movie based on the novel—the stuff that dreams are made of.

The Maltese Falcon firmly established Dashiell Hammett as the leading writer of hard-boiled detective stories. For the previous half-dozen years he'd honed his craft at *Black Mask* magazine, producing reams of pulp fiction, often featuring the anonymous, slightly over-weight Pinkerton agent called simply The Continental Op. In one of Hammett's other great novels, *Red Harvest* (1929), the Op cleans up the corrupt town of Poisonville by playing off its various factions against each other. (*Red Harvest* provides the template for any number of subsequent tough-guy stories and films, most notably Akira Kurosawa's *Yojimbo* and Sergio Leone's *A Fistful of Dollars.*) Several of the Op stories display elements eventually reworked for *The Maltese Falcon;* "The Whosis Kid" might almost be a twenty-page first draft of the novel.

Still, this hard-boiled American classic fundamentally belongs to the "satanic" Sam Spade. Throughout the novel, the detective remains essentially a cipher: The reader is never allowed into his mind. As with Gutman, the effeminate Joel Cairo, the young gunsel Wilmer, and all the other characters, we see Spade, and hear him talk, but we never know what he's actually thinking or feeling. On a purely technical level, Hammett's narrative displays a virtuoso control of point of view. In particular, the wholly external third-person approach allows him to keep the reader constantly intrigued about the meaning of Spade's actions and utterly in the dark about how things will finally play out. The sheer unexpectedness of the novel's climax duly takes our breath away. While Gutman and Spade may drink to "plain speaking and clear understanding," there's absolutely none of either in the novel, at least until the very end—and perhaps not even then.

In these pages Hammett pioneers the affectless, deadpan narration of the classic tough-guy crime story. There's nothing fancy about his deliberative prose, or that of his successors like James M. Cain (*The Postman Always Rings Twice*), Edward Anderson (*Thieves Like Us*), Paul Cain (*Fast One*), or even George V. Higgins (*The Friends of Eddie Coyle*). Hammett, like Hemingway, simply tells us what we would see if we were there, stressing nouns and actions rather than modifiers, going easy on any noticeable or witty phrase-making:

A switch clicked and a white bowl hung on three gilded chains from the ceiling's center filled the room with light. Spade, barefooted in green and white checked pajamas, sat on the side of his bed. He scowled at the telephone on the table while his hands took from beside it a packet of brown papers and a sack of Bull Durham tobacco.

Compared to Hammett, his rival and successor Raymond Chandler is a softie. Early on, Chandler recasts his detective in a frankly romantic mode, that of the world-weary knight traveling down mean and lonely streets. Instead of being transparent, his prose draws attention to itself, and we admire its diction, rhythm, and even its grammar. Chandler repeatedly tosses off gorgeous similes and descriptions that ask us to linger over their beauty: "A tall handsome blond in a dress that looked like seawater sifted over with gold dust came out of the Ladies' Room touching up her lips and turned toward the arch, humming." Not surprisingly, the author of *The Big Sleep* and *The Long Goodbye* once remarked, "I live for syntax."

Hammett would never have said that about himself or his work, yet he is superb in unobtrusively creating distinctive speech patterns. When oily Joel Cairo enters Spade's office, his first words are, "May a stranger offer condolences for your partner's unfortunate death?" Then, a moment later, "More than idle curiosity made me ask that, Mr. Spade. I am trying to recover an—ah—ornament that has been—shall we say?—mislaid. I thought, and hoped, you could assist me."

Such unctuous formality is exceeded only by the phony bonhomie of—by gad, sir—Casper Gutman, and the unprinted obscenities and murmured gutturals of the whey-faced punk Wilmer. Of course, Spade himself displays his own verbal tics: Women are seldom called by their names—indicating their fundamental unimportance?—and instead are universally and unsentimentally addressed as "angel," "sweetheart," or "precious."

In keeping with its highly dramatic character, *The Maltese Falcon* imagines each chapter as a scene, usually set on the small, empty stage of Spade's office or within the confines of a hotel room. Within such restricted areas take place verbal sparring, fist fights, lying cross-talk, seduction, and final confessions. The drab surroundings provide a frame for the often violent action and highly colored conversation. What, after all, is more like a fantastical tale from the Arabian Nights than Gutman's history of the black bird? What more tantalizing than Brigid's occasional references to Constantinople, Marmora, and Hong Kong? In certain ways, the characters of the novel might have wandered in from one of Eric Ambler's near-contemporary spy thrillers (*A Coffin for Dimitrios; Journey into Fear*), in which Greeks, Russians, and Turks try to outfox one another somewhere in central Europe or the Levant. *The Maltese Falcon* is a San Francisco murder mystery—who killed Spade's partner, Miles Archer?—fastened onto an international caper plot, the kind in which all the gang members end up turning on one another.

When Dashiell Hammett started writing his mysteries, S. S. Van Dine's Philo Vance was America's most famous detective. Hammett once said that Vance was "in the Sherlock Holmes tradition and his conversational manner is that of a high-school girl who has been studying the foreign words and phrases in the back of her dictionary." After novels like *The Maltese Falcon,* detectives and criminals grew laconic, cynical, and brutal. In other words, they became truly American.

Encyclopedic Visions

Everything, said the poet Mallarmé, exists to end up in a book.

In this final category of *Classics for Pleasure* one finds masterpieces of vast scope—a history of antiquity and a survey of bizarre rituals, an inquiry into human psychology and a guide to English usage, a visit to the world's "museum without walls" and a handbook of ancient mythology. Here, too, is a poet who took all literature for his province, and a visionary science-fiction novelist who revealed our probable future—a rain-sodden world where nothing works and people are gradually losing their minds.

Through such magisterial surveys and summas, humankind has always tried to make sense of things, to discern the pattern in the carpet, to uncover the secrets of history and life. Many of these monumental works are surprisingly lovable, idiosyncratic, and even a bit crotchety. They also fulfill that old Horatian artistic ideal and provide instruction as well as considerable pleasure.

OVID (43 B.C.–A.D. 17)
Metamorphoses

If one had to pick the single most influential poem in world history, a good choice would be Ovid's *Metamorphoses*. For two thousand years it has provided subjects for painting and opera, inspired poets and playwrights, and suggested ceiling and wall decorations for both ducal palaces and the bedrooms of courtesans. Sensuous and dreamlike, these tales of mortals transformed into all manner of flora and fauna haunt our cultural history: Narcissus, Perseus, Medea, Orpheus, Andromeda, Pygmalion, Arachne, Europa, Proserpina, Pasiphae, Philomela, Ariadne, Semele . . . Where would our museums and concert halls be without them? This great bible of classical myth appropriately opens with the creation of the world and ends with the apotheosis of Ovid's near contemporary Julius Caesar, as the emperor's soul is set in the heavens as a star.

Ovid's particular gift lies in his singularly flowing style, hurrying one famous story into the next without pause. The *Metamorphoses* is, appropriately, an altogether restless poem, for *"Nihil est quod perstet in orbe"*—"there is nothing in the world that does not change." Though abundant with scenes of violence (often rape), it nonetheless maintains a quicksilver lightness, a teasing wit (which has been called Nabokovian), and an atmosphere of high comedy reminiscent of *A Midsummer Night's Dream*. Striking tableaux, such as Daphne transformed into a laurel or Phaeton vainly trying to control the horses of the sun, also make the poem intensely visual, at once pictorial and dramatic.

But the *Metamorphoses* isn't simply filled with pretty or shocking pictures. Ovid shows us people in crisis, people racked with passion, desire, or fear, people torn apart by the conflicting claims of reason and emotion. He is a master psychologist. *"Video melora proque deteriora sequor*—"I see and approve the better course," says Myrrha, tormented by incestuous desire, "yet choose the worse." No Latin writer is more insightful into human psychology, especially that of women.

While Virgil and Horace may be the high-minded poets of official Rome, Ovid remains its bad boy. Instead of more pastoral eclogues and odes, he writes *Ars Amatoria* (The Art of Love), nothing less than a guide to seduction, sexual attractiveness, and lovemaking techniques. It is flippant and urbane, and sometimes as insightful as any cynical maxim by La Rochefoucauld: *"Casta est quam nemo rogavit"*—"Only she is chaste whom none has invited." When the Emperor Augustus unexpectedly and mysteriously banished the poet to a distant town on the Black Sea (from where he sent back plaintive verse letters), it may have been in part because of this endorsement of sexual license by "Venus's clerk Ovyde" (Chaucer's phrase).

Ovid neatly ends the *Metamorphoses*—this carnival of mutability—by proclaiming that it will outlast "the gnawing tooth of time" and that his name shall live for all eternity. Such immortal fame is, of course, every poet's secret dream. But Ovid made it a fact: *"Non omnis moriar"*—"I will not wholly die."

There are many translations of the *Metamorphoses,* including Arthur Golding's Renaissance version, named by Ezra Pound as "the most beautiful book in the language." Certainly, Shakespeare thought it good enough to borrow from. Among modern versions, those of Mary Innes (in prose) and Rolfe Humphries and Charles Martin (in verse) stand out.

ROBERT BURTON (1577–1640)
The Anatomy of Melancholy

The Anatomy of Melancholy (1621) resembles a great medieval encyclopedia, but instead of being devoted to abstruse questions of religious dogma like Thomas Aquinas's *Summa Theologica,* or to Biblical interpretation like Gregory the Great's exegetical *Morals on the Book of Job,* it offers a guided tour of our mental and emotional life, with an emphasis on neuroses, depression, and "love-sickness." Burton pillages all the previous writing he knows to explore these themes, mixing quotations and classical tags, anecdotes from history and literature, and his own humane reflections to create one of the best and most beloved browsing books in English literature. The prose can be famously knotty, rambling, and Latinate, but surrender to its seemingly wayward rhythms and you will understand why Samuel Johnson used to say that it was "the only book that ever took him out of bed two hours sooner than he wished to rise."

Burton's masterpiece is, at heart, a humorous treatise—humorous because its psychology is based on the four physiological "humors" that were believed to determine our personalities (blood, yellow bile, phlegm, and black bile, a preponderance of the last giving rise to melancholy), and humorous because it is slyly, dryly, pervasively funny. Sometimes it's more "funny peculiar" than "funny ha-ha," but one gradually comes to love the magpie mind and personality of this learned, endearing, rather bumbling Oxford scholar. Who else would blithely exclaim, "If you like not my writing, go read something else."? Burton is, or so he insists, "a loose, plain, rude writer, & as free as loose, I call a spade a spade." He even tells us that he's terribly disorganized, that all his reading has been "to little purpose, for want of good method; I have confusedly tumbled over divers authors in our Libraries, with small profit, for want of art, order, memory, judgment." Even reading itself comes in for the occasional remonstrance: "What a glut of books! Who can read them?" What college student hasn't sometimes felt this way, or nodded agreement with Burton's own *cri du coeur*, "We are oppressed with them, our eyes ache with reading, our fingers with turning."

The Anatomy of Melancholy is not, in fact, a volume to read through so much as to live with. Open to any page at random, like an ancient practicing the *sortes Virgilianae*, and your eye will light on some telling phrase or apt observation. Of battles, Burton writes "nothing so familiar as this hacking and hewing, massacres, murders, desolations." Of lawyers and courtrooms: "So many tribunals, so little justice, so many magistrates, so little care of the common good, so many laws, yet never more disorders." The only goddess mankind adores, he says, is "Queen Money, to whom we daily offer sacrifice . . . the sole commandress of our actions, for which we pray, run, ride, go, come, labour and contend as fishes do for a crumb that falleth into the water." Indeed, this world is but "[a] vast Chaos, a confusion of manners, as fickle as the air, a crazy house, a turbulent troop full of impurities, a mart of walking spirits, goblins, the theatre of hypocrisy, a shop of knavery, flattery, a nursery of villainy, the scene of babbling, the school of giddiness, the academy of vice."

Burton's book covers every sort of passion of the mind, from depression to hypochondria, from the belief in ghosts to religious fanaticism. But the most celebrated and consulted section of his anatomy of melancholy is surely that devoted to sexual infatuation, love, and jealousy. He can range from Plato's lovely phrase defining beauty as "a lively shining or glittering brightness" to a chronicling of perverse sexual couplings and the monsters that sometimes result from these encounters. Once, he tells us, some young philosophers were debating which was the most pleasing part of a woman's body, whether her lips, eyes, teeth . . . The controversy was referred to the celebrated courtesan Lais of Corinth: "She, smiling, said they were a company of fools; for suppose they had her where they wished, what would they first seek?" (That "smiling" is a lovely, human touch.) Speaking of the caloric power of sheer sexiness, he tells us of "a cold bath that suddenly smoked and was very hot when naked Caelia came into it."

Before long Burton goes on to describe all the "artificial allurements of love," the cosmetics and apparel and lascivious ways of women, their "meretricious kisses" and bare breasts, all their "nods, jests, winks, smiles, wrestlings, tokens, favours, symbols, letters, valentines." Nor does he spare men in his descriptions of their stratagems of "heroical love," which is really unassuaged lust: "He loved Amy, till he saw Floriat, and when he saw Cynthia, forgat them both; but fair Phyllis was incomparably beyond them all, Chloris surpassed her, and yet when he espied Amaryllis, she was his sole mistress . . ." and on and on.

Burton regularly quotes from the tradition that regards women as idols of perversity, vessels of corruption and sin. Indeed, he offers a horrific catalog of their physical infirmities and filths, then concludes by saying that none of these ever matters in the eyes of a besotted lover. *Facilis descensus Averni*—it is an easy passage down to hell. For the most part, though, the bachelor Burton honors marriage despite its ordinary miseries and discontents (ungrateful children high among them), yet sees sexual desire as the cause behind much of humankind's inner torment. Jealousy itself earns its own subsection. The jealous lover or husband suspects everyone and thing:

> Is 't not a man in woman's apparel? Is not somebody in that great chest, or behind the door, or hangings, or in some of those barrels? May not a man steal in at the window with a ladder of ropes, or come down the chimney, have a false key, or get in when he is asleep?

In short, says Burton, quoting Balthasar Castiglione (author of *The Courtier*), "A thousand years will scarce serve to reckon up those allurements and guiles that men and women use to deceive one another with." Bitter wisdom, even from so humorous a writer. Quoting the church historian Eusebius, he adds, "He that will avoid trouble must avoid the world." But when that world is too much with us, we can turn to Burton's never-ending, indispensable book. Here we will find a refuge, a metaphorical equivalent to "wax candles in the night, neat chambers, good fires in winter, merry companions"—in short, a quite passable medicine for melancholy.

―――――⟫•⟪―――――

EDWARD GIBBON (1737–1794)
History of the Decline and Fall of the Roman Empire;
Memoirs of My Life and Writings

Edward Gibbon divided his celebrated *History of the Decline and Fall of the Roman Empire* into six volumes ("Another damn'd thick square book! Always scribble, scribble, scribble! Eh, Mr. Gibbon?" as the Duke of Gloucester observed). The first three cover, roughly, the Roman world we study in school and conclude about 500 A.D., with some "General Reflections on the Fall of the Roman Empire in the West." The second three are devoted to the Byzantine empire of the East. Volume IV, for instance, treats the reign of Justinian (with some deliciously salacious pages about his empress Theodora), Volume V charts the rise of Islam, and Volume VI touches on the Crusades.

In Gibbon's three opening chapters to Volume I he lightly surveys some two hundred years of history. Of the later second century, he memorably writes that "if a man were called to fix the period in the history of the world, during which the condition of the human race was most happy and prosperous, he would, without hesitation, name that which elapsed from the death of Domitian to the succession of Commodus." After this, there follows an almost year-by-year account of a series of weak or colorfully bad emperors, nearly all of them brought to power not by the senate but by the army, and usually by the elite Praetorian Guard. In one shocking instance, the soldiers actually sold the imperial power at an auction.

Volume I aggressively concludes with the notorious fifteenth and sixteenth chapters, in which the deist Gibbon outlines, with considerable ironic relish, the early years of a heretical Jewish sect that will gradually develop into a powerful and fanatical mystery religion.

Here, Gibbon applies his most honeyed style to Christian miracles and martyrdoms with a wickedness that even Voltaire might envy:

> The lame walked, the blind saw, the sick were healed, the dead were raised, demons were expelled, and the laws of Nature were frequently suspended for the benefit of the Church. But the sages of Greece and Rome turned aside from the awful spectacle, and, pursuing the ordinary occupations of life and study, appeared unconscious of any alterations in the moral or physical government of the world. Under the reign of Tiberius, the whole earth, or at least a celebrated province of the Roman empire, was involved in a preternatural darkness of three hours. Even this miraculous event, which ought to have excited the wonder, the curiosity and the devotion of mankind, passed without notice in an age of science and history.

Gibbon's second volume continues his account of the empire's political fortunes, but slows down to expound on, compare, and contrast the reigns of Constantine, who advanced the Christian religion as a means of social control and domination, and Julian, the learned if somewhat fanatically austere and mystical "Apostate," who hoped to restore the pagan gods. In Volume III, Gibbon takes up the growing pressure of the barbarians, particularly the Germans, who under Alaric will eventually overwhelm Rome itself.

Critics have complained that Gibbon nowhere expressly states exactly why the Roman Empire of the West fell (nor why the tottering Byzantine Empire of the East somehow managed to hang on for another thousand years). But he does point to contributing causes of its decline: the corruption of government (especially the investment of all power in a single supreme leader, whose character might vary from saintly and ineffectual to vicious and destructive), the destabilizing force of a mercenary army, the unending pressure of the barbarians, and the replacement of an easygoing religious syncretism by a bigoted and otherworldly Christianity riven by faction and theological wrangling. (This English rationalist particularly loathed monasticism and described its "numerous vermin" as sterile, fanatical, and downright antisocial.)

Throughout his masterpiece, Gibbon's main hope is to understand and portray the forces behind history, which he admits often appears as "little more than the register of the crimes, follies, and misfortunes of mankind." Yet the writer's own humanist views grow apparent in the subtly more personal later volumes. Gibbon values a pluralist society rather than a totalitarian state, one where commerce, competition, and mobility will assure the citizens of freedom, material progress, polite intercourse, and the advancement of knowledge. In this sense, his history may be viewed as "Whiggish," one that conceives the past as leading up to the best of all worlds—that in which its author now lives.

However much we may learn from the *Decline and Fall of the Roman Empire,* we often turn to it simply for the pleasures of Gibbon's style—for his brilliant pen portraits, the artful balance of his periodic sentences, the vignettes of debauchery and excess (the tyrannies of Caracalla, the follies of Elagabalus), the dramatic narrative pacing, and his notoriously amusing and often licentious footnotes (eight thousand altogether). Here is a particularly splendid one, part of the description of the Emperor Gordian II:

> Twenty-two acknowledged concubines, and a library of sixty-two thousand volumes, attested to the variety of his inclinations, and from the productions which he left behind him, it appears that the former as well as the latter were designed for use rather than ostentation.

Edward Gibbon has sometimes been regarded as a one-book—one very big book—author, but this isn't so. His *Memoirs of My Life and Writings* is among the most appealing autobiographies ever written, even if he never finished it and left various drafts to the care of later editors. In these pages he relates, for instance, his courtship of the poor but beautiful Suzanne Curchod, a romance cut short at the insistence of his father: "I sighed as a lover, I obeyed as a son." (Suzanne, though treated shabbily, did all right: She eventually married Jacques Necker, who became finance minister of France. Their daughter Germaine grew up to be honored as one of the outstanding intellectuals of the age, Madame de Staël.)

In appearance Gibbon was short, corpulent, and pudgy-faced (to my eye he looks the very image of Porky Pig). He lived in and through his library, and after he finished his history at the age of fifty-one had only five years left to enjoy his scholarly triumph. Suffering from longstanding intestinal and urinary problems, he died three days after an operation because of infection from dirty instruments.

J. G. FRAZER (1854–1941)
The Golden Bough

J. G. Frazer's *Golden Bough* (1906–1915; thirteenth volume, 1936) is one of the great monuments of eccentric scholarship, harkening back in its scope to such earlier grab bags of lore and legend as Pliny's *Natural History,* Robert Burton's *Anatomy of Melancholy,* and Jacob Grimm's *Teutonic Mythology.* Of these, none measures up to contemporary standards of scientific investigation, but all proffer hours of what one might call learned entertainment and page after page of romantic erudition.

From the opening paragraphs of this "study in magic and religion," any reader will recognize that Frazer is as much a poet as he is an anthropologist, classicist, and student of mythology:

Who does not know Turner's picture of the Golden Bough? The scene, suffused with the golden glow of imagination in which the divine mind of Turner steeped and transfigured even the fairest natural landscape, is a dream-like vision of the little woodland lake of Nemi—"Diana's Mirror," as it was called by the ancients. No one who has seen that calm water, lapped in a green hollow of the Alban hills, can ever forget it. . . . Dian herself might still linger by this lonely shore, still haunt these woodlands wild.

In antiquity this sylvan landscape was the scene of a strange and recurring tragedy. In order to understand it aright we must try to form in our minds an accurate picture of the place where it happened; for, as we shall see later on, a subtle link subsisted between the natural beauty of the spot and the dark crimes which under the mask of religion were often perpetrated there, crimes which after the lapse of so many ages still lend a touch of melancholy to these quiet woods and waters, like a chill breath of autumn on one of those bright September days "while not a leaf seems faded."

Well until Roman times, Frazer tells us, a grim figure might be glimpsed prowling about a certain tree in this sacred grove: "In his hand he carried a drawn sword, and he kept peering warily about him as if at every instant he expected to be set upon by an enemy." Dubbed the King of the Wood, he has gained his mystic title by killing his predecessor, and will retain it until such time as he himself is killed. Such is the method of succession to this sacred honor. "This strange rule," Frazer adds, "has no parallel in classical antiquity, and cannot be explained from it. To find an explanation we must go farther afield."

Farther afield indeed. In the ensuing pages Frazer examines the myths, folklore, traditional customs, and festivals of ancient India, aboriginal Australia, and contemporary Africa; he gleans material from the beliefs of the Russian peasantry and the practices of the

Aztec priesthood; he draws on the Hebrew Bible, Scandinavian myth, Greek poetry, Middle Eastern scripture, and Celtic romance. Volume after volume proceeds as he piles up anecdotes; interprets bizarre folk beliefs; retails stories of Corn Gods and May Queens; studies the meaning of tree worship, sacred prostitution, child sacrifice, and voluntary castration; analyzes the legends of Adonis, Attis, and Osiris; probes the notions of the scapegoat and the totem; explains the "death of Pan"; and eventually works himself back to the doomed priest-king who guards the Golden Bough.

In essence, Frazer is trying to understand how people think about the world around them. He sees mankind as having evolved through three stages—those of magic, religion, and science. (He speculates, near the end of the book, that science may itself eventually be replaced by some fuller explanation of the cosmos.) At the heart of his great study lies the deep similarity between the life of a man—birth, maturity, old age, and death—and the seasonal planting and harvesting of crops. He shows that a king is the vessel of the sacred, indeed in some sense personates the god of his cult. So long as he is young and vigorous and strong, the corn will grow, harvests will be abundant, children will be healthy, and the people will flourish. But if he should sicken or become decrepit, the fertility and sexual power he embodies will decline throughout the community. Frazer writes, "There is only one way of averting these dangers. The man-god must be killed as soon as he shews symptoms that his powers are beginning to fail, and his soul must be transferred to a vigorous successor before it has been seriously impaired by the threatened decay." Whether at an annual springtime ceremony or merely at the first sign of a gray hair, and whether through voluntary sacrifice or in conflict with a candidate for his succession, the king must die to assure the greater good. As Frazer writes, *"Le roi est mort. Vive le roi."*

Such speculative anthropology is fascinating in itself, but Frazer also hints throughout his book at the similarity between ancient cults and the Christian religion, particularly as manifested in a common belief in the birth, death, and resurrection of a hanged god. Such provocations scandalized early readers, and in later life Frazer backed away from what he was saying when he compared, for instance, sacred prostitutes with nuns. One can see this caution in his 1922 one-volume condensation of his twelve-volume original, which is why most readers should look for the recent abridgment by Robert Fraser: In its eight hundred pages, the modern editor fully represents these more controversial sections. Alternatively, one might acquire a reprint of the most famous portion of the complete text, the two volumes titled *Adonis, Attis, Osiris,* which T. S. Eliot long ago recommended as background reading for students of *The Waste Land.*

Today, J. G. Frazer is commonly dismissed by anthropologists as being overly speculative (not to say fanciful), failing to ground his conclusions in actual fieldwork, and preferring a grand synoptic vision to the more mundane or localized meanings of various cult practices. But like Freud, whose work has been similarly viewed as parochial and time-bound, Frazer is fundamentally a great imaginative artist and an inspiration to imaginative artists of all kinds. From *The Rite of Spring* to movies like *The Wicker Man,* from Robert Graves's *White Goddess* to Joseph Campbell's "creative mythology" and Northrop Frye's archetypal literary criticism, we find aspects of *The Golden Bough* everywhere. It is a key text for the twentieth century, and still a lot of fun to read in the twenty-first.

H. W. FOWLER (1858–1933)
A Dictionary of Modern English Usage

Henry Watson Fowler was the eldest son of a clergyman, attended Rugby, lost his faith at an early age, and spent the first seventeen years of his working life as a teacher at Sedburgh, an English boys' school. He appears to have been ill-suited to classroom pedagogy, being shy, somewhat awkward, and a bit pedantic. Eventually, he quit the profession—in part because he wouldn't teach Christian doctrine—and in middle age traveled to London to become a freelance writer. There he penned rather sentimental effusions about literature, composed equally sentimental poetry, and eventually came up with the notion that the world needed a new translation of Lucian. He wrote to the Oxford University Press, which agreed that such an undertaking would be welcome—those were the days!—and eventually both publisher and author brought out a four-volume edition of the works of that charming Greek author.

Fowler worked on that translation with his much younger brother Francis, with whom he later went on to produce the superb "English composition manual" called *The King's English* (1906), followed by the *Concise Oxford English Dictionary* (1911). Both books remain classics of grammatical counsel and lexicography. When World War I broke out, the two men enlisted—Henry falsifying his age considerably (he was fifty-seven). The younger Fowler eventually died of tuberculosis aggravated by conditions in France—where the brothers saw, to their frustration, only limited action—and Henry was left to soldier on alone. He dedicated *Modern English Usage* (1926), his guide to correct diction and grammar, to Francis, "who shared with me the planning of this book, but did not live to share the writing. I think of it as it should have been, with its prolixities docked, its dullnesses enlivened, its fads eliminated, its truths multiplied. He had a nimbler wit, a better sense of proportion, and a more open mind, than his twelve-year-older partner. . . ."

When *Modern English Usage* first appeared, it was widely acclaimed for its common sense, slightly old-fashioned standards, and highly individual style. The *Methodist Recorder,* no less, described the book facetiously but with considerable accuracy as "a volume on table-manners, good breeding, purity of mind, cleanness of habit, self-respect and public decency," then went on to praise its humor as "broad, sly, dry and quaint."

As indeed it is. Take the compact entry "illegible/unreadable": "The illegible is not plain enough to be deciphered; the unreadable is not interesting enough to be perused." Or consider the conclusion to the short essay "Unequal Yokefellows" (in his longer entries, Fowler generally indulged his taste for enigmatic titles):

> To shape one's sentences aright as one puts them down, instinctively avoiding lopsidedness & checking all details of the framework, is not the final crown of an accomplished writer, but part of the rudiments; if one has neglected to acquire that habit in early days, one has no right to grumble at the choice that later confronts one between slovenliness & revision.

Throughout *Modern English Usage* one can discover unexpected brief essays on such topics as the "Position of adverbs," the complexities surrounding the words "the" and "that," the types and uses of metaphor, and technical terms in rhetoric. Most pages, however, are taken up with sticky or ticklish points of usage, such as the distinction between "childish" and "childlike" or "farther" and "further," and the pronunciation of words (technical term: orthoepy); there is even the occasional tabular grid, as that in which the various kinds of humor (wit, sarcasm, invective, etc.) are listed, along with their motive or aim, province, method or means, and audience.

Like *Roget's Thesaurus,* the phrase "Fowler's *Modern English Usage*" has now passed into the language, even as the book itself has been updated, Americanized, and amplified by other hands. Nevertheless, it's worth searching for the unadulterated original—easy enough to find in second-hand book shops—to savor Fowler's forceful dicta in their purest state. Be warned, though: *Modern English Usage* isn't easy reading, in part because the author's style is so compact, so relentless in analyzing solecisms and pointing the way to sound prose. But it is, to those of the right temperament, a bedside bible and a desktop companion. Fowler himself was more modest in his estimation of his work: "If I can aspire to expertise in anything," he once wrote to the poet Robert Bridges, "I suppose it is in split infinitives."

That remark alone testifies to the scholar's idiosyncratic and endearing personality. Fowler, reclusive by nature, spent much of his adult life in a cottage on the island of Guernsey. Each morning, well into his seventies, he would go for a half-hour run, followed by a swim. He said, "I cook and sweep and scrub for myself, as a hermit should." He read no fiction, only newspapers, and would often work ten-hour days at his dictionary-making. Notwithstanding his many decades associated with Oxford University Press, the eminent scholar visited its offices only twice; nearly all his work was submitted by mail. Because he lived so simply, he often asked his publisher to reduce the amount of money it wanted to offer him for his labors. Even then he would usually take his pay in lump sums and later be "naively grateful" for small Christmas bonuses. At fifty, he unexpectedly fell in love and married a large, plain woman. They were almost deliriously happy with each other for twenty-two years.

As he grew older, Fowler suffered from high blood pressure, glaucoma (eventually he had one eye removed), and, worst of all, the painful death from cancer of his beloved wife. Yet his spirits remained amazingly high, and he was at work almost to the end on a new dictionary devoted to contemporary English. (It was never completed.) In most respects, Henry Fowler seems to have been a man of almost Buddhist equanimity, serene and saintly, wanting little out of life but the chance to work hard on his "grammar and idiom." It seems only just that he should have created in *Modern English Usage* one of the most beloved, and authoritative, reference books of all time.

‹——⇒›•‹⇐——›

EZRA POUND (1885–1972)
Selected poetry; *Literary Essays; The Spirit of Romance;*
The ABC of Reading; Letters

Ezra Pound once defined great literature as "language charged with meaning to the utmost possible degree," and that word "charged" seems the *mot juste* for the man himself. Pound jump-started artists of every sort, crackling with a personal electricity that powers every page of his letters and essays. Imagine a combination of a carnival barker, a Hollywood super-agent, and the Godfather. "It is after all a grrrreat littttttterary period," he once shouted, and then made it so by getting James Joyce into print, taking T. S. Eliot under his wing, teaching the old Yeats to write more boldly and Ernest Hemingway the virtues of conciseness.

Throughout his youth and early middle age Pound was a one-man literary revolution, writing and translating, editing, haranguing, and beating the modernist drum. He started poetic movements (Imagism), composed a not-bad opera (*Le Testament de Villon*), guided Laurence Binyon and W. H. D. Rouse in their translations of Dante and Homer, and himself tackled Japanese Noh drama, Anglo-Saxon fragments, Chinese lyrics, Provençal songs, Latin classics, and Egyptian love poems. Sculptor Gaudier-Brzeska transformed his head into a Vorticist icon, Wyndham Lewis painted his portrait, and James Laughlin founded the publishing house New Directions at his instigation. Not least, the most famous poem of the century, T. S. Eliot's *The Waste Land,* was dedicated to him, *"il miglior fabbro,"* the better craftsman who chopped and sharpened a handful of rambling pages into a masterpiece. (Is it any wonder that Pound even built his own furniture?) But years later, when Nobel laureate Eliot was still thinly smiling at the superficial honors of this fallen world, ol' Ez found himself locked up, first in a cage, then in a jail cell, and finally in an insane asylum.

During World War II, Pound not only supported Mussolini but also made broadcasts to America filled with poisonous rants. In the 1930s the poet had adopted eccentric economic theories that eventually led him to detect an international Jewish conspiracy everywhere—inciting war, reaping profits through usury, exploiting, manipulating, double-dealing. He not only promulgated these views in letters and speeches, he also inserted them into his magnum opus, *The Cantos*.

It is this shameful anti-Semitism that keeps Grampa' Ez—he liked to refer to himself in folksy ways—from settling quietly into the *Norton Anthology of Modern Poetry*. It also raises a perplexing general problem for any student of literature. Can a beautiful poem be made in praise of a hateful doctrine? Is Leni Riefenstahl's film *The Triumph of the Will* a work of art? Do Paul de Man's anti-Semitic essays invalidate his mature scholarship? How much wiggle room, if any, should we allow great writers and artists for what we now judge as racism, sexism, religious prejudice, and homophobia? Every reader will eventually have to confront this heart-wrenching issue. An African-American must face it in *Huckleberry Finn;* a devout Catholic in Renaissance gibes about papists and the Whore of Babylon.

As for Pound, his early greatness as a teacher and artistic campaigner has never been in question. His literary essays and letters, his study of Provençal poetry *The Spirit of Romance,* the exhilarating *ABC of Reading*—all these still deliver a real wallop: They are at once scholarly, iconoclastic, and fun, as in the assertion "France assumed the intellectual leadership of Europe when it reduced the academic hour to 50 minutes."

Matters get tricky, though, when we turn to Pound's actual poetic achievement. Most readers would agree that the pre-*Cantos* Pound is a superlative poet, with a matchless ear for sound and rhythm. He could take a genteel form like the sestina and give it the equivalent of a hip-hop rap—"Damn it all! all this our South stinks peace"—while in *Cathay* he might be as delicate as a miniaturist: "O fan of white silk, clear as frost on the grass-blade/ You also are laid aside." Exquisite, but so too is his spot-on parody of A. E. Housman: "O woe, woe./ People are born and die/ We also shall be dead pretty soon/ Therefore let us act as if we were dead already."

Pound's most ambitious early poem is *Hugh Selwyn Mauberley,* an acid overview of the English literary scene, with a famous opening: "For three years, out of key with his time,/ He strove to resuscitate the dead art/ Of poetry; to maintain 'the sublime'/ In the old sense. Wrong from the start . . ." Most enjoyable of all, though, is the swaggering translation, really an "imitation," called *Homage to Sextus Propertius,* with its "devirginated young ladies" and sexy talk: "If she plays with me with her shirt off/ We shall construct many *Iliads.*"

Virtually all the shorter poems were gathered together in *Personae,* which first appeared in 1926. After that, *The Cantos* sucked up everything like a vortex. Using a form of collage derived from Chinese ideograms, Pound juxtaposed autobiography, random reading, and political ravings in an attempt to construct a *Divine Comedy* for our century. Admirers judge the result a demanding and maddening masterpiece that rewards a lifetime of study, the verse-equivalent of Joyce's *Finnegans Wake.* Other readers find it a broken bundle of mirrors, as did Pound himself when he finally called his life's work a botch. Still, anyone interested in poetry should read the first seven or so cantos, most of the *Pisan Cantos* (about the poet's imprisonment after the war; they were awarded, in a controversial decision, the 1948 Bollingen Prize), and such dazzling set pieces as the "with usura" aria of Canto XLV and the "pull down thy vanity" climax of Canto LXXXI.

Whether one regards Pound as a genius or crackpot (or something of both), it's impossible to come to any real understanding of twentieth-century modernism—"the Pound Era," in Hugh Kenner's phrase—without reading the work of this encyclopedic gadfly and live wire. "Make it new," he famously commanded, and all the arts listened.

———→•◦•←———

ANDRÉ MALRAUX (1901–1976)
Man's Fate; Man's Hope; The Voices of Silence

Near the end of his life, André Malraux appeared on French television in a series of conversations entitled *"La Légende du Siècle."* A grandiose title—The Legend of the Century—but who has a better right to it? Certainly it would take some fantastic—or *"farfelu,"* to use one of the writer's own favorite words—mixture of Ernest Hemingway and Erwin Panofsky, of Indiana Jones, T. E. Lawrence, and Henry Kissinger, to approach Malraux in his diversity, to match the sheer charismatic aura surrounding his name.

Still, some younger readers may need to be apprised of the man's astonishing career. Here are just a few highlights:

Rare book scout at eighteen, prowling the book barrows of Paris in search of first editions of the Marquis de Sade. Adventurer in Southeast Asia, pillaging art from temples on Cambodia's Royal Way. Editor of *L'Indochine,* a newspaper devoted to the cause of freedom for a people later known as the Vietnamese. Novelist of renown, especially after the Goncourt Prize–winning *Man's Fate (La Condition Humaine)*. Committed fellow traveler in the communist 1930s (and then an ardent Gaullist in the 1950s and '60s). Freedom fighter and aviator during the Spanish Civil War. Award-winning moviemaker (*L'Espoir*). Commander of the Alsace-Lorraine Brigade during the Resistance. Theoretician of art in *The Voices of Silence* and its sequels. Autobiographer, who in the multivolume *Le Miroir des Limbes* hoped to rival Proust. And, not least, France's minister of culture. André Malraux accepted no limits—and was, moreover, electrifyingly attractive to women.

Man's Fate (1933), about a communist insurrection in Shanghai, and *Man's Hope* (1938), about airplane pilots during the Spanish Civil War, are ambitious, politically engaged novels, true art in the service of social causes. It is hard to forget the opening of *Man's Fate,* as the assassin Ch'en stoops over his intended victim asleep in bed: "Should he try to raise the mosquito-netting? Or should he strike through it?" Or that novel's heartbreaking last sentence: "'I hardly ever weep any more, now,' she said with a bitter pride." As for *Man's Hope*, this prose epic's terrible scenes of siege and plane crashes bring home the Spanish Civil War as vividly as Hemingway's *A Farewell to Arms* or George Orwell's *Homage to Catalonia*. At least to me. But then I read the book as a young man, bunking in a youth hostel in Barcelona while the generalissimo Francisco Franco still lived. Every morning I could look out at a nearby park and watch rank upon rank of youthful cadets marching and training in the dewy mist. At such times, 1937 seemed like yesterday.

After Spain and World War II, Malraux essentially stopped writing fiction and devoted himself to politics and art. His masterpiece of the second half of his life is a multivolume series of illustrated books about the psychology of art, the most famous of which is the first, *The Voices of Silence* (1951). These volumes consolidate a lifetime of reading, looking, and remembering.

To borrow poet Randall Jarrell's words, *The Voices of Silence* is "a long, lyrical, aphoristic, oratorical, wonderfully illustrated Discourse on the Arts of this Earth, with space for Celtic coins, Van Meegeren's [forged] Vermeers, any artist who ever was, fairy tales, religions, a history of taste, the drawings of the insane, best sellers, the influence of Tintoretto on cameramen: it is a kind of (very elevated) Flea Market of the Absolute, with room even for a remark about paintings at the Flea Market."

In its pages Malraux approaches sculpture and painting from a comparative point of view, in the widest and best sense of that sometimes controversial word. Throughout he emphasizes the importance of transfiguration and metamorphosis: "Great artists are not transcribers of the scheme of things, they are its rivals." The result is, at first glance, an overwhelming tome, providing a synopsis of art's dominant forms, zeroing in on African carvings and Gothic cathedrals,

Renaissance portraits, theater, the novel, and even audiovisual media, for our global culture has resulted in what Malraux calls a "museum without walls."

The Voices of Silence remains a dazzling book in every sense—but with Gallic nonchalance, Malraux never includes footnotes or references to other critics, a cavalier approach that allows him the speculative freedom of the amateur but is the despair of the student and scholar. Moreover, he sometimes declaims in a lofty, orotund style, with lots of capitalized words (Death, the Irremediable, Man, Art), and it's soon clear that the one important gift he lacks is a sense of humor. However, Malraux does possess a flair for brilliant maxim-like observations, tossing out ideas that—in Stuart Gilbert's translation—make him sound like a Parisian precursor to Marshall McLuhan or Harold Bloom. Television is "the intrusion of the planet into the salon." While "the reader of a newspaper was informed, the television viewer is engaged." (Remember, this was written at the very dawn of the TV era.) A few other examples:

> Each genius that breaks with the past deflects, as it were, the whole range of earlier forms.

> Artists do not stem from their childhood, but from their conflict with the achievements of their predecessors; not from their own formless world, but from their struggle with the forms which others have imposed on life.

> To be a musician does not mean liking music, it means going out of one's way to hear it.

> The supreme power of art, and of love, is that they urge us to exhaust in them the inexhaustible.

Toward the end of Malraux's life, he speculated more and more about the key concept of metamorphosis. He is uncertain how a modern world that recognizes mutability in all things will develop; the positivism of the nineteenth century has vanished, to be replaced by the random, uncertain, and chancy. Audiovisual culture strikes him as infantile, lacking the novel's ability to penetrate the essence of man by conveying his inner thoughts. He concludes that humankind will develop some new civilization actually based on metamorphosis, but wonders what form it will take. Had he lived a few more years to observe the rise of the computer and the Internet, he would have known the answer.

André Malraux remains an altogether inspiring esthetic crusader. Readers enthralled by *The Voice of Silence* will want to go on to some of the other grand syntheses of the past century, such as Erich Auerbach's magisterial *Mimesis: The Representation of Reality in Western Literature,* Northrop Frye's stylish *Anatomy of Criticism,* Kenneth Clark's urbane *Civilisation,* and Claude Levi-Strauss's various structural studies of myth, starting with his autobiographical *Tristes Tropiques.*

—————

PHILIP K. DICK (1928–1982)
The Man in the High Castle; other novels and stories

Fictionalizing philosopher, gnostic visionary, pill-popping California dreamer, "our own home-grown Borges" (Ursula Le Guin), author of dozens of paperback novels and as many short stories, "the most consistently brilliant science fiction writer in the world" (John Brunner), a legend in his own time and a myth ever since—Philip K. Dick changed the way we look at the future, the world, and ourselves. Throughout his work this literary shaman returns, again and again, to the same pair of existential questions: What is it to be human? What is real?

"Fakery," said Dick, "is a topic which absolutely fascinates me; I am convinced that anything can be faked, or anyhow evidence pointing to any given thing. Spurious clues can lead us to believe anything they want us to believe. There is really no theoretical upper limit to this. Once you have mentally opened the door to the reception of the notion of fake, you are ready to think yourself into another kind of reality entirely. It's a trip from which you never return."

Many people, outside of devotees of science fiction and fantasy, first heard about Dick as the author of *Do Androids Dream of Electric Sheep?*, the loose inspiration for the film *Blade Runner.* The man himself was already dead, but this movie, a shallow version of the original's metaphysical density, nonetheless revealed to a general audience the hallucinatory universe of PKD. The future was bleak, polluted, overcrowded, and dirty. It looked gimcrack and tawdry. There were so few animals left alive that a man's greatest dream might be to own a real sheep. When machines broke down, no one could fix them. Paranoia wasn't merely rampant; it was the only reasonable attitude to adopt in a world where nothing was certain, where drugs, technology, or government mind-control might create fantasies so convincing you could never be sure of the reality of anything or anybody.

Little wonder that half of Dick's characters are either insane or think they are. Yet they also tend to be quiet, ordinary people—in his most accessible masterpiece, *The Man in the High Castle* (1962), the chief characters are a Japanese trade official, a divorcée who teaches judo, an insecure jewelry designer, an antiques dealer, and a middle-aged fantasy novelist. In *Martian Time-Slip* the most powerful man on a planet desperate for water is the head of the plumbers' guild. Other works feature musical instrument–makers and tire-retreaders. As Dick once confessed, "I like to take employers that I've had who've owned small stores and make them the supreme rulers of entire galaxies."

Time and time again in Dick's fiction, a man will suddenly discover that everything he believes is suspect. The very cities we live in may be Potemkin villages. All information may be, and probably is, manipulated by some elite for purposes of its own. Perhaps that man or woman next door is really an android and only apparently real.

The demonic cyborg Palmer Eldritch, the global purveyor of the consciousness-altering drug Chew-Z, brings in his wake only "alienation, blurred reality, and despair." In Dick's view anything could be ersatz, the solid always melts into air, and we exist in a controlled Matrix-like environment of distorting mirrors and smiling simulacra.

How does one continue living with such total uncertainty, surrounded by the void? Dick's answer is the most humane possible: Kindness, generosity, and love are the signs of the real and truly human. Stubbornness and persistence also count, as does a sense of humor. After all, despite their darkness and narrative vertigo, Dick's novels are often extremely funny. In one, a talking taxicab advises the hero not to leave his wife. The universe may be crumbling, but people still worry about losing their jobs or their girlfriends. Even the cosmos can be seen as something of a joke. As Dick once wrote:

> What we have in the universe is obviously badly constructed. I mean, it doesn't work well. The entire universe and all the parts therein continually malfunction. But the great merit of the human being is that the human being is isomorphic with his malfunctioning universe. I mean, he too is somewhat malfunctioning. And when he recognizes that he is part of a malfunctioning system instead of succumbing to the realization and just lying down and saying, well it's all hopeless, you know, there's nothing to be done—he goes on trying. He goes on trying.

The core of the "phildickian" achievement can be found in a half-dozen or so books, among them *Martian Time-Slip, Dr. Bloodmoney, Do Androids Dream of Electric Sheep?, The Three Stigmata of Palmer Eldritch, A Scanner Darkly, Flow My Tears, the Policeman Said,* and *Valis.* Dick's writing, like one of his imaginary drugs, is addictive, and once you start reading him you won't want to quit. *The Man in the High Castle* (1962) is the place to start.

In this alternate history, Germany and Japan have won World War II and divided the United States between them. But there exists a banned book called *The Grasshopper Lies Heavy* that suggests that America actually defeated the Axis. At one point, the gentle Mr. Tagomi mystically crosses over into our world and is nearly driven mad by what he sees. Could this be the true reality? With good reason, the Germans send an assassin to kill the author of this insidious work. Who knows how much damage its perverted message might have already caused?

The Man in the High Castle touches on nearly all of Dick's major themes but follows a relatively clear plot line, which is surprising since it was written with the divinatory help of the *I Ching*. Though in some sense a science-fictional spy thriller, the novel is also quite charming. Clipped English and formal modes of address neatly convey a subtle sense of the Japanese domination. That the book's heroes are the Taoist Mr. Tagomi and Juliana, the ex-wife of a small-time jewelry-maker, only adds to its spell: Here are fragile people trying to lead benevolent, responsible lives in a world they cannot understand, let alone control. And yet Dick's protagonists somehow manage to cope with every sort of madness. In the end, battered or redeemed, they go back to their ordinary and very human lives.

Philip K. Dick is arguably the greatest of all American science-fiction writers. Only Robert Heinlein, Alfred Bester, and perhaps Ursula Le Guin can match him in importance, and none of these authors possesses his current cultural influence. Once upon a time, Kafka imagined the world as a cold-hearted and incomprehensible bureaucracy. His successor, Philip K. Dick, goes even further: He drops us directly into a madman's brain and whispers, "Here is reality, here is your home."

ENVOI

Now that *Classics for Pleasure* has drawn to a close, I can already hear the grumbles. "You've left out my favorite writer!" I am sorry, but as Judy Garland might say, we can't sing them all in one night. In some instances, I may have talked about that favorite in one of my earlier books, such as *Readings* or *Bound to Please,* where you can find pieces on, say, *The Arabian Nights* and *The Tale of Genji,* as well as the work of Charles Baudelaire, Algernon Blackwood, E. F. Benson, Isaac Babel, Djuna Barnes, Samuel Beckett, Jorge Luis Borges, Lord Berners, Elizabeth Bishop, and Thomas Bernhard, just to mention some of the Bs.

As long as it is, *Classics for Pleasure* might easily have been longer. In the end, I decided to cut out my introductions to Boethius, *The Nibelungenlied,* John Meade Falkner, Lord Dunsany, Kenneth Grahame, and eight or nine others to make room for authors who seemed more essential. All these pieces were, at least, written. Despite my good intentions, I never quite got around to starting essays on Goethe's *Elective Affinities,* Casanova's memoirs, William Beckford's *Vathek,* Byron's *Don Juan,* Arthur Machen's *The Three Impostors,* Stella Gibbons's *Cold Comfort Farm,* Hope Mirrlees's *Lud-in-the-Mist,* Eric Ambler's spy thrillers and Robert Heinlein's science fiction. Oh well, perhaps some other time.

Right now, though, I hope that you've enjoyed *Classics for Pleasure* and that you will pursue some of its recommendations at your local library or bookstore. Ralph Waldo Emerson once said that "There are books . . . which rank in our life with parents and lovers and passionate experiences." I certainly believe that.

APPENDIX

A Chronological Index of the Authors

Originally, *Classics for Pleasure* opened with the great works of antiquity and proceeded up to the end of the twentieth century. Upon reflection, though, I decided that a categorical approach—even a very loose one—would be more reader-friendly and might forestall any wholesale skipping of books written before the modern era. After all, I do want people to recognize that an old writer may speak to our modern condition better than a new one. The following chronological index should help convey the historical sweep of *Classics for Pleasure* and make it easy to locate essays on particular authors.

Denis Diderot   8

Samuel Johnson   116

Alexander Pope   156

Edward Gibbon   301

Xavier De Maistre   217

The Classic Fairy Tales   125

James Hogg   188

E. T. A. Hoffmann   128

Sören Kierkegaard   73

Mary Shelley   185

Prosper Mérimée   131

Elizabeth Gaskell   237

Thomas Love Peacock   11

Ivan Goncharov   241

Frederick Douglass   164

Jacob Burckhardt   168

Sheridan Le Fanu   192

George Meredith   76

Jules Verne   220

H. Rider Haggard   270

José Maria Eça de Queiros   244

J. K. Huysmans   224

Émile Zola   52

Frances Hodgson Burnett   134

H. G. Wells   280

Bram Stoker   196

Rudyard Kipling   277

Henry James   170

Max Beerbohm   14

Arthur Conan Doyle   274

E. Nesbit/John Masefield   136

M. R. James   199

Anton Chekhov   248

J. G. Frazer   304

William Roughead   203

Ernst Jünger   55

Jaroslav Hašek   18

C. P. Cavafy   81

G. K. Chesterton   283

H. W. Fowler   307

Ezra Pound   311

Jean Toomer   251

Anna Akhmatova   88

H. P. Lovecraft   206

Walter de la Mare   141

Agatha Christie   287

Louis-Ferdinand Céline   257

Willa Cather   254

Dashiell Hammett   290

Zora Neale Hurston   261

James Agee   60

Robert Byron   230

Ivy Compton-Burnett   22

Isak Dinesen   226

S. J. Perelman   25

Georgette Heyer   84

André Malraux   314

Daphne du Maurier   92

W. H. Auden   174

Philip K. Dick   317

Eudora Welty   264

Italo Calvino   29

Edward Gorey   32

ACKNOWLEDGMENTS

I want to thank André Bernard for suggesting this project and Ann Patty, my editor at Harcourt, for bringing it to fruition. Harcourt's editorial, publicity, and marketing staff—especially Jennifer Bassett, David Hough, Cathy Riggs, Vaughn Andrews, Van Luu, and Susan Gerber—deserve every plaudit. As always I am grateful to my agents Glen Hartley and Lynn Chu and to their associate, Farah Peterson. Once again Andy Solberg kindly lent me his Chesapeake Bay condominium as an occasional refuge. Barbara Roden, with assistance from Christopher Roden, agreed to read over the manuscript and more than once has, as we say in journalism, saved me from myself. (Any remaining mistakes are mine, all mine.) My family and friends, especially those in the Half-Pay Club and The League of Extraordinary Gentlemen, endured my constant litany that "I've got to finish my book."

Classics for Pleasure is entirely my own work but, in some instances, I have drawn on or adapted material from essays and reviews written for the *Washington Post Book World* or other publications. Though *Classics for Pleasure* is obviously a stand-alone title, I have long viewed it as capping the series of "books about books" that I have brought out since the year 2000: *Readings: Essays and Literary Entertainments; An Open Book: Chapters in a Reader's Life; Bound to Please: Essays on Great Writers and Their Books;* and *Book by Book: Notes on Reading and Life.* Each of these differs in its approach to books and reading, but in all of them I have tried to remind people that novels and poems and plays and great works of history and biography only continue to live when they are read or reread. In other words, they need you. Keep turning those pages.

INDEX